THE
WETHERILLS
OF THE
MESA VERDE

THE WETHERILLS OF THE MESA VERDE

Autobiography of Benjamin Alfred Wetherill

Edited and annotated by
Maurine S. Fletcher

University of Nebraska Press
Lincoln and London

920
W532

First Bison Book printing: 1987
Most recent printing indicated by the first digit below:
1   2   3   4   5   6   7   8   9   10

Library of Congress Cataloging-in-Publication Data
Wetherill, Benjamin Alfred, 1861–1950.
  The Wetherills of the Mesa Verde.
  Reprint. Originally published: Rutherford [N.J.]:
Fairleigh Dickinson University Press; London:
Associated University Presses, 1977.
  "Bison books."
  Bibliography: p.
  Includes index.
  1. Wetherill, Benjamin Alfred, 1861–1950.
2. Pueblo Indians—Antiquities. 3. Mesa Verde National
Park (Colo.) 4. Colorado—Biography. I. Fletcher,
Maurine S. II. Title.
[E78.C6W47 1987]   978.8'27 [B]   86-14606
ISBN 0-8032-9719-X (pbk.)

Reprinted by arrangement with Maurine S. Fletcher

This book
is dedicated with love
to the memory of

STEVEN KEITH FLETCHER

who brought it about

Contents

Acknowledgments

It seems that all library and historical society representatives are immediately interested in any project brought to them and enter into the research with gusto. To all of them I express my thanks and appreciation for their kindness and considerate treatment. Although some librarians were unable to make personal search when contacted by letter, they all regretted their inability to assist due to personnel shortage. Others, however, were able to spend considerable time with me to substantiate Al's records.

In Denver, Laura Ekstrom, Librarian of the Colorado State Museum, gladly contributed her time in finding some of the Wetherill-related material. Alys Freeze, Director of the Western History Collections at the Denver Public Library, enthusiastically undertook the problem of locating excerpts from government documents that corroborated Al's records. She searched on her own initiative until she found, copied, and mailed to me several pieces that I needed. Mrs. Judd, Colorado State Services Library Director, Velma Churchill of the Colorado State Archives Department, and Dolores Renze, Colorado State Archivist, along with others, brought forth a considerable amount of printed matter pertaining to the World's Columbian Exposition of 1893. Mary Martner, a friend, assisted in running all the warrants issued against the World's Fair Commission and became so interested in the Wetherills that she went back for more research that added a great deal of information.

Ilvah Mosby, of the Department of the Recorder of Deeds in Durango (Colorado), helped in locating records of Wetherill deeds. Mrs. Marion Lundell at the Durango (Colorado) Public Library provided the microfilm of old newspapers of the area. Contact with Dr. Robert Delaney at Fort Lewis College led to an interesting interview with Hans Aspaas at Ignacio, Colorado. From an article written by Art Ballantine of the *Durango Herald,* Mary Bachman Phelps contacted me and I later talked with her in Bayfield where she allowed me to copy some photographs in her collection of Wetherill memorabilia.

In Pueblo, Colorado, Mr. Ralph Taylor sent me to Mrs. Fred Orman, who invited my husband and me to visit her and to see her collection of Mesa Verde history.

L. K. Scheie, Assistant Librarian of the Hennepin County (Minnesota) Historical Society, located extremely important evidence in a private library and sent copies to me.

At the California Academy of Sciences, Margaret Campbell, Library Associate in the J. W. Mailliard, Jr. Library in San Francisco, undertook with verve the reconstruction of the period of time Alice Eastwood was closely associated with the Wetherill family. Through a three-month period of time, she laid on my (really HER) desk stacks of material, amassing it faster than I could possibly keep up. In addition to her intensive contribution, most of the library personnel displayed keen interest in the proceedings and stopped often for a progress report.

Only one National Park or Department of the Interior member assisted with the research. Keith Anderson, Park Archeologist of Navajo National Monument, tried to help in identifying some of Al's unidentified photographs.

Several Wetherill descendants willingly related as much as they could recall of family matters. Luella Mason Dunkelberger permitted me to copy several documents and photographs from the reposit of Anna Wetherill Mason and Charles Christopher Mason, her parents. From all the sources, new areas of search opened up.

But it was Martha Wetherill Stewart on whom I depended most. Every situation that drew me into a morass of puzzles was usually solved by a call to her. Nearly always she managed to extricate me in short order. The credit for collecting, saving, and preserving the Wetherill records has to go to Martha. Without her there would be nothing to publish.

Introduction

It should not be surprising to find that one of the Wetherills left an account of his activities during his life span. Every year several pieces of interest concerning American history are found in someone's attic. The remarkable factor in any discovery is that the pieces have been preserved until brought to public view.

In Al Wetherill's case, the material became a trunkful of papers and photographs, including the negatives (both glass plate and "instantaneous," as the first celluloid negatives were called) of the first pictures made of the Mesa Verde cliff dwellings and the ruins of the Four Corners area. The Wetherill family also saved stacks of letters, notes, receipts, deeds, and so forth, of the Alamo Ranch and kept pertinent records of their life there.

Especially carefully kept was their cashbook, where even such small items as "shoe strings, 10¢," "soda, 20¢," and "ink, 10¢" were meticulously recorded. The original Alamo Ranch records are, for the most part, in Benjamin Kite Wetherill's handwriting. Benjamin Kite, Al's father, had been a Trail Agent for the Osage Indians in what is now Oklahoma, and was accustomed to keeping exact accounts. Following him, Al kept an account of all activities and transactions. In turn, his daughter's determination to preserve everything pertaining to her father's records produces another segment of Western Americana.

At what point Al Wetherill decided that a record of the Wetherills should be published is uncertain. Originally, he probably recorded only pertinent dates, for many of them are entered singly in the ledgers that also contained his narration. In 1948 he wrote that he had recorded many pages written over a period of nearly fifty years, adding that the original material consisted of memos made for reference and later enlarged into short articles to keep the information fresh in his memory. In addition, he once wrote in a letter that he usually wrote up his trips "soon after the making" of them, during his years at the Alamo Ranch below the northern prominence of the Mesa Verde.

The Mesa Verde, in southwestern Colorado, almost where the four states of Arizona, New Mexico, Colorado, and Utah meet at a common point, thrusts a golden-crowned profile eighteen-hundred feet above the valley floor. Like a subject curtsying to the north star, the sides swing away like arms encased in green, gently sloping southward into the desert behind it. Behind the profile, called *Point Lookout,* the mantle fans into an accordian-pleated green-velvet cape that swirls from east to west. In early morning light a gossamer web of clouds drifts, lifts, and returns in a shimmering veil to envelop the chiseled outline. When the sun rises and shines fully on the rocky point, dispersing the mists, it glows with an invitation to seek the mystery of the cañons hidden in the darkness of the velvet folds, folds broken here and there with cliffs that gleam like gold-and-white filament in the woof of green. In the evening the lofty crown turns into soft and muted shades of mulberry and gray, while the folds of the cape turn into deeper colors as they blend to form an unbroken cloak behind the crest, and the whole mesa settles into the quiet and the silence.

There is little wonder that the Mesa Verde concealed its treasures for so many years, for it holds itself aloof from the surrounding land and enfolds the silent cities of the cliffs deep within the crevasses of the cañons. It is difficult to understand how any place that was once a beehive of human endeavor for a long period of time could disappear into complete oblivion. Yet the people who built the complex community houses in the caverns of the nearly sheer cliffs left only mute testimony of their dwellings to mark their place on earth. After their departure, the mesa reclaimed the land with a thoroughness that defied the white settler to find even a trace of their occupation.

For many years the mesa defied even the Wetherills, although the Ute Indians permitted them, and only them, to use the cañons of the Mesa Verde for their cattle range. The Indians, always reluctant to discuss the ancient cities, readily admitted that they did exist. Refusing to reveal the location of any cliff dwellings, they explained that they would die if they disclosed the locations and the Wetherills themselves would die if they ever succeeded in finding any of the cavern cities.

Once the Wetherills did find the major ruins of the cliffs and those locations were soon after known to others, white settlers and others swarmed into the mesa, bustling in and out and about as actively as the cliff-dwelling peoples themselves must have done when they inhabited the lofty heights. Until the mesa was declared a National Park, the area was the scene of considerable activity, some commendable and some deplorable. After it became the Mesa Verde National Park in 1906, four long years after the last Wetherill had departed, those in charge sought to blame everybody but the federal government for the condition of the houses and for the loss of the artifacts they had contained.

Questioning Al's daughter Martha about the date the material was written produced no clues. According to her, "Papa was always writing something." Not only did he record his own life, but he also wrote lengthy papers expressing his opinions of historical figures as well as contemporary events of his own time. In all probability, he wrote some short experiences for the local Mancos, Colorado, newspaper and, in later years when he was living in Tulsa, Oklahoma, he did write an article or two for Western magazines.

Al had a habit of writing an account, then later adding comments in the margin, and even of rewriting portions to bring it up to date. In several instances he incorporated later developments into subsequent drafts so that they carried a reflective attitude. Most certainly this is true of the final draft of his discovery of Cliff Palace, for it revealed that he was well aware that his credit for the discovery had been deleted from Mesa Verde chronology. That omission was first contained in the 1935 Mesa Verde National Park publication, so his last account includes his reaction to the knowledge.

It would seem that the first time he used the present tense in recording was in 1891 when he and Gustaf Nordenskiöld made their trip to the Grand Canyon. Since the account is a mixture of present and past tense, it indicates that he wrote when he could find the time. Part of the narration is contained in a hard-backed ledger selected, no doubt, because it could be packed in a saddlebag. The latter part was written on writing paper and, before it could be found, provided a suspenseful interlude, for the first portion had left the party at the bottom of the Grand Canyon with no food or water. Later drafts added material pertaining to Nordenskiöld's book, which was not published until 1893.

When writing about the cliff dwellers of the Mesa Verde, he again used the present tense, which would place the time before 1902. Commenting about irrigation systems on the mesa, he wrote that the "hurry-up-quick tourists never notice the terracing walls." In another passage he remarked that "we still find so many cliff-dweller sandals in the trash heaps." Again, he noted that "quite often we find stockings or leggings. . . ."

Other remarks indicate that he then revised the material about the cliff dwellers, for he had added in parenthesis, "All that is passing now, [since] the Indian trader usually marks out a design that he thinks will be a good seller," when he wrote of rugmaking. Again, he disclosed a revision when he included the speculation that there was a possibility that the cliff dweller still existed as a race "now living within our range of vision." The period of time when the two expressions mesh, point to around 1918 when he was the Indian trader at Salane (Tselani) in the Chinle Valley in Arizona. As an additional consideration, his journal shows that he was probably far too unsettled or was too overburdened with work to have had the time to write constructively much before that date.

From the foregoing it would be reasonable to assume that the section *The Mesa Verde and the Ancients* was the first material prepared for publication. If that was his intent, nothing came of it. Then in 1922 he moved his family to Arkansas and all his papers were evidently put aside for many years, for no mention of them was found in either his journal or his letters.

Apparent in his compilation pertaining to the ancient peoples of the Four Corners area is the fact that he did not change his opinion after he made his revisions. His comparisons included in the section establishes that he had done a great deal of research and study in order to make his comparative analysis.

In addition, he had access to the knowledge of scientists who came to the ranch and used that knowledge for his evaluations. The conclusions he reached at that time satisfied him and subsequent archaeological findings were insufficient to change his mind, although numerous brochures of archaeological development were in the Wetherill library and had been well marked by him.

It is definite that his family lineage was written in the mid-1930s, for the correspondence is postmarked during those years. At that time he actually seemed to be trying to write an autobiography and felt that it was not complete without some reference to his background.

Always he was concerned with presenting his narration in an interesting manner for "punk" or "rotten" was scrawled across the tops of some drafts, words written in critical rejection of his efforts to express himself. A note found within the pages states: "A person needs considerable imagination, as well as facts, to write anything, and lacking either your story is flat even if you write the way you feel. It is necessary to have the reader see things as you have seen them."

Had he worked at it, Al might have become a Western poet, for he often broke off writing the details of an incident to include a few lines of verse, and many completed poems were interspersed throughout the material. His expressions concerning the cliff dwellings, the Cliff Dwelling peoples, and his possessive attitude toward the Mesa Verde's ancient inhabitants, and the country itself signify a great depth of feeling for that area. Each section of the autobiography is prefaced by one of his poems.

During the 1930s and early 1940s Martha tried to interest at least two writers in assisting her father so that the autobiography could be finished or in writing a biography while he could help with the details. She failed to interest either. After Al's death, she put the records away, feeling that no one was really interested in Wetherill factual material. She then vowed that nobody would ever have access to any Wetherill records in her possession.

Over the years her resistance wore down and in June 1964 she permitted the accumulation to be used to prepare Al's belated autobiography. At that time the papers were retrieved from boxes stored in the attic, under the bed, in trunks, on closet shelves, and even in bureau drawers. Originally in good order, the papers had by that time become separated and shuffled so that a great deal of sorting became necessary. Disconcerting was the discovery that only a page or a torn portion of a page remained of some accounts. Several boxes were known to have been lost in moving from place to place, but sufficient material remained to provide historical facts. The Wetherill library, however, was untouched by time and many of the annotations are taken from the publications found on the home library shelves.

Of humorous interest is the fact that burning eyes and sneezing accompanied the reading and sorting of papers. When Martha was told about the irritation, she erupted with a rippling laugh and explained the problem. Al had read once that bugs would never attack paper that had been sprinkled with black pepper, so he liberally dosed his boxes of records. His precautions proved the theory correct, for not one piece had deteriorated from insect or mouse raids.

A puzzle developed concerning the photographs. Nothing is recorded in the Alamo Ranch expense accounts about the purchase of a camera or who taught Al photography. An album of pictures taken in 1889 establishes the fact that they had a camera at that date, although it probably was the glass-negative type. Photographs of the ruins show a box-type, hand-held camera within the photos, a camera that no doubt contained the first celluloid film they used. Notable is the name "Kodak House" in the Mesa Verde that was named for their "instantaneous" film camera, although the spelling then was either "Kodac" or "Codak" in the account books.

Prints from the numerous negatives are strikingly clear and sharp, evidence of expert photography at an early date. A photography account, in Al's handwriting, kept the costs and income for picture making and selling. Another section listed requests for photographs as early as 25 October 1892. From 1893 to 1898 charges for lantern slides were entered in the account. In addition, Marion Mason Brandt, Anna Wetherill Mason's daughter, in identifying the ranch buildings in one of the photographs, pointed to the blacksmith shop that also contained "the darkroom where Al made the pictures." Only a few of the glass plate negatives remain unbroken, but they prove the Wetherills made the first Mesa Verde photographs.

In order to preserve Al's tone of writing as closely as possible, his excessive use of "and" has been curtailed. A half-page sentence connected with ands was not at all unusual, either with him or others around the turn of the century. Eliminating the "and" necessitated adding periods and capitalizing letters. Occasionally a sentence needed clarification, so words have been added in brackets. If several drafts of an incident were found, the most interesting, detailed, humorous, or expressive rendition was selected or combined. Otherwise, no attempt has been made to interpret what he may have intended to convey. His sometimes quaint way of expression, either of Quaker or Pennsylvania origin, adds much color to his narrative. He always spelled easily as "easilly" so that has been corrected. Other unfamiliar spelling and word usage is found in the words: arroya, sympathise, barbwire, hopple, realised, appetising, utilise, civiliser, divers (for diverse), and finely (to express a satisfactory condition). Most of the terms have been changed, reluctantly, to current spelling so that they will not present a distracting note to the reader.

Chronology

BENJAMIN KITE WETHERILL FAMILY, DECEMBER 1832–FEBRUARY 1902

1832   December (12–24–1832): Birth of Benjamin Kite Wetherill in Chester Township, Delaware County, Pennsylvania. The farmhouse, now within the city limits of Chester, Pennsylvania, was still standing in the 1960s at the 200 block of West 24th Street.

1835   February (2–18–1835): Birth of Marion Tompkins.

1856   May: Marriage of Benjamin Kite Wetherill and Marion Tompkins in Clear Lake or Iowa Falls, Iowa.

1858   June (6–12–1858): Birth of Richard Wetherill, probably at Leavenworth or Diamond Island, Kansas.

1861   June (6–25–1861): Birth of Benjamin Alfred Wetherill, probably at Diamond Island, Kansas.

1865   January (1–24–1865): Birth of Anna Wetherill at Diamond Island, Kansas.

1866   September (9–24–1866): Birth of John in Leavenworth, Kansas.

1868–   Clayton and then Winslow were born between the two
1872   dates. Another child, Alice, was born sometime during the period between 1858 and 1872, but died while still an infant.

1870   The date scratched in the frost on a pane of glass by Alfred. Discussions about Quaker dissatisfacton with government management of Indian problems overheard by him.

1871   January: Beginning of plans for a Yearly Meeting House for the Religious Society of Friends in Kansas developed for Lawrence, Kansas. Benjamin Kite Wetherill appointed secretary.

1872   B. K. Wetherill appointed Trail Agent for Osage Indians in present state of Oklahoma. The family remained in Leavenworth.

1873   October: The Yearly Meeting House at Lawrence completed.

1874   Great Grasshopper Year in Kansas completely destroyed the grasslands.

1876   B. K. Wetherill left Indian Service and, with the family reunited, settled in Joplin, Missouri, to work a mine purchased earlier.

1879   B. K. left Joplin for Colorado. The rest of the family was relocated in Atchison, Kansas.

1880   B. K. sent for Richard to assist him in farming the homestead site on the east side of the Mancos River below the settlement of Mancos, Colorado. The rest of the family remained in Atchison.

1881   Spring: Wetherill family, minus Al, moved to homestead site in Colorado.
        Fall: Al arrived at the homestead site.
        Winter: Log cabin constructed; two 16'x16' rooms with 12'x16' open space between.

1882   Cottonwood slips set out on each side of the irrigation ditch near the log house to establish the name of Alamo Ranch, meaning Cottonwood Ranch. The ruin later named Sandal House located and explored by Al.

1883   Exploration trips down the Mancos Cañon to view ruins of ancient peoples who had built homes in the cañons coming into the Mancos Cañon on the southern side of the river.

1884   The homestead site enlarged to permit hay production on a large scale. Barns and outbuildings constructed.

1885   December: Anna Wetherill married to Charles Christopher Mason on the 27th. Possibly the year Al first viewed Cliff Palace from the bottom of the cañon.

1886   Building boom at Alamo Ranch; enlargement of ranch house and construction of more outbuildings. Start of cattle ranching in partnership with merchants in the area who had been forced to accept cattle in payment of debts. Search for the larger cliff cities the Ute Indians had told the Wetherills about continued when time permitted.

1887   Al wrote a letter to a friend reporting finding artifacts in the Mancos Cañon ruins while conducting soldiers from Fort Lewis on sightseeing trips. A few people began to come to the ranch to be shown the mysterious ruins of the homes of an ancient race of people.

The camp in the Mancos Cañon at the mouth of Johnson Cañon established by the Wetherills. Exploration of other cañons when time permitted.

1888   Ranch work and cattle herding occupied most of the time of the whole family. "Grubstake men" (McLoyd and Graham, and later Patrick) made some excavations in the cañons.
December: Cliff Palace rediscovered by Richard Wetherill and Charles Mason.

1889   First collection of artifacts taken to Denver by McLoyd, Graham, and Patrick. Register of Tourists to Cliff Houses started.
Summer: First Alice Eastwood and F. H. Chapin signatures recorded.
Winter: Second collection of artifacts from Mesa Verde and cliff dwellings made. Tourists to the cliff houses came from as far away as Pennsylvania and Connecticut.

1890   Summer: Second collection taken on tour of southern Colorado. It was acquired in Denver later in the year by H. Jay Smith. Tourists to the cliff houses came from as far away as New York, Pennsylvania, and Connecticut.

1891   July: Gustaf Nordenskiöld from Stockholm, Sweden, arrived to sightsee but stayed to make a major collection of artifacts from the Mesa Verde cliff houses.
November: Al, G. Nordenskiöld, and Roe Ethridge left on a trip to the Hopi Villages and Grand Cañon.
Signatures in the tourist register included Dr. W. R. Birdsall and J. R., E. M., and Julia Cowing.

1892   March: Alexis J. Fournier and H. Jay Smith stayed at the Alamo Ranch while studying the construction of cliff caves and dwellings for an exhibit at the World's Fair of 1893 in Chicago.
April: D. W. Ayres arrived at the ranch to notify the Wetherills that the Colorado exhibit at the World's Fair would include cliff-dweller relics.
May: Al and Alice Eastwood collected plants from Thompson's Springs in Utah to the Alamo Ranch.
June: Mrs. Robert Coleman, a member of the World's Fair Board of Managers, and the wives of members of the historical exhibit were guests at the ranch. A. F. Willmarth signed the register.
August: F. E. Hyde, B. Talbot B. Hyde, and F. E. Hyde, Jr. entered their names on the register.
December: C. D. Hazzard and Alice Palmer Henderson's signatures joined other notable names on the register.
Far points of residence went to New York City, Pennsyl-

vania, and Delaware, with California represented for the first time.

The house was enlarged to make a solid building incorporating the original log house to and including the smokehouse, which then became the summer kitchen for the huge hotel-size stove and cooking facilities. The icehouse was constructed next to the irrigation ditch. Spare time in the winter months were spent whittling pegs to hold together the huge barn planned for the following year, for the price of nails was "out of the question."

1893   The Alamo Ranch Museum was completed and the huge barn finished. Signatures from Stokes Poges, England, and Braunschweig, Germany, were entered in the register.

November: Hyde Exploring Expedition account charges for the trip into the lower San Juan included 400 lbs. flour, 120 lbs. potatoes, and a supply of medicine. Richard, John and Al were more-or-less permanent members of the work force, with Charles Mason joining the group part of the time.

1894   January: Continuation of the Hyde Exploring Expedition with additional charges for supplies entered in the account. Included were 300 lbs. flour and 100 lbs. pork.

May: Putnam signatures in register, along with the Frederick O. Vaille family, and C. Whitman Cross, U.S.G.E. of Washington, D.C. Massachusetts was the place of residence most remote from the Alamo Ranch.

1895   January: Money borrowed by B. K. Wetherill to finance a gold-gathering expedition on the San Juan River below the Goose Necks.

July: Al and Alice Eastwood collected botanical specimens from the Alamo Ranch to Willow Springs near Grand Gulch in Utah.

September: The Palmer Family from Larnard, Kansas, arrived at the Alamo Ranch. Signatures in the register included T. Mitchell Prudden and Francis E. Leupp. Providence, Rhode Island, held the distance record until three signatures from England were recorded in November.

October: The first trading post at Pueblo Bonito established by Al Wetherill and Oscar Buck "not fifty feet from Threatening Rock."

1896   March: John Wetherill and Louisa Wade were married at Mancos.

May: Richard began excavations at Pueblo Bonito, with Clayton and Al helping at times, for the Hyde Exploring Expedition. Charges in the H. E. E. account included 4 horses for 38 days, 3 men, board and room for 13 weeks, 720 bales of hay, and 150 feet of lumber.

December: Richard Wetherill and Marietta Palmer married in Sacramento, California.

A family from New Haven, Connecticut, came the longest distance to sign the tourist register at the ranch.

1897   January: C. E. Whitmore and George P. Bowles financed an expedition into Grand Gulch. Richard and Marietta Wetherill conducted the journey and Clayton assisted. Al and Charles spent some time there.

A signature from Berlin, Germany, marked the greatest distance traveled.

July: Al, Clayton, and Dr. Prudden made their long trek to the north rim of the Grand Cañon.

1898   A tourist from Amsterdam, Holland, won the longest distance honors for the year.

November: Death of Benjamin Kite Wetherill after a lengthy period of ill health.

1899   Anna and Charles Mason moved to Creede, Colorado, and were joined in December by Marion Wetherill.

December: Al Wetherill and Mary Tarrant were married in Atchison, Kansas.

The greatest distance traveled to the Alamo Ranch came from a Los Angeles, California, signature.

1900   The John Hays Hammond family from London, England, came the longest way to visit the cliff houses and to sign their signatures in the register.

1901   July: Birth and death of Benjamin Alfred Wetherill, Jr.

A signature from Boston, Massachusetts, claimed the distance record.

December: Marion Wetherill and Debby Mason returned to the Alamo Ranch to assist Al and Mary in their departure from the homestead.

1902   Exodus from the Alamo Ranch by Al and Mary.

EDITOR'S NOTE

Tell 'em, Pops. Set them straight, *commanded one of the two young men who had straightened to erect attention at the words they had just heard from the uniformed guide for the National Park Service.*

It's no use to tell them. Nobody'll hear what he doesn't want to believe, was the dispirited reply from the frail old man standing between them. I have heard what I thought I would hear. Although the sun shone with blistering intensity that still August day in 1946, the pale, nearly bald, elderly man in the tourist group grew a little whiter and his cheerful blue eyes dulled to an opaque gray as he meditated upon the statements they had just heard.

In 1888 two cowhands, Richard Wetherill and his cousin Charles Mason, discovered Cliff Palace. They must have been reading German fairy tales to have used such a misnomer as "Cliff Palace" for this ruin, for it was never a palace in any respect, just a community house, the guide had blithely stated. That date marks the beginning of the sad history of the Mesa Verde ruins. The early explorers almost completely rifled the contents of all the buildings in the Mesa Verde and left the walls in a very dilapidated condition. The vandalism done by those who dug into the ruins has destroyed much data and has greatly reduced the possibility of determining the culture of the cliff dwellers, he had concluded.

Such was the greeting the discoverer of Cliff Palace received when he returned to the Mesa Verde. Benjamin Alfred Wetherill was eighty-five-years old when he stood with the tourists to hear the words that would have crushed a much younger man in good health. Al (Alfred) Wetherill's return to the ancient cities of the cliffs was the desire, in Western parlance, of an old range horse to get back to the locale of his colthood days before he dies. Only when age and infirmities had claimed their toll, could he bear to consider viewing again the land he had turned his back on just after the turn of the century and closed for all time, he thought, the memories of his life at the Alamo Ranch on the Mancos River at the foot of the Mesa Verde.

For some years previous to 1946, friends of the Wetherills, upon their return from vacation trips to the Mesa Verde National Park in southwestern Colorado, had made cautious mention of the information they had received there about the role the Wetherill family had played in the history of the cliff ruins.

All had gained the impression that the Wetherills had been a most undesirable element in the history of the discovery and excavation of the major ruins in the cañons of the mesa.

The desire to once again view the land of his youth had grown stronger as Al's physical self grew weaker. Then there was added another ingredient: to learn for himself what the Department of the Interior personnel actually stated about the Wetherills. So, unannounced, he returned with his grandsons and fell in with the rest of the tourists as they made their way down the cliff front to the Cliff Palace. There, for the first and last time since his departure from the area, he stood in front of the cliff dwelling that was the dearest of his memories, and listened to a recitation not only erroneous in content, but also full of implied denigration of the Wetherill name.

Upon their return home, they were too humiliated and indignant to discuss the incident immediately. It was more than two years before a letter was sent to the Department of the Interior, a letter objecting to the discredit given the Wetherills both by speech on the part of government employees and through the National Park Service publications.

In reply, the office of the Secretary of the Interior requested that Al point out what the Wetherills considered erroneous information and to present his own story for consideration by the Department's historians. From his records, Al compiled a summary of the years between 1879 and 1902, and on 16 June 1948 sent it to the Secretary. The first paragraph began:

The sentences that make up this article are not new ones. They constitute portions taken from many pages written over a period of fifty years. . . .

Those sentences, written so long ago, are presented on the pages that follow.

THE
WETHERILLS
OF THE
MESA VERDE

PART 1

WESTWARD-MOVING PIONEERS AND THE HOMESTEAD

PROCRASTINATION

Haven't done a thing today but fool my time away.
Don't know a single thought to write, nor anything to say.
My head, it sure gets hazy. I guess it needs a boss.
Nothing doing in its empty rooms; its rent a total loss.
Some other day, with brighter skies and sunlight shining 'round
Some high-brow stuff will come to me and then I'll write it down.

Benjamin Alfred Wetherill

1
Leavenworth

IT may have been the pioneer instinct, or the, "Go west, young man, go west" advice of Horace Greeley, that started my father, Benjamin Kite Wetherill, from Chester, Pennsylvania, when he was a young man. Or, it may have been the dreams of perfect health under the invigorating skies of the Golden West that induced him to be a would-be pioneer.[1]

Accepting all the conditions of hardships, my father was one of the early seekers for the fulfillment of daydreams and air-castles that just grow and grow if you do not attempt to sidetrack them.

His first stopping place was in Clear Lake, Cerro Gordo County, Iowa, but that only seemed to have been a resting place, although it must have been a romantic one, for it was there he met and married my mother, Marion Tompkins [born 18 February 1835].

That was the day of small things in the frontier settlements and wedding garments did not hang on the hazel shrubs. Benjamin was short in this respect, and, as the young couple was sighing like a furnace in the warmth of their love, a postponement of the wedding until the bridegroom could order a wedding suit from the far-off East was not to be thought of. Fortunately, there was a city-bred young man of his acquaintance who took pity on Benjamin's straits. This friend was Joe Hoag and it was he who had the suit of regulation broadcloth—spring-bottom pants, cut-a-way jacket, and claw-hammer coat—and he sold the outfit to Benjamin at a fair margin of profit.

The ceremony took place at Mr. Talbott's house and after the regular Quaker formula. Both arose, joined hands, and each repeated to the other, in the presence of the congregation of witnesses, the simple ceremony of the Society. Whereupon both subscribed their names to the marriage register and several other persons added their names as witnesses on 22 May 1856.[2]

To just follow up the name you now bear seems simple enough, but if you follow up just one branch you would lose a great deal of good, or bad, from the other side of the family. Just one hundred years does not seem to be any time at all, but to go back along the line of people before your time, in name, color, or nationality, is entering upon a task. It requires a study of what your name actually is, or what it may have started from, and what circumstances gave the reason for the name.[3]

Grandfather Richard Wetherill was born in 1788 at Mulladry, County Armagh, Ireland, the son of parents from Yorkshire, England. (They were probably with the linen mills in Ireland.) Upon reaching manhood in 1812, he came to America and embarked upon a commercial venture in this country, manufacturing woolen goods in Concord township [Delaware County, Pa.]. He married Ann Henvis, daughter of Robert Henvis and Deborah Kite. The Henvis family was descended from Joran Kyn, which is pronounced *George Keen.* In 1664, the Swedish Crown patented to Kyn the territory upon which the colonial village of Chester, Pennsylvania, was located. There is a whole lot more about the family ancestry [in the family tree], but I skip the unnecessary bouquets. My father was born on 24 December 1832 at Chester, Pennsylvania, and named Benjamin Kite, the twelfth of thirteen children. When father came out to Iowa, his father gave him six hundred dollars, which was all he ever did get from him, or the estate, at Grandfather Wetherill's death.

It is said that every Tompkins or Tomkins in the world is descended from a family in County Sussex, England, until about three hundred years ago when a branch moved to County Essex, England. The name, which is believed to be Saxon, has many variations. A theory of the origin is that it signified the kin of Tom. The suffix "kin" is also a diminutive, so Tompkin, or Tomkin, may have once been "Little Tom." One of the first Tompkins in this country was Micah Tomkins who, with his wife Mary, came from England about 1639 and settled in Wethersfield, Connecticut. The women of the Tompkins family have possessed beauty, grace, and polished manners, if we may credit old records; nor is all this placed in the past. Nearly all have been well educated, some have possessed wealth, and the name has always been noted for musical ability. Mother's maternal ancestors were Canadians named West, while her father's ancestors were the New York Tompkins. Daniel D. Tompkins, who was Governor of New York, was also Vice-President of the United States from 1817–1825 when Monroe was President. The [Tompkins] family in Iowa were Quakers.

Later in the year of 1856, my mother and father moved to Leavenworth, Kansas, and then on to Diamond Island, about ten miles south of Leavenworth. Father had a saw mill and a grist mill there, both of which were pioneer-type products.

I guess I was born a few days after the Civil War was well on its way, 25 June 1861, the second from the top (brother Richard, born 12 June 1858, being the oldest). Father was not drafted, or else he bought off, for at that time it was allowable, if Quakers were drafted, to find a substitute if you could pay as much as three hundred dollars for one.

My rusty memories of Diamond Island are that it was a strip of land cut off from the main part of the Missouri River by a slough, deep and dark, while the Island (as it was called), was all overgrown with the most monstrous growth of cottonwood timber that nature ever produced. I remember it was said that the lumber from this timber would shrink and warp so much that within a short time it would work itself back into the forest from whence it came. Some of the logs brought in to the mill, I remember, were far over my head in diameter.

The men at the mill were always having fun at my expense to hear me come back at them. One sample was when they said they were going to throw me in the river and I told them, "Then I'll thwim down to Thaint Louith."

I remember, too, a rather ancient woman that I did not think much of would want to kiss me once in awhile. If she did, I would run to my mother and say, "Wipe it off! Wipe it off!"

Perhaps my sister, and brother John were born there. One of them was anyway, because I was present when a small square of cloth came into the room where I was and was weighed on some kitchen scales. The square contained one of the aforesaid children.[4]

Somehow I do not remember much about Richard in those days, perhaps because he might have been off with the men, thinking he was a man himself. In fact, I do not remember much about either Richard or John, or of sister Anna, because I was always snooping around by myself. I would come up missing at night and no one would recall seeing me for some time. But, they would look in my little nest and there I would be, sleeping soundly. That habit holds good even now.

One time a rabbit running across the yard looked like a round, furry ball to me. Of course I wanted it, so took chase as fast as my short legs would carry me. It was just a bit too speedy for me and I stumbled over a rock and, in some way, tore a fingernail all but off. I was not in the habit of making much of a fuss over such things, but I went to my mother and she just tied a rag around it. When it got well, I had one dickens of a nail on that finger. (I always kept it from sight—the middle finger, right hand.) We did not have lock-jaw or any such animals in those days and no doctors within ten miles of the mill.

Business must have been bad after the war, because the mill ceased to operate and back to Leavenworth we took our weary way. There was no railroad and we had no wagon, but the river was big and wide and steamboats were going up and down all the time. We had our household goods on board a pretty large boat and landed at the levee at the main part of Leavenworth. Those days the large business houses were in close to the landing place, which was a long, sloping place of rock, and here the drays met the boat. They were drawn by just one big powerful horse and the loads they could get away with would make most modern horses blush with shame. I do not remember any railroad at all and do not remember when it came in, but I do remember the large, twin-bottomed snag boats, sidewheel and sternwheel boats.

On the levee were great hogsheads of sugar, brown and almost juicy. The kids would be around them digging the sweet, sticky stuff out of the auger holes in the side of the hogsheads, holes that were probably put in to drain off any of the molasses [from the moistened sugar] that might ooze out.

Fort Leavenworth was just a couple of miles further up the river and a great part of their freight landed on the levee. Quantities of Northern and Western products were unloaded, as well as products going back to the West. I remember one big sign on one of the largest buildings near the levee, which read:

HIDES FURS BUFFALO ROBES LEATHER WOOL.

Father then had a grocery store, but I guess that he was not a success at it, or the customers did not have any money those days. After that he was probably a commission man, or a fruit buyer, since one winter took him up in Nebraska to buy apples.

For the time, we had a house that was already furnished. In one of the rooms there was a sort of a penny bank, but it seemed to me to be a rattle-box. I rattled it and it kept me busy for a spell. Then, when a penny (or maybe it was a nickel) dropped into my hand, I thought that I could make a rattle-box of my own. Anyway, when father came around and saw me so busy, he wanted to know what it was all about. When he saw the coins, he wanted to know where I got them, so I showed him the rattle-box. He just took the money and dropped it back into the bank and then and there I got the first and last spanking he ever gave to any of us. That must have been my first course in honesty, even if I was too small to see that side, but it was a lesson to leave other people's stuff alone. After that it seems to me that mother looked after the honesty part of childhood education.

Mother and father were strict Quakers and I suppose that I was toted along with them to Church (or Meetings, as it was called) until I could waddle along on my own legs. Meetings were held whenever the Spirit moved them or the day demanded it. At home, we had family prayers, Bible reading, and silent grace at the table.

We moved, after a time, to a house on a high bluff, south of the main part of town, [one that had] a large cistern near the back door. We were too high on the bluff to have a well, so we had to drink flat-tasting rainwater in lieu of good old Missouri River running mud. The cistern had a low curbing around it, and we could drop a bucket, attached to a rope, down into it and get water as wanted. One day, as mother was getting up water for washday, she left the cover open and Anna, looking into the depths, just took a header right down into the water. The water must have been fully seven feet or more deep. Mother came out the door in time to see Anna topple over and go down. She shrieked and father took a high dive down into the cistern while mother rushed out to the alleyway where some men were working. She could not talk, she was so scared, but motioned to them to come quickly. They came and let down the well rope and father anchored the small girl to it while he paddled around waiting for his turn.

He said afterward that he could not hold Anna up and stay up himself, so he had to hold her up to get a breath and then let her go under the water while he took his turn at getting air. He kept repeating the operation until the men pulled him out. I do not know if they rolled him over a barrel or not, but neither of them seemed to have been anywhere near drowned. Father lost his watch in the depths and it laid in there for a long time, but did not seem to be effected at all when he got it out.

When I was in my seventh or eighth year of age, and useful, a woman in the "higher-ups" said she would like to get a boy like me to help around the house and yard. So, I was loaned to her. If I had an hour's rest during the daylight hours, I do not remember anything about it. The worst was pumping water from the cistern to a tank in an upper-story room. When Sunday came around, I beat it home and no talk or arguments had any effect on me. I would not go back.

During the year 1870 (I remember that because I scratched the date in the frost on the windowpane), there were many complaints about the way the Indian Service was being handled and how a cleanup of the whole affair would be made if the entire business was turned over to the Quakers, or Friends, as they called themselves.

Out in South Leavenworth, where we lived, was a large frame Meeting House where all of us had to go on Sundays. There were plenty of others who were not Quakers who came, since it was the only church out that far from the center of the city. The yard around the building was quite large and trees were thickly scattered around. It was an ideal place, so cool and inviting on the hot summer days. Quaker boys, just like the other boys of the same ages, are good mixers and fit in with any other Sunday-school groups. But "boys will be boys." In Sunday school, the boys' class had a corner of the Meeting room and when spoken to, or spoken of, we were called "the boys in the scalawag corner."

But there must have been some little devil in our midst all the time. The leader of the class was larger and perhaps older than the rest of us and he always had ideas and schemes that kept us all busy. All of us had "bean shooters" and anything was a target for our company. One hot afternoon we were all sitting or lying around in the shade of the trees, when our chief told us that we could shoot shot through the windows of the church and it would not break the windows: it would just make a little round hole. We all tried out the scheme, with the result that our fathers had to pay five dollars each to replace the broken glass.

Another episode, not so funny, was that we dug a big hole (perhaps three feet deep and about eight feet by ten feet) and, after a big rain, it was full of muddy water. Of course we had to go swimming in it, but the fun did not last long, because mother spied us and here she came. All the boys flew for the barn, but I was left alone to face my fate, which was that I was marched up the street to the house, maybe one hundred fifty feet away, with no clothes on and muddy water dripping from me. I tried to wrap the skirt of mother's dress around me, but the neighbors laughed at me just the same.

The Quakers around Leavenworth and nearby cities thought it was time they had a centrally located Yearly Meeting House and father was chosen [among others] the go-getter-of-money to finance the proposition. He went back to Philadelphia, Pennsylvania, and rounded up all his kin, and any of the Quaker people who were so plentiful there, and soon all had the necessary funds to build the stone Meeting House at Lawrence, Kansas.[5] It was so substantial that it probably is still used to this day.

At Leavenworth I had, for a time, a rather old sort of woman teaching me. I must have done better under her teaching than I managed to do in later years. I remember the examination I had in which I spelled all the words but one in the speller I had. I do not remember having arithmetic; it must have been just learning to count or such like. She gave me a present, a book, and signed herself as "Sere Leaf" that would indicate that she was getting along in years.

In 1872 father became Trail Agent for the Osage Agency in Indian Territory [now part of Oklahoma], where I. T. Gibson was Agent at the time. His duties were to follow up reported depredations by the Indians against the whites or by the whites against the Indians.[6] All were at times what you would naturally expect them to be in a new country.

While father was gone on his Indian job, we were good-sized kids and settled down to big-kid thinking that was about guns, fishing poles, and such. One day, brother Richard and I were out in the barn and were examining a double-barrelled shotgun we had annexed to our belongings. We were seeing if we could let both hammers down at the same time. Richard did it alright, but I did not. The gun was not loaded (?) but both barrels went off. As it happened, only two or three shot went through Richard's hat, which was on his head at the time. I just dropped the gun and beat it. I did not want to associate with such a reckless sort of a machine.

And once Richard kicked me. We were going to the store for some stuff and I was to carry the basket, but set it down about halfway there. That was when he kicked me. Another time, Richard was going to ride the pony and I wanted to go along. He did not see it that way and started off. I shied a rock and caught him in the back of the head. He never told mother, or I would have been awful sore about it.

At that time, too, great herds of cattle were moving north-ward from Texas to shipping points on the railroads or to the wide-open ranges of northern Kansas or Montana, or 'most any-where on what was known as the Great American Desert. The buffalo were already being classified as "has beens." Still, there were miles and miles of grassland as far as the eye could see, just like an endless meadow where the howl of the coyote could be heard and the fleet-footed antelope and jack rabbit ranged without fear of an early death by, or at the hands of, trappers.

That was about the time of the Great Grasshopper Year, 1874. They came in from the west and the sky was darkened the same as a heavy raincloud would have done. Wave after wave of the 'hoppers arrived and landed in that portion of Kansas. They were said to have been blown over from the islands of the Pacific or Asia.

Every green thing was cleaned up until the ground was as barren of vegetation as in early spring. They left no leaves on trees, no corn in the fields, or garden patches of anything. The dead 'hoppers choked up the streams. Deep furrows were plowed around the fields to sort of check the travels of the things. I do not know how the farmers managed feed for their animals.

In the spring the 'hoppers started hatching out to make more damage. Then came to us thousands of small sparrow like birds that fed on the grasshoppers and were just Heaven-sent to clean up the evil. The sorry part was that hunters and any-one who could shoot a gun came out around the open spaces back of our home and shot the birds. If a hunter could not get more than a hundred birds at one shot he was not considered much. I am sorry to say that we were guilty, too, of shooting them. There was no law against such a deed.

The open range had been a solid mat of bluegrass that could be taken up in strips and used to replace barren spots and was what the early settlers further west used to make their sod houses of. The spring following the grasshoppers, no bluegrass could be found, and so the bluegrass days were over forever. A small, curly, buffalo grass took its place.

Two narrow escapes I had still come up in my mind. Both were in the wintertime. There were a number of houses around us on the bluff and right at the edge of the cliff, a high board fence had been built around the last one. There was about an eighteen-inch space left, so that the fence would not topple over onto the rocks below. That narrow strip in the summertime was alright for us to sidle along and, by doing so, we would save some distance in getting home from town.

In the winter, it was a different proposition, for the ice and snow formed on that narrow strip and it was best for us to keep off. I was rather a smart-guy and would tackle the impossible if it happened to come my way. This one came near to being my last impossible. Brother Richard took himself home around the long way, but for me that was "nothing doing." I started bravely (or foolishly) along the icy trail until I was about half the distance across. There the trail sloped a little downward and was a little more icy. It was impossible to turn around and go back. I believe I was actually scared stiff. Maybe I thought of the little prayer mother had taught me. I felt some braver and inched along and finally landed beyond the scarey place, but I do not think I said, "Thank You," to the power that helped me.

The other time, I wanted to go over to the Missouri side of the river to see how the place where we went in the summertime looked in the winter. I could have crossed on the bridge, for I had the nickel, but the ice was so thick and heavy along the shore, that I had no idea it would be any different out in the middle of the river. We sort of live and learn by experience, if we survive the various attempts. Soon after starting out on the ice, the water seemed (or really was getting) wiggly, and would sink some under my feet. I did not think of turning back, thinking it would soon be better. But it really got much worse and I thought again of my little prayer and forgot to be scared. Soon the ice seemed to be harder and the water had all left.

When I got to the other shore, I did not even go to see how things looked where we went in the summertime. The bridge looked good to me and I used it to get back on the home side of the river.

I never was very good as a swearer and even yet do not have much faith in such a course. I never was much of a scrapper, either, but neither was I much afraid. Two boys met me one time just at the bottom of the hill in plain sight of the calaboose and one of them wanted to fight. The sight of that hoosegow looked too close, so I beat it. The kids caught me, still in sight of the jail, and jumped on me. I bit, scratched, and kicked my way out and beat it again. They did not follow and I was not bothered any more.

NOTES

1. In preparing his material, Al had noted that the definition of *pioneer* as found in their dictionary and encyclopedia was a "military laborer employed to form roads, dig trenches and make bridges, and so forth, as the army advances and to preserve cleanliness in camp when the army halts." This did not correlate with the popular use of the word *pioneer*, but he evidently decided there was no other word to use.

2. There has always been some confusion in the Wetherill family about the place of marriage. Al uses the location of Clear Lake, Cerro Gordo County, Iowa, but the family roster of the eastern Wetherill clan states that it was the first wedding in Iowa Falls, Harden County, Iowa.

3. The Wetherill genealogy correspondence was dated during the 1930s thus making it certain that the family history was written last.

4. Anna Wetherill was born 24 January 1865 at Diamond Island, Kansas, and John on 24 September 1866 in Leavenworth, Kansas.

5. At a meeting of the committee of the various Quarterly Meetings in Kansas on the 4th of 1st Month, 1871, Benjamin Kite Wetherill was appointed Clerk of a committee to consider the construction of a Yearly Meeting House in Lawrence, Kansas. On the 5th, 1st Month, Benjamin Kite Wetherill and William G. Coffin were appointed, among others appointed to other Quaker groups in the U.S.A., Canada, Britain, and Ireland, to attend the Philadelphia Yearly Meeting and to bring to the Society of Friends the matter, including the contribution expected. The 10th Month, 1873 concluded the activities of the committee that reported receipts, subscriptions, and donations of $29,593.37, of which Philadelphia Friends contributed $2,887.72. After deducting the costs of the House and improvements, the payment on the lot, miscellaneous, and interest, the Balance on Hand amounted to $175.91 (Minutes of the Meetings of the Religious Society of Friends to consider a Yearly Meeting House at Lawrence, Kansas, 1st Month 1871 to 10th Month 1873. From Anna Wetherill Mason memorabilia).

6. Al did not develop his notes sufficiently to determine just how the Quakers became involved in Indian affairs. Aubrey L. Steele gives a history of the events in, "The Beginning of Quaker Administration of Indian Affairs in Oklahoma," *The Chronicles of Oklahoma* 17, no. 4 (December 1939). Following agitation among the Southwestern Indians after the Civil War, sympathy for the Indian aroused the interest of several organizations, among them the Society of Friends. The Society (whose interest in the Indian had begun with George Fox in 1672) noted that, at their 1867 conference, the care and civilization of the Indians should be given to them, citing as reference the William Penn treaties, their conduct between the Seneca Indians and the U.S. government, and offered their services in behalf of the Indian. The Yearly Meeting of the Friends of Iowa that same year appointed a "Committee on Indian Concerns." In 1869 the Friends gained the support of Ulysses S. Grant who, when elected President, awarded control of part of the Indian tribes to the Quakers. The Kansas and Indian Territory Indians (except the Five Civilized tribes) were placed in the hands of the Orthodox Friends in Iowa. B. K. Wetherill, no doubt in good standing with the Iowa and Kansas Quakers, became a prime candidate for appointment to aid the Indian tribes.

2

Joplin and Atchison

THE newly discovered rich bodies of lead and zinc in south-west Missouri beckoned to father and, in 1876, he left the Indian Department. He traded a horse he had for a mining claim and a considerable amount of undeveloped land out north-west of the new mining town of Joplin, Missouri. The unde-veloped land could not be worked because of the water that could not be kept down with such prehistoric methods as whips for horsepower and tubs for manpower. There might have been pumping equipment available, but it was out of his reach finan-cially.

Finally, he sent to Leavenworth for the rest of us, which by then consisted of mother, five boys, and one girl.[1]

The railroad came only as far as Baxter Springs, Kansas, and the balance of the trip was by the wagon route. It was a couple of years before the railroad was built into Joplin. When it did, the natives came from miles around to see what it was all about.

There was no water fit to drink in the town on account of the minerals so near the surface. A man by the name of Mason had a spring out east of town a few miles and hauled water into Joplin and delivered it to people for 10¢ a barrel. Everyone had a barrel handy to be filled. Later, when the railroad came in, his business was done for, so he picked up his family and went west.

Teams came in from out in the hills around Joplin hauling wood, or hickory-hoop poles, or whatever was raised near there. Numbers of strangely matched teams could be seen almost any day on the streets and one in particular was a donkey and a cow. I think their load, which was not very big, consisted of apples, peaches, and maybe hog and hominy.

We got along fairly well for a time, but the mine was about worked out when father got it and we could not afford to go down after the deeper veins. Then, it was slow sledding for us. The bunch of us six kids were not an asset, by any means.

Brother Richard and myself scouted around town picking berries or sawing wood (no coal in Joplin then), cutting ice in winter, and picking stray pieces of ore out of old dumps or sluice boxes and selling it to the smelters. The prices were low, but it helped out in the commissary department.

Then Richard got a job in a machine shop and I went to school until I went to work at the machine shop, too. In the machine shop, the men were always up to some scheme to get a joke on any of the other shops. Across the way was a foundry and a man from there came over to our shop about every day. The boys in our shop told me to heat a pair of tongs and hang them around my neck. I did just that and was waiting for him as innocently as a yearling the next time he came over.

When he spied me standing near the forge with the tongs around my neck, he casually walked over my way and grabbed the ends of the tongs and was going to squeeze them tight around my neck. Did he ever let go of them! And did the boys let out a yell! I am sure he would have landed all over me if the boys had not been there to back me up. I was some scared, but nothing ever happened—except the blisters on his hands.

Finances began running low and father took a position in the white-lead works. The smoke from the smelters goes through a series of long, cotton bags suspended from overhead beams. As it cools, the fine blue dust settles and is then taken out in bins at the bottom of the bags. The blue dust is then burned in a sort of an oven, losing the blue coloring and leaving the finest grade of white lead. The men at the works had to go through the rooms where the bags (from one to three hundred of them, each twelve to fifteen feet long) were hanging and give each one a shake to loosen the powdered lead inside. At the same time, of course, the men breathed the fumes of sulphur. Smoky dust was everywhere. Some of the men wore heavy sponge masks, but they were of little use against the dust and fumes.

During the time we were there [Joplin], I got my first call to do cooking, the reason being that one of our friends and a pretty close neighbor had been drinking too much of that rotten water. All running water of the streams was saturated with iron and nearly every other mineral you could name. Even if the water did not have it naturally, it was acquired when the lead was washed to free it from rock and dirt before being sent to the smelters, and all the dirty water from the washing let back into the creeks.

I happened to be the one who was called on to help out, and I do not believe I even knew how to build a decent fire. But, that made no difference, because the man could talk and tell me what he wanted and how to fix it. I started with biscuits. He told me to take just so much flour, so much salt, milk enough to make a thick dough, and last, the stuff he used to make them puff up: bicarbonate of potash, or saleratus. Too much made the biscuits a beautiful golden color and even more made them a yellowish green. I got the stuff mixed and cooked and you can just imagine what the results were. But, after awhile, I got there and was a good cook.

It was always sunshine to us while in Joplin, for we had games of ball, marbles, and tops; nut gathering and hunting; skating in winter, and fishing and swimming in summer.

One time, two families of us went out to Shoal Creek, about ten miles south of town, for a joy ride and a general swim. We had all day for it and had a swell dinner in the hills. We rested up a bit and then all prepared to either paddle around in the shallow water or to go in for a sure-enough swim in the deeper parts below the falls.

There were a couple of young ladies there, along with their boyfriends. The boys in our bunch had on Nature's bathing suits and we were supposed to stay in the deep water and let the rest of the gang do the paddling around near the shore. For some reason, I came rather close to the bank just as one of the young girls made a slip and went over backwards in the shallow water. Her hands could touch the bottom of the creek bed, yet still leave her nose and mouth high enough above the water [for her] to get her breath and shriek for help.

"Oh, Walter, Walter. Help! Help!" she yelped. But Walter was too busy to help her, since he was trying to keep his lady love from fainting. I happened to be nearer her than anyone else, so rushed forward, splashing the water high in every direction. I rescued her from her perilous position, but that bunch howled, then and later, every time I showed up with any member of the party. It was even in the paper, but no names were given. Ever after that, I would manage to dig up a pair of overalls to go swimming in, but never again had I occasion to rescue a maiden in distress.

After about two years at the white-lead works, father caught up a case of lead poisoning from the gassy fumes of the works. So, in 1879, he just had to get out and leave that part of the country. There was another man with a family who had to leave the district for the same reason, so they put their heads together and decided to go to the mines in southwest Colorado. The sunny skies and the possibilities of the Silver San Juan beckoned to them. This friend had some sort of kinfolk thereabouts who would look out after him and his family. It did not take the men long to get ready for the trip—the other man had a good team and father had a saddle horse. Father said later that they had a glorious trip across the alleged desert and were not molested by Indians or wild animals, although they were a full month making the trip. From the start, they acquired health and fat.

Rico, Colorado, was their destination, since that was the center of the silver-mining operations, but the other family decided to go on to a relative's place on the San Juan River near the Utah line, the only place in the United States where four states meet. Red Mountain, Silverton, Telluride, Ouray, and Rico were the roaring mining camps then. Telluride was the main attraction, but the mines were all too high up and not very conducive to long life and prosperity.

Father met up with an Old Timer by the name of Clements and they entered into a partnership that worked out finely. Father ran an engine at one of the mines and Clements did the prospecting that first summer.

There were no Quakers in the mining camps that father ever heard of, except for one old man and he did not advertise himself. (After I arrived in Colorado, this old man was fairly near us and I used to go over once in a while and cook him a mess and make coffee, since I think I am an expert at such industries.)

While father went on to Colorado, we were located at Atchison, [Kansas]. Mother's brother, Uncle Caleb Tompkins, had lost his wife a short time before and that left him with four small children on his hands, or mind, or both. He wrote us to come on to Atchison and get into railroad work. He was a railroad man and got us passes, so we shook the lead dust from our shoes and [coughed] the smoke of Joplin from our lungs, and moved to Atchison.

We were a welcome bunch when we arrived there by train from Joplin, even if we did make ten head of children in the gang, ranging from around twenty years of age down to squalling brats and yearlings. Brother Clayton was carried all the way to Atchison on a pillow—just a handful of humanity—but he soon snapped out of it and became quite a husky lad.

"Of all sad words of tongue or pen, the saddest of these 'it might have been.' " There are more regrets expressed and more tears shed over lost opportunities than for any other single cause the human race is heir to. At the machine shop in Joplin we [Richard and Al] were in a position to step right up the line and become master mechanics or better, for there was every class of mechanical work required of employees as soon as they were capable of handling it. To proceed, opportunity number one was lost when Richard and I left Joplin and the machine shops.

As soon as we arrived in Atchison, Richard and I went to work in the freight house at the railroad. There was no railroad bridge across the Missouri River at the time, so freight was taken across by teams and transfer wagons.

In the winter, out in Colorado, Clements and father came down out of the snowy heights to the more desirable climate of the Mancos Valley. Clements had a piece of farm land with a little cabin on it on the Mancos River. They spent the balance of the season there in comparative comfort until the "back to the soil" epidemic struck them in the spring [of 1880]. They decided that one of them would do the farming act and the other go back to the mines. It was my father who stayed behind on the rented farm and, in the meantime, filed on one hundred sixty acres on the opposite side of the river.[2] Within a short time, Father wrote for Richard and so he left us to go help father.

Soon after Richard left, I was put on carwork as an inspector and all I had to do was just look forward for an advance in work and an increase in pay. We (that is, the rest of the family and myself) got along fairly well on what salary I was getting. The youngsters were all going to school and there were not any children's quarrels. The grown-ups did not do quite so well, so we finally moved out and then everything was lovely.

When spring came along again [1881], father thought he and Richard needed the family out in Colorado.

But I was left behind. It was a sorry day for me and I still do not know why unless it was for a little ready cash to be used between seasons. But, when we left Atchison, that was our second lost opportunity to reach "Easy Street."

Two of the cousins went with mother and the rest of the family, the youngest of the children being about seven. It was easy for a railroad employee to get passes anywhere at any time, so, the expense of getting them all out to the end of the line was just a matter of packing up the duds and picking out the train.

The railroad extended only as far as Alamosa, Colorado, and that left three hundred miles to be trekked via the wagon route. (They probably went to Pueblo first and transferred to the Denver and Rio Grande [Railroad] line to go on to Alamosa.) The trip was a near-heavenly journey for the kids and they had to be corralled at night to keep them from wandering out of the camp grounds when they should have been sleeping. The children were always wide awake to the new and strange surroundings that were met up with and passed each day. The wonderful clear skies at night showed the stars so much closer than they had ever been seen from the thick atmosphere of the Missouri bottomlands.

Father's long trek to Alamosa and back set the agricultural deal a hard blow for awhile. The main part of the ranch had been a gravel-bar, roundup ground for cattle before it was taken up and was piled high with loose cobblestones. But, farming was ace-high if anyone had the nerve to admit he was a nester, as farmers were called, or classed, by the miners and stockmen.

It was months later that I was sent for and had the advantage or disadvantage of coming through on the train, arriving on a cushioned seat. The railroad had been rushing their lines on to southwestern Colorado from Alamosa to get the great quantities of ore being produced in that district. The line to Animas City was completed by the time I arrived and the railroad was rushing to get in a line up the Animas River Valley to Silverton.[3]

Animas City was the original city on the Animas River, but Durango was the terminal of the railroad. The City had no chance at all and was soon absorbed into the friendly circle of Durango's growing fold. Durango had an abundance of coal and sites for smelters and mills. Miners were coming in from everywhere to be in on the ground floor of the Silver San Juan. Speculators, farmers, businessmen, and sightseers were oozing in out of the pioneer stage with the settlers. Great herds of cattle were driven in and were spread out over the grassy ranges for miles in all directions.

And, over the mountains to the west, everything was looking up for the Wetherills. Mancos is about thirty-five miles almost due west of Durango and it was just a day's horseback ride for me to reach the ranch. Another day's ride on to the southwest would put me where the four states corner.

NOTES

1. The children were Richard, Alfred (or Al), Anna, John, Clayton (or Clayt), and Winslow (or Win), in that order. Another child, a girl named Alice, was born sometime before the family moved to southwestern Colorado, but died before she was two-years old.

2. The location was on the east side of the Mancos River about two miles below the present town of Mancos, Colorado. The origin of the name puzzled F. H. Chapin (*The Land of the Cliff Dwellers* [Boston: W. B. Clarke & Co., 1892], p. 97) as well as others. In *A History of Montezuma County* (Boulder, Colorado: Johnson Publishing Co., 1958, p. 26), Ira S. Freeman states that the name came about as the result of an accident that crippled a member of the Spanish exploring party of Juan María de Rivera during camp near the confluence of the three forks of a stream they named "Mancos" as a result. Bolton, however, states that Rivera's report of the trek has never been located, although its contents have been referred to by later traders and trappers along the same route (*Pageant In The Wilderness*, [Salt Lake City: Utah Historical Society, 1951, 1972], p. 6). Escalante's diary records (p. 140) that they camped on the Rio de San Lázaro, also called the Rio de los Mancos. Bolton translates the term as meaning *skeletons with hands cut off* or *Indians with hands cut off* that had been seen or heard of in the vicinity, but concedes that he might be making a bad guess (p. 27). At any rate, near the old Spanish campsite, the American settlement on the Mancos River was named *Mancos*.

3. The Denver and Rio Grande Railroad completed its lines to a point just

south of Animas City, Colorado, in July of 1881, according to Robert W. Delaney, "This Is the Four Corners," (*Durango Herald* annual *Four Corners Magazine*, Durango, Colorado, 1964, p. f) . Al could not have arrived earlier than that date and in all probability did not arrive until some time in the fall.

THE ALAMO RANCH ON THE MANCOS

Where the snowy peaks reach upward to the skies
And cañons cut the world in two,
Each glen and nook is filled with flower fragrance
In night clouds of purple hue.

Below the slopes with the towering pines,
We love the thought that surrounds us here,
With the breath of Heaven on the evening breeze
We've the blessings of God and nought to fear.

Benjamin Alfred Wetherill

3

The Alamo Ranch
on the Mancos

FROM the time the family arrived at the ranch, it was a case
of work from daylight until dark, day after day, but nobody
seemed to get tired. I suppose the atmosphere at the high alti-
tudes had an exhilarating effect on everyone. We all took to the
pioneer life [as if] it had been born in us, and, aside from working times, there was hunting, fishing, and exploring "places
where the hand of man had never set his foot."

I was twenty years old when I arrived at the ranch and had
in my possession an army Springfield rifle .45–70, so I was capably equipped to meet all comers, man or beast.[1] (I did not have
a name for it early in the game, but I do remember one Winchester [that] we called *Sure-git-'em*. It was a real hummer and
got mad if we failed to get what we shot at.) The first day on
the ranch I was parading around, trying to look the perfect Wild
West to trees or bushes that might cross my path and to my
brothers. In starting across a field, we saw a large sandhill crane

50

standing on the opposite side with his head up watching us. I kneeled down and pointed the gun in his direction and pulled the trigger. The crane lost its head then and there, and, even if it was an accident, no one knew but myself. The distance was at

Benjamin Alfred Wetherill
Al had this photograph made of himself in Topeka, Kansas, at the Leonard Studio on one of the occasions he "escaped" from the ranch during the winter months while looking for the opportunity to make his fortune elsewhere. "During the winters we sometimes would fall into a serious case of the blues for the reason that often we were snowed in and did not even get mail. . . . When such times occurred, we would have feelings like the little birds have before they begin drifting south," he explained.

least a couple of hundred yards and, at that range, it could not have been done again in a hundred, or even a thousand, shots. The bird might have thought he heard a bug coming and opened his mouth to catch it. Just the same, my reputation was established as an unusually good shot.

We were living in the partner's one-room cabin (with dirt floor and roof) and large, round tents known as *Sibley tents*—about eight feet in diameter and about the same in height. They looked like Ute wickiups. For heat, we had a little circular sheet-iron stove that had to be fed frequently with chips or little sticks and it was fairly comfortable [inside the tents] if you had enough blankets or sheepskins to roll up in.

We had to get busy and get logs enough for our own house before winter came along and caught us getting up mornings out of a snowbank. Richard and I went up in the pines to get out house logs for the ranch house.[2] We took plenty of meat (venison), some salt-side bacon, tallow for grease, spuds, some flour, and maybe corn meal (there was a flour mill over on the Animas River). Perhaps we had sugar, but it was the light brown kind.

The pines were easy to cut and all the proper size. They seemed to have grown for the sole purpose of being made into a cabin for the people who were the first to occupy the land. Whenever I think of the thousands of acres of heavy, monstrous pines where men had never set foot except to cut out a trail, I just blow up. Deer and wild turkey were all along the edges of the cañons and no mining—nothing to mar the beauty Nature had left.

While at work with the logs, a heavy snowstorm came up. In the morning we scraped away the snow from in front of our sleeping quarters and, while we were getting our breakfast, a fine large deer came up out of the cañon near by and stood looking at us, scarcely seventy-five yards away. He was broadside to us and taller than a yearling calf. Here was meat for us if—so I promptly started firing away at him. I shot away six to a dozen cartridges and the deer started on about his business, never having been touched. (I found out that no matter how big or how close the object might be, I could not fill the air full enough of lead to bring in the meat.) I followed his tracks for a time and gave him up and started back to camp, for he had vanished into thin air.

Apparently something was amiss, for I soon thought someone

else was in the woods. I did, that is, until I had made two circles of tracks and decided that I had made them and that I was turned around. It did not make any difference which way was north, south, east, or west, and when the sun showed up, it was in the wrong place. The moss run all the way around the trunks of the trees. The timber was so thick the mountains were not to be seen and, anyway, they would have been in the wrong place, too. I continued on around the circle until I came to the place where I had started to make pinwheels and took my back track. They did not seem headed right, but there were no others. I did know enough to hang close to my back track. In the course of hours, the camp showed up, much to my surprise and wonder. Was it dog instinct [that brought me back to camp] or was I born to hang?

We never told what poor marksmen we were, for my brother did some shooting, too, with the same results I had. We lost our reputations as hunters between ourselves.

Father, Richard, and myself proceeded forthwith to cut and put up the pine logs for a two-room house. Each room was sixteen feet by sixteen feet inside. Between them, there was a roofed-over open space twelve feet by sixteen feet that was to be closed up later.[3] The name of lumber and shingles for the roof was out of the question, so we used dirt. The floor was dirt, too, for a long time.

We made a big fireplace in the west side of the house, made pine blocks for chairs, and the biggest kids still slept in the army tents, or else we all tried to sleep under the center ridgepoles of the roof to keep from getting wet when it rained. Clothes and bedding were kept in boxes. The house was kitchen, dining room, sitting room, and general workshop in the wintertime. On the fireplace mother cooked us many a feed of venison, trout, wild duck, or turkey and we had wild fruit sauce to go with the meal. Cooking could be done out of doors and the Dutch oven was the main standby for cooking bread, meat, and vegetables, or come-after of any sort. Mostly, the come-after [dessert] was some sort of dried fruit.

Then came the making of the ranch out of the river-washed gravel and cobblestone bar. Oh the cobblestones we did haul! Thousands of loads were hauled by the whole bunch of kids, big and little.[4] What a world of work for all of us, with the boys under father's guidance and with mother, sister Anna, and cousin Ida keeping us all fed, clothed, patched, and clean. They also

Anna, the Keeper of the Hearth
"Sister Anna, along with mother and cousin Ida, did their part
[toward making the ranch a success] by keeping us fed, clothed,
patched, and clean, as well as looking after the milk and chickens,"
Al recorded. Anna had another goal. She had determined in Joplin,
Missouri, that one day she would be grown up to twenty years of age
and would then marry Charles Mason. On cue, Charles showed up at
Mancos and worked for other residents there before marrying Anna
a month before she was twenty-one.

looked after the milk and the chickens, but the boys did the milking and looked after the stock. All the time, too, the younger children did their part.

The garden and flowers were under mother's supervision. The smaller children saved mother many a step, although she could not have made many more than she did, unless she was going at a run all the time. They went down to the river and dug up cottonwood trees not much larger than sumac bushes and set them out on each side of the irrigating ditch that ran in front of the house for a distance of about one hundred feet. It was those very trees that gave the place its name: Alamo Ranch, meaning Cottonwood Ranch.

View in the Yard at Alamo
Benjamin Kite Wetherill and Julia Cowing are seated, while Anna Wetherill Mason stands, in the shade of the cottonwoods in front of the house that grew from the log cabin (right) into the rambling ranch house of 1893.

And the sagebrush we did grub out! But, after it was cleared, how the alfalfa, timothy, wheat, oats, and potatoes did grow with irrigation. The rock pile produced five to six tons of alfalfa to the acre and, at the lower end of the meadow, the timothy grew higher than a horse's back. The Valley of the Nile was never better nor more productive than this land redeemed by irrigation.

Always, the irrigation ditches had to be cleaned out and, as our crops increased, to be extended. Rails had to be cut, fencing had to be done and always there were those cobblestones to be hauled off [as more fields were added].

Between stretches of work building fences and digging ditches for irrigating, we ranged around the valleys and over the fields to fish for the beautiful trout. Deer were everywhere, even coming into the fields at nighttime to sample our grain or the sweet-smelling alfalfa.

We could have had Thanksgiving every day if we had cared to look up and shoot the grouse and turkeys. They certainly were fat in the fall of the year from feeding on piñon nuts. Piñon nuts were good after the first frost, for the cones then opened up and the nuts fell to the ground.

The piñon nuts were also the bears' favorite diet; they would gulp them down, dirt and all. We knew that bear were thick in the high places just a few miles from where we lived and that they kept the stock scared stiff all the time. But sometimes they could be had for the taking and we managed to take one once in awhile. Most frequently, they were met up with along the side fence nearest to the chunk of the Mesa Verde [that was] cut off by the Mancos River. Fortunately, they were usually on the run when we met up with them, or else the bear might have done the taking bit.

The first bear we ran across was on a very dark night when no moon was visible. They had come down to the lowlands in search of a change of diet, which in this case was a recently deceased horse. A bear trap was set there to see how they would take it. One took it all right, but fooled us to a certain extent, for when the bellowing began we thought one of our calves had been caught in the trap.

We always had a gun or two for emergencies and took them along when three or four of us went to release the poor calf, since a bear trap is no child's play to either set or unset. When we got near enough, we could hear the sniffs and grunts and could barely see three or four bear. One was in the trap and was making all the racket. Not fifty feet from the bear, we all opened fire at what we saw moving. The bears all took to the hills except the one in the trap. We tried to trail the others, but could not. Anyway, we got enough grease out of the one in the trap to grease our saddles.

While I talk of bear grease, we killed a pretty good-sized fellow out in Arizona country one time and were going to have some nice grease for table use and harness and saddle grease, too. We put a large can of fat out into a tree to render it out and got it down in a few days and brought it to the house to filter out the dirt. As it worked out, it was the rankest smelling stuff that ever met up with our smelling apparatus. The reason was that the bear had just recently come out of winter quarters and [was] too poor to provide fat.

There were many [mountain] lions, too, and one time when we killed a beef and hung it up in a tree to cool overnight, we found it pretty well chewed up the next day. The balance had been covered over with dirt and leaves, probably for the lion's next meal. We did not even get the lion's scalp, which was worth ten dollars at the County Clerk's office. Such prowlers as lions were a terror to young stock, especially horses and colts. Burros were the most terrified of them, though.

We could always find wild berries in the hills in season, but the pick of them all was the so-called buffalo berries that grew on small trees along the streams. The Indians would put a blanket under the trees, give the trees a shake, and down came the berries. In some places they were scarlet red and at other places yellow. Wild currants were also a gift from the gods and there were no berries to be had that were better. Lots of raspberries grew along the streams, also just delicious.

Through all of it, I do not remember even one word of complaint from mother and, always, there was encouragement for our few dark days. It took real pioneers to keep in good humor all the time, regardless of inconveniences and discomforts. With the eight of us we seldom, if ever, had a dull or gloomy day. Mother used to tell us one story that was handed down for ages:

A young man went to see his girl (or so he thought) and she set out milk and mush. Just then her favorite suitor dropped in, so she rushed around, put those refreshments out of sight, and stirred up some dough and made tea. When they sat down, she even had the best dishes out. The first young man was told to ask the blessing, so this is what he said, "Oh, Lord, I am amazed to see how things have ended. Shortcake and tea for supper when milk and mush was intended."

This one of father's is just as old:

A young woman was asked to go to a dance but refused because "when I dance, I sweats, and when I sweats, I stinks."[5]

Horsebreaking, or rather kid-breaking, was one of the requirements of early ranch life and my first attempt at that came soon after my arrival. The horsebreaking fell to me for the time being, because I had ridden quite a bit when in the papoose age 'way back in Kansas.

We had a fine young horse, perfectly gentle to handle, but had never been put to use yet, since we did not wish to stunt his growth. Finally, we felt it was about time we were getting some use out of the beast. Just below the house, on a piece of bottomland, was an ideal place to break him. We had an old government saddle (a muley, or henskin, as such a saddle was called), and this we put on him and tightened it up. He seemed to wonder what it was all about, but let me get up in the saddle all right. Then the fun was on for him. With just one big grunt and one big jump, I was left alone in the air. Although I had grabbed for his mane, it was just a bunch of grass that I held in my hand when I came down.

We tried to save a horse and colt once. The horse was caught in barbwire in the river during high water. We cut her leg off to get her out and made a sling, but she struggled so hard she died anyway. We kept her colt because he was pretty, but he was no good as a cow horse because he was always afraid of ropes.

I speak of work, happiness, and peace, but that passes when I mention Indians. All this section of Colorado was occupied by the Southern Ute Indians. They were the ruling power of the San Juan [River] drainage. The reservation reached from where the four states corner north along the Colorado-Utah line for fifteen miles, then east for one hundred, all lying within the state of Colorado. All the time, Southern Utes and Uinta Utes were traveling back and forth through our area. There were also Pah Utes, or Pi-Utes, as they were called. Originally, all were from eastern Colorado.

The Utes held the mountains as their own personal property, but they did not dare to be found out on the plains or they would be going home without their scalp-locks. Still, they did have to go out on the plains for buffalo. The Cheyennes paraded close to the mountains to get a few horses or scalps. Both tribes finally met up with Uncle Sam's real fighters and were put on reservations. A soldier, probably long since dead, told me that when the soldiers went after the Indians following the Civil War, they made a clean-up because the chief had told his gang that it was not possible to get soldiers who could make seventy miles a day. Chief Ouray must have been bought off, for, in the 1880s, he was considered the only chief who was favorable to the whites; but even then there were occasions to call out the troops.

The Pah Utes were mostly renegades from Utah, and northern and southern Colorado, and I think that a goodly portion of them were quiet and well behaved, especially as the days of rations and money came around. The Utes were getting annuities and so were equipped with all the latest firearms and ammunition. At a Ute camp, I once saw more than a bushelfull of cartridges for all calibre guns. They were extravagant buyers and could not keep money. At hungry times between paydays, they would hock the cartridges and the guns, as well as everything they possessed. And, even then, they would ask for a stand-off. One time I took out more than two candy pails full of silver dollars to them. On the way out, in crossing over a divide long after dark, I heard a rustling in the brush. My hair stood straight up, but when the brush gave way, it was just a bunch of range horses crossing over.

Along about this time, Durango was besieged by Ute Indians located on the hills surrounding the newly made railroad town.

It was the Northern Utes who were responsible for the Meeker Massacre. But all this is history that can be looked up. It is just our immediate locality that I know about—incidents that did not make the history books.

Occasionally the early settlers had to hide out in the sagebrush and piñons on the Mancos River. Most had heavy log walls on the houses and around the schoolhouse—about two-and-a-half miles up the river toward the mountains—a twelve-to fourteen-foot stockade had been built. The schoolhouse was one of the first cabins built and it was to be used as a port of refuge if necessary. The children were taken to school by adults for a long time. (In the course of time, there was a school district made a short distance down the river from the ranch, but school was for only a few months, anyway.)

The people in the valley were always looking out for trouble and bunching up in some strongly built house. Among these was the Morefield house. Their claim was on a point of land about a hundred feet above the river, where the Mancos Valley begins to close up. On the opposite side of the ranch was a dry wash, ordinarily, but when it rained, it took on the name of Mud Creek. The ranch house was on the edge of the mesa looking down the [Mancos] river into the Mancos Cañon. It was a beautiful view from there, looking up and down the valley, with the high mountains off to the northeast, and with peaks and timbered mesas on all the other sides. Anyway, the Indians got a number of settlers cooped up there and the settlers became short on water.

It was all a man's life was worth to try to get to the spring, which was not over seventy-five feet from the door of the house and down on the side of the riverbank. The Indians were just out of sight, but in daylight the gun barrels could be seen occasionally above the bushes. The folks were the unafraid sort, but they were on the lookout just the same, for no telling how many Indians were waiting to even up grievances of the past.

Finally, Mrs. Morefield said, "They'll hardly shoot a woman." So, she took a pail and walked boldly out and down to the spring and soon was safely back again. She could hear the Indians moving around and could see faces peering at her through the bushes. Help came down soon after and the siege was over.

This all seems weak in trying to tell it, but it was quite a different proposition at the time.

At a ranch in Montezuma Valley, north of the Mesa Verde, the Indians killed a rancher and burned the building, but his wife escaped in the dark. Next, we heard that seven Utes were found dead in one camp over on the Dolores [River] (or perhaps it was in Lost Cañon, which runs into the Dolores near the bend). No one ever knew for sure what happened. And then we heard that one of the chiefs of the Utes, Red Jacket or Colorow, was going to wreak his vengeance on the Mancos population.

That never happened, because, somehow, word got out that the Utes were on their way on a certain night. Knowing the regular trail ran along the west side of the valley, there were perhaps a dozen or more men posted on Mud Creek where they could do the most good. While they were getting located properly, one of the men decided his family at home should be looked after, so he quit the more hard-hearted bunch and beat it back to town.

Chief Colorow of the Pyutes (Wetherill caption):
"Taken at the Alamo Ranch about 1890" is written on the back of
the original print. Reluctant to have his picture taken without just
compensation, the price for posing was set by the exchange of a sack
of flour. One of the Wetherills' closest friends, he was taken aback
when accosted by Mary Tarrant Wetherill in later years and forced
to dismount his horse in order to let his wife ride, for she was walking
behind carrying a burden. From their other encounters, he never did
understand Mary and her ways.

In a short time, the Indians could be seen coming along the old trail and one of the Mancos men got so excited that he let his gun go off. That was the last of that hostile bunch. The way those natives beat it for Point Lookout was a caution! There were no casualties to report on either side and all were thankful to get off with whole skins for the time being.

To be sure, we had cattle killed and horses stolen, but who did not? We had cattle; the Utes had cattle; we both ran them in the cañons and on top of the Mesa Verde. Perhaps we ate Indian beef and we knew they ate ours. The worst I ever knew, though, was when I was riding along a ridge and found where a steer had been killed and only his tongue taken out. But, when the Utes told us to keep out of a certain branch cañon in the Mesa Verde, we always did what they told us to do and asked no questions. They would help us work over the rough part of the high range and, as a result, many of them would come in at the home ranch at any time and be perfectly at home. We would make their camping places just the same as ours, as though they were part owners in everything, and it worked out fine.

Staying on the good side of the Utes did not require much effort, since we had lots of wheat for flour, plenty of beef, and pasture. Indians were expensive friends, but it was a good policy. And too, perhaps it was because of our father's years among the Indian Territory tribes that we got along with them. We maintained a friendly attitude and accepted friendship in return.

Actually, Ute boys were scarce—kept at the Agency school, I suppose. Ordinarily, it was the young married folk who worked in our supplies and pasturage, but that was all right, since we ran our cattle on their reservation. The old timers, Ignacio, Mariano, Red Jacket, Colorow, and occasionally Mancos Jim (a renegade Ute, or Pah Ute, just as it happened to suit him) never failed to be around when beef and money were being handed out.

One of our first holdups by an Indian was when we were bringing a bunch of cattle across country from Farmington [New Mexico] to the Alamo. We had managed to get over the most of the mesa country when an Indian rode up and wanted us to turn back and not go that way.

"My grass, my water; you pay," he said. Father happened to have a fifty-cent piece in his pocket, so he handed it out to the Ute and we were all right. (I met that same varmint years after

The Camp

The log cabin reportedly built and used by the Wetherills while wintering cattle down the Mancos Cañon was actually only a cluster of wickiups. The arrangement was probably intentional to establish rapport with the Ute Indians, for Al wrote that "we would make their camping places just the same as ours, as though they were part owners in everything and it worked out fine. They would help us work over the rough part of the high range and, as a result, many of them would come in at the home ranch at any time and be perfectly at home." Charles Mason wrote of the camp that Richard and Al and a few other cowboys were in the camp a greater part of each winter, Al spending more time there than anyone else and doing more exploration of the side cañons than any of the rest of them.

and he had a laugh on me because, as he said, "Me no land; no grass." He was a Pah Ute and did not belong anywhere, although he ranged from the Uinta country far out in Utah to the Southern Ute Agency at Ignacio on the Pine River [southeast of Durango, Colorado].)

Getting off the high mesa and into the valley of the Mancos was some undertaking, since it was midwinter and the ice and snow made traveling very slow. One cow slipped down the icy trail and lodged headfirst in the forks of one of the scrubby trees that cover the hillsides, and it broke her neck. One horse fell off a ten-foot ledge, but was not hurt at all. I guess it was because he was sort of a chunky build and his bones were too deep under the skin to get broken.

While on the way to the top of the mesa, we ran short on eats so I took my saddle horse and beat it back to the La Plata [River] where there was a store. It was nearly nighttime when I started back, but as long as I could see the tracks of the cattle, it was easy going. After the darkness got so thick I could not see, I had to camp. The horse would have gone on regardless of the darkness, but he could not tell me where there was a low bridge where I might get raked off and left behind. None of the trees at that altitude are more than twenty feet high and most are less. There was plenty of wood and the fire was easily kept up. I ate a bite, gave the horse a smell of oats, and anchored him to a tree. Then I dug a hole in the accumulation of needles under another tree and soon made a nest. With the saddle blanket over me for a covering I let myself believe I had gone to bed.

Where we camped at the top of the hill [above and south of the Mancos River Cañon], we could see dozens of holes around over quite a patch of country and smoke, or gassy vapor, was blowing out all the time. It was evident that a heavy body underneath was burning out. The rocky formation was all broken up and a great part of that region showed the effects of having been under an intense heat at some earlier period. All down the mesa to where it is cut off by the valley of the San Juan, it shows the burning of the coal. The cowboys who know of the smoking holes call it the Volcano District.

The snow was not so bad as we got further down and when we got nearly to the [Mancos] river, we met up with a neighbor who was down there with a team "looking for a claim." He did not say whether it was a land claim or a beef claim he was looking for.

We got home late that next P.M., happy and smiling.

The Utes had no inferiority complex in their make-up and always wore a sort of superior bearing, or attitude, when in contact with other people, be they other tribes or mere white folk. Yet, they get a kick out of any sort of joke they can put over on anyone. Once, as we were coming up from the San Juan, we came by the way of a spring but had no occasion to stop. After we had gone about a hundred yards, I looked back. There were three Ute heads peering over the bank with their rifles trained on us. I was on top of a load of wool and whispered to the boss but he did not seem to take any notice; just whispered back to me to slide the rifle to him. This I did without any apparent movement, but the Indians must have seen our play, for they jumped up with loud "haw-haws." Of course, we had to join in.

Another time we stopped at that same spring overnight. When we pulled out in the morning, we left an axe and a hatchet where we were cutting up brush for our fire. We did not miss them until noontime and so had to get along without. Perhaps it was a week later, on the return trip, that we found them—still laying where we had used them, although there were Utes around about all the time. I might say that there were no Navajos around, or it would have been too bad for axe and hatchet. The Navajos usually stayed on the south side of the San Juan [River] at that time, and the Utes stayed on their side.

There was not much more trouble around our part of the country, but out toward the Blue Mountains [southeastern Utah] and the Navajo Mountain [northeastern Arizona] country, there seemed to be some sort of a scrap going on all the time. The troops from Fort Lewis, Colorado, a small military post over on the La Plata River, were called on to settle the cause of any unpleasantness. Many times there were false alarms, the troops being rushed to some far-away point in order to sell them something, or to get the extra supplies the soldiers may have had.

One case of a rush order to the troops was either from Bluff City, Utah, or Monticello, Utah, where most likely some of the Mormons had a mix-up with the Indians, but the Indians got a head start on them and beat it for the White Cañon. Perhaps they planned to get over to the north and into the Uinta Agency, where they could mix in with the Indians there and be all innocence. They were overtaken by the soldiers, however, and the Mormons and cowboys, and treed on a high plateau about eight or nine hundred feet above the valley, at the head of White Cañon. They felt they were perfectly safe, since the risk of getting up to them was too great for anyone to tackle. The way up the side of the plateau was strewn with slide rocks, but the troops tried to make it anyway. The first try was a failure and, at another attempt, two of the boys were killed: Wormington, a soldier-scout, and Higgins, a Mormon cowboy. They were buried right along the side of the trail with their names scratched on rock headstones. (Brother Clayton and I passed that way a few years later and there was nothing to show where they were buried.)

It must have been the lack of water, or the impossibility of getting at the Indians, that retreat was in order. The Indians had plenty of feed and water where they were, but the soldiers perhaps did not know of the water around at the end of the mesa, just a few miles from them. There was quite a bit of it there, even if it was mighty strong with alkali. In the summer-time that place is certainly a hot and dry piece of the world and the further you go down White Cañon the hotter it gets. There is very little vegetation there—just hot rocks.

Those first few years at the ranch I was always looking for an opportunity to make my fortune elsewhere. During the winters we sometimes would fall into a serious case of the blues for the reason that often we were snowed in and did not even get mail for days and days. The trains to Durango did not arrive for long periods. Mail came via horseback from the Santa Fe railroad one hundred fifty miles away. When such times occurred, we would have feelings like the little birds have before they begin drifting south.

At such a time I thought that, as soon as I could get out, I would be on my way to Holton, Kansas, to go to a sort of high school and college. I always had an idea that I was in need of a higher grade of education than just the rule-of-three and knew I could work my way through the school. However, I stopped over to visit at Topeka and that was as far as I got that time, for there was a railroad job just to my liking awaiting me. I hung on until the birds and flowers started to arrive from their winter hide-outs and my thoughts went back to the freedom of the West. By then I had been sent out along the [railroad] line where I knew no one and there was nothing to see except freight and passenger cars. So, I just unhung those ambitious thoughts [concerning further education that] I had acquired and back to the ranch I went.

The next winter I got as far as Trinidad, Colorado, where I again met my old railroad friend [from Topeka]. He proved to be a jinx to my high hopes because he had been fired off the railroad for being the leader of strikers between the time he had written me and [when] I arrived. That left me out on a limb and I was forced to work along with him on odd jobs of carpen-ter work, in a stone quarry, and, for one day, in a coal mine. I never saw the color of any payday money, but finally got a horse in payment of what I had earned. I boarded with my ex-friend and slept in the barn loft, because there was no room in the little house they had. I was fairly comfortable because I had brought my bedroll with me but, even at that, it was something fierce to get up in the winter mornings.

All this time there was no chance of success being just around the corner, for he just did not happen to reside in that immediate neighborhood.

A postal card brought me the carfare home. After I bought the ticket I had ten cents left for eats until I got back to the ranch. I bought bologna sausage and, while waiting for the train, a big dog smelled the stuff and came around for a handout. I did not feel I could spare any but he kept insisting, so I had to go out and walk around town until train time.

Shortly after [arriving at home], I just picked up and, with a pack on my back, beat it over to Durango. The railroad was building a line up the Animas River to Silverton and I got a job all right, but it was merely a job. Even that was ended before too long, for the reason that a case of inflammatory rheumatism laid me out on my back and I could not even wiggle a finger for a couple of weeks. I was toted over to a downgoing grade, put on the train, and carried into the hotel at Durango. Word was sent to the ranch to come and get me.

It was only a few days after getting down out of the high altitude that I was working away the same as if I had not been away at all.

My friend at Trinidad soon left there because he was blacklisted so far as the railroad was concerned. His daughter wrote me that he had had an accident while out hunting and died from the effects. I could not help but think that it was not an accident, but that he was discouraged and gave up and shot himself.

Before long, I went with an Indian trader who was located on the San Juan [River] near the four corners. I did not know anything about Indian trading. In fact, I was an all-around tenderfoot. Needless to say, I absorbed knowledge in chunks. I soon learned enough store talk and signs enough to get by, as well as the pawning part of the game. It is safe to say that all Indians were gamblers, and when one had played a losing game, he would begin to shed his jewelry and blankets, and hock them to the trader; sometimes redeeming them, sometimes letting the pawn go dead. What a supply of silver, blankets, saddles and bridles, and other stuff a trader would have!

While I was still new to the business, the owner of the store had to leave the whole works in my care for two weeks while he was away down the river thirty or forty miles where his father-in-law had a store.[6] (His wife was there because she and the trader were expecting an increase in the family. The father-in-law was something of a yarner, as numbers of old timers get that way in spite of themselves. The Mitchell of the Mitchell-Merrick prospecting expedition was a son.)

Generally, things went along smoothly, but one day an Indian came in and wanted to see a saddle blanket he had in pawn. I let him have it and he went out to get a better light on it—to be sure it was his, I thought—while I was selling some coffee or sugar. As soon as I had the order filled, I went to take a look. I saw him streaking down the valley and the other Indians tried to tell me something. It might have been Greek, or any foreign language they were speaking. There was nothing I could do until he came around again.

In three or four days, he showed up. He left his horse just a little way beyond the door with the blanket under his saddle. There was a gun standing under the counter, quite handy, so I gathered it up and sauntered out and yanked the blanket from under the saddle and went back to the store with it. About that time the old man let out a bunch of yelps and a string of jargon. The other Indians just helped themselves to me: set down on me; took the blanket; removed my gun and hid it behind a tree; put me back on my feet, and went on about their business. And that was all right with me! I do not believe I was a bit scared, but just took things as a matter of course. Later, he paid out what was due on it. The report they sent in to the trader was that he had a crazy fellow there at the store.

Of course, there are rascals among Indians, but you will soon find them out. Usually, they appreciate you when you are accommodating to them.

The trader had a boat to use and a bunch of the natives [Navajos] from across the river had me take it over for them to bring across their wool and pelts. The river was high and the ford was impassable on account of the heavy sand rolls. The Navajos bought what they wanted and had me take them back over the river. After depositing them and getting back to the store side, I heard one of them yelling, "Bel-de-clish, bel-de-clish" ("Indigo, indigo"). He had left his indigo on the counter in the store.

They were afraid to come over after it and I did not want to cross over again with the boat, since it was too hard a job to keep from drifting down into the sand rolls. It was too far to throw the package across, so I finally slid out of my clothes, tied the indigo around my neck, and swam across. I swam overhanded, which was a new one on the Indians, and, after that, they tried to imitate my swimming by waving their arms around in the air whenever they saw me. We had a big dog at the store and he tried to swim across with me, but got caught in the rolls and was tumbled and rolled for nearly half-a-mile downstream. Ever after that, he was afraid of the water.

Later, when I was working there again, I left the San Juan [Noland's Four Corners store] one nice, warm, sunny winter day with eleven sacks of wool, going on the road leading through Montezuma Valley and over the divide into the Mancos Valley and to Durango, the nearest shipping point. Durango was more than a hundred miles from where the four states corner. (We had to haul supplies that same route, coming back from hauling the wool and pelts to the railroad.) The solitude and loneliness of the route was broken only when night came on and I could camp, using sagebrush and rabbitbrush for campfires. Having been away from home and family for what seemed like a very long time, it was a great relief to reach the Alamo Ranch and talk United States language again. At that time, the home ranch was still the two-room-and-roofed-over-space log house.

I left the ranch early the following morning and made good time to the top of the divide between the Mancos and La Plata Rivers, but, just as I made the turn to start down across Thompson's Park, the side of the wagon ran over the edge of the grade and over we went. As the wagon turned over, the horses, the wool, and I went along with it. None of the outfit was damaged, except for a part of the wagon that I easily fixed. I loosened up the sacks of wool, turned the wagon back on its wheels, and took the wagon and horses down the hill to a cattle ranch below. [From] there I had to drive back up the hill to just below the wool, where I rolled half of the load into the wagon. Then I had to take that half down to a bench on the hillside, unload, drive back, and go through the same process with the balance of the load. Then I had to get it all back on the wagon, bind the load, and go carefully on my way.

It snowed during the following night, and part-way up Fort Lewis Mesa the wagon bogged down in the deep mud and snow. So, I had more grief in having to unload part of the cargo, take what was left to the top of the mesa, and then go back for the rest of it. It would bring tears to your eyes to mentally go through the time I had. Those sacks of wool weighed close to one hundred fifty pounds apiece, and in the middle of winter to have to break trail——! But, after that, it was an uneventful downhill run.

There was practically no travel over the roads in winter and the only vehicle that passed me was a buggy with my own mother driving it! She never seemed to worry about us—worrying was not a Western custom.

NOTES

1. In the fall of 1881, which was perhaps the time Al arrived, Benjamin Kite Wetherill was 49; Marion Tompkins Wetherill, his wife, was 46; Richard, 23; Al, 20; Anna, 16; John, almost 15; Clayton, either 13 or 11; Winslow, either 11 or 9. In addition, the two cousins, Ben and Ida Tompkins, were members of the family but their ages were not positively determined.

2. Benjamin Kite Wetherill made an inventory of their equipment at the time of the homesteading. They were: 1 wagon, 1 sett harness, 1 saddle, 2 pcks, 2 shovels, 2 pitchforks, 1 snath, 2 scythe blades, 1 scythe stone, 2 hammers, 2 paulins, 2 log chains, 1 sett lead chains, 2 axes, 1 rifle, 1 shot gun, 1 tent, 1 spade, 3 mattock, 1 square, 2 saws, 1 sett bitts, 1 brace, 1 sett augers, 4 auger handles, 2 pack saddles, 1 sett planes, 1 cartridge belt, field glasses, 1 14" plow, 1 pair single trees (broken), 1 quirt (worn out), 1 grind stone, 1/2 mower and rake, 1 tape line, 1 black snake-whip (worn out).

3. A photograph made in 1889 shows the 12' x 16' space still open but a shingle roof had replaced the dirt roof and siding had been used to extend the upper part of the fireplace above the gable on the west end of the cabin.

4. Early photographs show that the "fences" between various divisions of the ranch yard were actually walls of rock about three feet high, evidently putting to good use the abhorred "cobblestones."

5. These incidents would indicate that the family always had a sense of humor, although many reports have stated that they were "rather stiff." Luella Mason Dunkelberger, B. K.'s granddaughter, relates a story of his college preparatory days when he was nearly expelled from Westtown School, Chester County, Pennsylvania, for fastening walnut shells on a cat's feet and turning it loose to go tapping down the hall.

6. Although Al hesitates to identify by name many of the people around Mancos, the trader was Oen E. Noland, who carried an account at the Alamo Ranch. Al's income was entered in the Noland account on the one occasion as "staying at store" and a similar entry carried "hauling wool" as the reason for the income.

4
Cowboy Days

IN the course of time, the ranches in the district were pro-
ducing more hay and grain than could be used and so prices
went to the bad. We got into the cattle business in spite of ourselves. We had the range and the husky kids just the right age
for cowpunchers, so, when the merchants were getting stuck
with cattle in payment of debts, the cattle really were forced
on us.

We were able to hold our own, regardless of the various cow
outfits in the surrounding territory, because we were all five
good riders, broncobusters, and all that goes to make the cattle
business a paying proposition. When we started in, some of the
outside outfits thought they had the laugh on us, for they
thought we would go wrong side up within a short time. But
we did not go as we were expected and got along fine, finan-
cially and physically, for years.

The average cowboy is not tough or anything of the sort,
but he does have to hold his own.[1] Would-be terrors were usually killed off by others of their kind, so cow camps were seldom overrun by undesirables. The name *cowboy* does not mean

71

a boy any more than the name *cattle* means cows. Any boy, after his eighteenth or nineteenth year in a cattle country, could be classed as a cowboy. Until cowboys have a good bunch of cattle, they are called *cowboys;* after that, he is always a *cowman.* And, in the early days, the making of a cowman was to own a good horse, a long rope, and a branding iron.

To begin with, every cowboy ran his cattle independent of any other cattleman and, if he happened to run across a maverick (or long ear), it was his meat. Later, the cattlemen formed pools, or companies, and would get together and cover miles and miles of range, driving everything before them. These roundups are necessary in the cattle business, to get the stock that stray off their home range back to where they can be seen occasionally, and to have the calves branded before they get old enough to leave their mothers. On such drives, in all the dust stirred up, large handkerchiefs were necessary, especially to wipe the dirt out of your eyes—cowboy handkerchiefs were never for display and the silk ones were the best ones to use. The drives would have a day crew, which herded the cattle and the unbranded calves, yearlings, and strays, and at night, a night crew. At the railroad, where the stock was sold to the highest bidder, the money was divided among the men. All this was a rather loose way [of management], but the money kept up a part of the winter expenses.

During the roundups, or on long drives, the would-be tough guys would be kept too busy to display their rough dispositions and at winter camps they were seldom held over or given responsible leadership. The ones held over were always those who were constantly looking out for the interests of their companies.

Branding time is also the time when rustlers got in their best work. At all times the rustlers were dangerous, because there was very little law aside from the collective gathering by the real owners of the stock. Brands had to be large, plain, and easily named. In addition, some owners used ear marks (part of the ear trimmed off), and others used wattle and dewlap marks. A slice in the flap of skin over the brisket was an easy mark to see, even if the hair was long in the springtime.

On one occasion, a cattleman and myself were down in a cañon looking for stray cattle and came upon a couple of Utes looking at a fresh brand on a cow. One of the Utes and myself were back on the trail while the other Indian and the cattleman were examining the brand. Finally the Indian drew his six-shooter (everyone wore six-shooters; you were not properly dressed unless you had a long Colts Frontier within easy reach) and I thought it was all-day-gone with the cattleman. The Indian next to me had his rifle sort of trained on me, but that was all right, since my gun was in good working condition. But, just the same, I felt my hair go up and stay up. I do not know what the Indian beside me was thinking, but Indian number 1 shot his gun and the *cow* fell dead right where she stood. Then the Indian said, "My cow; my grass." That made it plain that the cow was the Indian's property. It was also an easy way out, even if it was an expensive settlement.

Another time a couple of us boys were drifting cattle out of the cañon country and out to the more level grasslands outside when we came across a yearling calf that had been killed by a bear. When we reached home and told our story, we were elected to get right back out there that very night and lay for the fellow. The calf had been killed alongside a little wash, or arroya, as it is called. We laid down on the other side of the gulch, not more than thirty feet away from the dead calf, and waited for the bear, which was not very long [in appearing]. We had brought a dog along and when he whispered a trembling bark, we could see the bear on the opposite side of the wash. We both opened fire on him and told the dog to go get him. That dog did not open his mouth; just sneaked in behind us and looked toward home. We stayed there until morning and saw where the blood marked both sides of the trail so thought we could follow the beast. Although we followed his trail until noon, he was still going strong, instead of weakening from loss of blood. We turned and beat it for the ranch, but I will bet that bear never wanted, or needed, any more veal.

Another time we had trouble that cost us a lawyer's fee. A sort of a Laddy Boy came to the ranch and wanted a job. We did not need him because he was too green for any sort of work. If we were moving cattle around on the range or bringing in stock from another county, this guy would play cowboy and try to cut calves out of bunches of other stock we passed and put them in our bunch. We were not used to such a course, so called him off and let him know that we were not doing any such thing. I do not know how long this Laddy Boy stayed around after he got to know our cattle, but the first thing we knew, he had us reported to a big cattle company.

The company had us brought up for a trial. It was easy enough to show him up as a—well, you know what—but he claimed to be a detective for the cattle company. He made a very poor showing, but it cost us a bit [for the attorney]. He pretty soon left the country, for cattlemen make it a rule not to have such varmints around very long.[2]

Mancos was a cow town and dances were all the go; some shooting going on, but seldom anyone killed. The first death I knew of was when George Frink (who was probably drunk) was making war-talk with one of the Rush boys. Mr. Rush shot off a rifle from his house. The ball went through the well curb, caught Frink in the leg, and, from lack of attention, he died of blood poisoning. Rush had been a Texas Ranger and was called, "Butt-cut," on account of his size, which was not much over five feet in height.

Frank Adams was the cow camp name of a mild-mannered kid whose name was Jacob at his Mormon home. He was mild-mannered but, like many another of his kind, could be stirred up to show a rough side, too. He had come with his parents to make a Mormon settlement in southeast Utah, coming over the old route as much as possible. They met up with what appeared an impossibility when they reached the Colorado River. But that did not stop them, although they were six months getting down and out the opposite side of the cañon. It was necessary to let their wagons down by ropes and handpower.[3] He was quite small and one time wandered away from their camp and was lost for three days.

All the time that I knew Frank, he never quarreled with anyone, but, at one of the dances, a would-be badman made him go out and climb a flagpole. He climbed it and was the laughingstock for awhile. The next time a dance was on, this man talked to Frank's girl in some ungentlemanly manner and our Frank just shot him so full of holes that it was hard to tell which part to save. There was nothing ever done about it, for everyone was in sympathy with Frank.

In all our wild and wooly cowboy days, none of our bunch was ever shot at, strange as it may seem. We were threatened a number of times, but it never developed into actual quick-draw action.

One time, if the man had been real sober and made the breaks he did, there might have been something happening. As it was, he went up town and got soaked up with whiskey and then came down the road shooting and making a great noise. Just before reaching our gate, his horse jumped the wide irrigating ditch and he fell off. Since I was near the gate, I rushed out before he got up. I grabbed his six-shooter and then had him coming *my* way. (I did not know it at the time, but brother Win was in the upstairs of one of the barns about a hundred yards away and had the heavy Winchester trained on the guy. So, he never could have got in a shot, anyway.) When I had him, he began talking and said I was the "bess' fren'" he ever had.

We took him over to the house and dosed him up with coffee and kept him around the rest of the day. That night we got out our light wagon and ordered him aboard. He objected, but we told him that we would hog-tie him and take him anyway. So then he crawled in and one of the boys rode his horse to town and, when we got to the front of the saloon, we made him get out and told him he could have his gun the next day.

A neighbor and I locked horns one time. His cows got in on one of the farms we had and I ran them off and up toward the mountains a couple of miles. The neighbor came down to pay me a call and had the wrong end of his quirt in his hand. He said nothing; just whacked me across the face with the heavy end of the quirt. I grabbed the quirt with one hand and poked my other fist at the bridge of his nose (which left him carrying two black eyes for a spell). I kept on punching 'til I thought I could throw him down and sit on him. But, since he weighed nearly two hundred pounds and I only about one hundred-fifty, he sat on me instead. I did not holler enough, so he choked me a bit, then let me up and began lecturing me about what he would do if I ever run his cows off again.

I said, "Let's just try it out again."

He didn't offer to, but said to the man he brought along with him, "Give me that, Benny." Benny handed him a little old pistol, which he poked toward me and said, "Will you ever do such a thing again?"

As he was waving his arms and hands around, a pocket knife fell from his sleeve. He picked it up and then asked if it was mine! I had a rifle in the next room and if he had felt like trying the shooting business, I felt I could go him one better. He finally satisfied himself with the conquest and beat it.

I went on home then, and, as I passed his house, the family came out to look me over. By that time, *my* eyes were black. I stopped the wagon and let them look and laugh at the whole works. He never bothered me again and managed to keep his cows somewhere else.

I did not love that old codger before then and still less afterward.

A hired man working with me on that farm at the time of the trouble took a saddle horse and beat it back to the home ranch. I do not know why—there was nothing to get excited about. The next day I went up in the mountains where I had some friends and stayed until I had no more black eyes.

One year we had an especially good and fat piece of meat [saved] for our Christmas dinner. But the aforesaid calf got away from us and followed a bunch of cattle we knew not where. We took our beds and eats along [while searching for the calf] and stopped at a winter cow camp where we knew all the boys. One of them went out with us a couple of miles away from camp, where we ran across a nice, long yearling. He rode up close to the animal and one shot made a wagonload of beef for us. I guess they were not particular about their own beef hides for, as I prowled around over the ruins, I ran across an especially good and fat calf hide. ([I pretended] I never saw it, though.) The boys were short on sugar and, since we had a pretty good supply, we did without sugar and they had a temporary feast on it.

All's well that ends well.

There was one time that a cowboy I knew of had some words with a so-called badman. (I think maybe they both got too much soothing syrup, or something.) Some of the boys who had been in town at the time heard the badman's talk about how he was going to go out to camp and clean up on the cowboy. When he came along at the camp, the boys were sitting on a log and taking life easy, because they had just made a hard drive.

The badman spied his supposed victim and went up close to him, gun in hand, and slapped the rim of the cowboy's broadbrimmed hat down over his eyes. As quick as thought, or quicker, there were two shots fired, but the shots were from the cowboy's .44 and the badman was no more trouble. He was hauled to town in a wagon and I do not remember ever hearing of his recovery. Maybe he just took passage to his Kingdom Come.

All this created no excitement among the boys, for they

were as one with their thoughts. It would have been no use to arrest the cowboy or even to try.

Where there is cattle, there also has to be horses. Anything on the range is called a horse, a cow horse or a cow pony. If cowboys get short of saddle horses, they will decide to make a wild-horse roundup. Talk of gathering a bunch of wild horses was quite common in cow camps or at ranches. The Southwestern country, for all its desert sands, in places grows rich and nourishing feed for horses and cattle. The cattle are easily taken care of but horses need special treatment to round up, to catch, to tame, and to put to man's use under a saddle or in front of a wagon. Man never started on the road to civilization until he had developed the horse to do his part. It must have been ages before the little Eohippus, with his five or six toes on each foot, was worked over into the most useful of all the animal kingdom's animals for man's needs: the horse.

Actually, there is no such thing as a wild horse at this late day. The so-called wild horses are just stock horses that have been turned out on the range and have just kept on going to live "in a state of Nature, untamed." Spanish horses that were brought to this country along with its discovery have ever since been escaping and increasing in numbers on the open range. Indians kill wild horses to eat (and horse meat is not half bad if you have to eat it), and cattlemen kill them to keep their saddle horses from joining the wild ones. No matter how gentle your horse may be, he will leave you if a bunch of range horses come around. When he gets in a wild bunch he turns wilder than the wild ones. And they will all forget to come back home in the springtime.

In different parts of the country the system of making a run on horses varies according to the way the surrounding ranges lay. Along the San Juan Valley, especially on the south side, there are a series of broad, grassy valleys called draws and the horses water at the river. (The alkali seeps are not fit for even hog wallows in that district.)

To make a run on a bunch of horses in that area, the horses are located and their time of watering made known. A long, narrow valley is an ideal place to make the run, or drive, on a bunch. There should be enough riders so that they can be placed on each side of the gulch or cañon the horses water in, not over a couple of miles apart, and all riding their best mounts. They sit around until the wild horses are all filled with water. Then the wild horses are started at a full run by the first relay of riders, and the rest is a dead run from start to finish. After the run is started, the next relay is ready to take up the chase and give the wild horses the best that their saddle horses can do.

By this time some of the mares and colts drop out and are taken over by the first relay of riders. They catch the mother and colt, brand the colt, and make a broomtail out of the mare by cutting off her tail until it looks like a broom. Or, they brand her if she is not otherwise marked. The mares are usually turned loose unless there is something special in the bunch.

(The mares are usually headed by a stallion and the saddle horses that try to enter the bunch have to take the sidelines or fight. A horse fight is sure something to see. An old horse has no business around a wild band, for, if he is too persistent, he is killed. The stallions fight for leadership and it is a case of the survival of the fittest.)

Occasionally a mare will desert her colt, probably with the thought that she can come back that way and pick it up, the same instinct that birds and other animals seem to have.

After five miles or so, at the best the wild horse can put in, he is about ready to desert his company or give up. The bunch has to be kept out of timber and rocky ridges, for they will dodge the chasers there. If in rocky ridges, they can dodge so quickly around the rough and rugged places that it would be the ruination of a saddle horse to try to keep the wild ones in sight. By the time the bunch of horses has slowed down they will try to scatter out—one or two at a time—and the boys will do their best to hold them together until they can get them into a corral.

The corral must be immense, with wings spreading far aside the wide gates. When the bunch is inside, the best of them are picked over and those that would make cow ponies are caught and rode once and then turned over to the cowboys to break.

Breaking a horse means staying on the top side of the horse when he is saddled. Any horse that is half-broken is called a *bronc* or a *broncho,* the name coming up from Texas. There are always those who make a business of taking the wild out of a horse, but horses broken that way nearly always have to be broken again about every time they are used. At some cow camps the cattle company has a man who does nothing but uncock, as the term is, every saddle horse before the outfit leaves camp for the day's work. The man has to be an expert rider and, when he saddles the horse, rides him until he gets the jumps out of the cow pony. All cowboys are not broncobusters and lots of them lose their nerve and get quite shaken before climbing into the saddle. Usually they will ask, "Has he been uncocked?" before mounting the horse.

To understand conversation in a cow country, it is necessary to know cowboy talk and expressions. Some words and their meaning are:

Gotch ear, an ear cut off or partly frozen off.

Palomino, a yellow horse with white mane and tail.

Horse wrangler, the boy who looks after the horses during roundup.

Broncobuster, a regular breaker of saddle horses. Some horses are never safe to climb on unless you know the business. To uncock those, you have to know their tricks but, usually, just a few hard jumps and they are ready for the day's work.

Ride-'em-straight, is to ride a bronc without trying to hang onto the saddle strings.

Hobbled stirrups, are stirrups tied to the cinches so as to keep your feet from flying out, for if you lose your stirrups you are lost and will be grabbing at bunches of grass instead of the mane.

Grabbing leather, is when you think the horse is going to get you and you reach for safety. When it comes to this, you are afraid that you are a goner.

Night horse, a horse that has better sight at night than in the daytime and is used especially during roundup for night work.

The Slush, the cook, and it is never a desirable job, even in the wintertime at permanent camp.

Greasysack outfit, is going out with a single pack horse, or none at all, carrying a very limited supply of grub and bedding at the back of the saddle.

Ride and tie, is two riding one horse, one at a time. One will ride ahead for a given length of time and then tie or hopple the horse and start on afoot. When the one walking gets to the horse he climbs on and rides far enough to pass the one walking until he is quite a bit ahead; then the operation is repeated.

On a small scale we became involved in a horse downfall

experience. Along the San Juan River there were a number of Indian trading stores and one of the traders, Noland, was quite a friend of ours. One time a man from the north, or northwest, came around with a bunch of fine-looking horses and it seemed that he had had all the horse education he needed and then some. He turned the whole bunch, maybe as many as a hundred head, over to the trader for twelve hundred dollars. Even at that it looked like a holdup, because the horses were too big in size for good cow ponies.

For a few months the horses could be rounded up and driven anywhere, but the bunch gradually got broken up and scattered in all directions. Possibly they were scattered by being chased by Indians or by their natural instinct to take care of themselves and to join up under different leaders. Anyway, they became a wild bunch and would begin to move and scatter as far as they could see a rider.

About a year after they had been turned loose, Noland wanted to turn the bunch over to us. We knew of the horses and had seen them at close range, so thought "here is some easy money." So, two of us rigged up an outfit to go on a horse roundup. We loaded a wagon with horse feed and an abundance of grub and away we went with our spirits 'way high.

Near Noland's store there was a corral and I think now that we bummed off him while we were getting in shape to get a herd of cow ponies mighty cheap. In a day or two we had several bunches in sight from the hillside above the store and, as long as we just stood on the hill and looked, it all appeared to be an early Christmas gift.

We had good saddle horses and the country appeared easy to work. The valley of the San Juan at the location of Noland's store was nearly thirty miles wide in places, for nearly a hundred miles up or down the river. We soon laid out our work and all we had to do was sail in and have the corral full of horse money before the first night came on.

The first night came and then several more and still there were no horses tied up, hoppled, or corralled, but we did not shed any tears or use any swear words.

We spent a week or more there and just worked our saddle horses to a standstill, ate up all our grub and horse feed, and, for results, had just four head of the culls from the bunch of wild horses (which could run rings around us).

If there had been forty of us we might have made a killing. We could not keep the horses away from the water holes because they had the whole of the San Juan River to drink from and miles and miles of little draws to hide in, thus leaving the whole range as free of stock as a jack rabbit's dooryard.

As the saying goes, we just dragged our tracks out as we sneaked back home; dirty, ragged, and mad at all the world.

In going out after cattle or stock, we would sometimes be gone for days and at times were thought to be lost. One time when someone said that, one of the smaller boys said, "No, they are not lost because they know every tree and bush and have them all named."

This was said about the occasion when a couple of us went on a stock-hunting hike on snowshoe skis (snowshoes about six or seven feet long) after a heavy fall of snow. We left home early one morning and went across the valley to the high table-land that was really a continuation of the La Plata Mountain system. From the bottom to the top of the mesa we had to work our way up through the heavy brush and rocks and snow. There was an occasional windblown bare spot and our thought was that when we reached the top, the snow would have been melt-ed so as to form a crust and then we could go skiing along like nobody's business. It did not prove to be that way at all; it had not thawed a bit, was waist deep, and dry. We just left our snowshoe-skis and wallowed across the top to the head of a cañon we thought we knew.

We went down the sunny side of the cañon, which was more exposed to the sun, was out of the wind, and had more bare spots than where we came up. We saw no sign of stock, for they generally drift out of the mountains as soon as the snow flies. Some of the stock, though, if they find a sunny hillside, will stop over and perhaps winter it through, because there is always plenty of feed along the slopes of the cañons if only it can be pawed out.

Not finding any strays, we struck down a little draw and, just before night, arrived at a little cabin, about eight or nine thousand feet in altitude, where we usually had some grub stored for emergencies. But the mountain rats had made a clean-up of everything except a very small chunk of bacon. Otherwise we were well fixed, there being plenty of wood everywhere, and so for the entire night we kept up the warming and drying process.

In the morning, an old plug of a horse was snooping around outside. He had drifted in during the night from a nearby gulch. He looked as hungry as we were, but also he looked, to us, like a free ride home. We tried to double up on him, but he would not see it that way and so we did as he suggested—ride and tie (but without a rope or wire). That is, one would ride him at a time and then leave him and walk on. The other one, when he caught up to the horse, would ride him past the one walking and leave him. And so on.

We got along very well until we got down through the bottom of the cañon and there met up with a neighbor who happened to be down in there at that time with a wagonload of hay, or straw, or so it seemed. (A beef, maybe?) But people did not ask questions those days and, too, we were well satisfied to just ride in the wagon, keep our mouths shut, and look the other way. We mooched a square meal off him when we reached his house and, since he did not live far from our place, we arrived home shortly [thereafter].

We were smiling and happy to be home, even if we found no stock except that lonely old plug. He wintered at our ranch and was happy, too.

In the course of time, we decided to look for another [cattle] range where we could not be pushed around so much. The Henry Mountain country looked pretty good to us—from our distance of a hundred miles or better—so a couple of us (Clayton and myself) got pack horses and a well-filled camp outfit and drifted along through the rough and broken country of southwest Colorado and southeast Utah via Elk Mountain and White Cañon.

Just around the point of the mesa where the Indians and the soldiers had their trouble was a narrow cañon and a waterhole with awful water in it. We went there to get a sample of it and found a yearling calf lying there, too weak to get up. We thought it would be a big help to get him on his feet, so we each took an end of the beast. He came right up and butted me down and stood spraddled over me, blowing through his nose every time I moved. There was no way for me to wriggle out, for he was looking wild-eyed at both of us. Brother Clayton just laughed and laughed and I did not dare to get mad at him, or there would never have been an end to the story.

The rocks along the edges of the deep gulch that carries away the water from the Elk Mountains were all cut up into bridges and caverns and all sorts of rocky scenery. The water works over and under the soft spots of the sandstone to make the pictures. How many there are who seem to think that beauty in Nature consists only of running streams, green trees, and waving corn! Let them but go over most any part of this country and they would be unable to express the wonder and the feelings that ever-changing scenery inspires. There is no monotony to it as there is in riding mile after mile in the alleged more favored localities of the East, where each mile is a duplicate of the previous one.[4]

We made more trips down that way than any other way, for we came over the Elk Mountains when we were scouting around for cliff dwellings, pasture for the stock, and so forth. Our trip back to the ranch was without anything of interest. Feed was scarce for our horses, but we had some oats for an emergency, so they stood the trip O.K.

Among other dogs we had at the home ranch were two of more-or-less Collie stock. One of them was rather heavy and we called him Sullivan. The other we called Spike, because he was born without more than six inches of tail. Those two dogs were a pair of perfection. We could send them for a bunch of calves as far as we could see the stock. Sullivan was a first-class heeler, while Spike would keep the attention of the beast, whether it be a horse or a cow, away from the heel dog. Sometimes we took them out into the heavy timber where we could not use a rope and have them catch the calves for us out of a bunch of wild cattle.

Those years had a few exciting things happen. Once, Clayton saved a boy's life in Grand Gulch. Another time, when we were running half-wild cattle off a high mesa, Clayton and I became separated. When I had my bunch out of the timber, he was nowhere to be seen. I circled back and, in an open space, saw his horse whirling around with Clayt hanging from a stirrup yet still holding a single bridle rein. In making a quick turn, his saddle had slipped down on the side of the horse, but, as long as he could hang onto the rein and keep the horse's head turned, the horse could not kick him, which he was trying to do with every jump. Before I could reach him, his foot came out of the stirrup and he climbed back in the saddle as though nothing was wrong with that kind of behavior.

Richard saved a cowpuncher's life in Grand Gulch when a cow had the man down. And one time John and the husband of a woman trailed a man up into the plateau country of the lower Dolores River and caught him, but then wasted three or four hours deciding whether to shoot him or just treat him rough.

About all I ever did was to save my own skin on several occasions among the wild cattle on the Mesa Verde, but did find some exciting moments during the San Juan "placer gold" experience.

We had known for years of the oil and gold possibilities along the lower San Juan [River] and were wintering our horses and pack mules on the uplands of the river, looking over the cañon sides for archaeological prospects, when there was a sudden boom to get placer-mining claims along the river. Fully a thousand would-be miners, prospectors, and others rushed into Bluff City within a two-week period of time, to reap a harvest of gold. Actually, very few miners came in, just city people who wanted to pick up the large gold nuggets that were never there. They soon got out of there and back to civilization, poorer and wiser, because no one ever made any rich gold strikes.

The entire five-hundred-mile length of the San Juan Valley is covered with mountain-washed-and-rounded cobblestones, sand, and gravel. All these persist in showing a few grains of gold in the pan for those who hunt for it. I never heard of anyone getting even as much as fifty cents for a single pan, although it is possible to get a showing of "shines" almost anywhere. There is a small stream coming in from the Blue Mountains, called Recapture, which has a gold seam along it somewhere, but I do not think any of it ever reaches the San Juan [River].

We were always on the lookout for things of interest and the stories of some of the more enthusiastic prospectors began to take effect. So, we had to take a bit of the supposed gold-gathering ourselves. We did not know just how the gold was to be found, but decided the gold-hunting game appealed to us, so packed up horses and mules, rigged up an outfit and a rocker, and were ready to start in business.

One of the first steps in gold hunting is to get an iron pan with sloping sides, [one] which is twelve to fifteen inches across the top and about two inches deep. It must be perfectly clean or burned free of any substance. (In an emergency, we have used our frying pans for the purpose.) Then, get a pan of gravel or sands from the bed of the creek, pothole, or any pool where the wash from the mountainside has been blocked by slides. When the dirt is in the pan, it is filled with water and given a whirling around with a jerky motion. As the movement goes on, the gold (if any) sinks to the bottom of the pan. Remove the gravel or coarser dirt from the top and, when a small space is free from anything, give the pan a slow movement to show a portion of the bottom of the pan. If the gold is there, it will show up as a little string of gold grains.

When the pan shows enough gold to justify it, the next move is to get a rocker. The main part of the rocker is a copper plate, of high grade, with a coating of quicksilver on it.

A framework of two-by-fours, large enough to let the copper plate slide in position under a rather close-spaced wire screen, makes up the rocker. Another screen goes in the bottom of the boxlike top of the rocker. Into the box is shoveled the gravel and, as this part is worked up and down by handpower, the gold and heavier rock settles and has to be cleaned out frequently. A handpump makes it easy to keep a stream of water running in the top over the gravel and rocks. The finer stuff, as well as the gold, goes on to the next screen and the gold goes on through the fine mesh screen to the copper plate. As the quicksilver gets washed or ground off, or if there is too much of a load of gold on it, the plate has to be cleaned. Cyanide of potassium is used for the cleaning. The result is called *amalgam* and has to have as much of the mercury cooked off as can be cooked off. If you have a baby retort, you do not waste, or lose, any of the quick or the gold.

We made our rocker and hauled it via wagon as far as we could go that way, going through Bluff City and on down to the Mexican Hat. From the Mexican Hat, you look across a very historic section of that part of Utah. You can not actually *see* all the country where weary feet and hopeful minds were forever trekking back and forth seeking betterment of conditions. You have to stretch your neck some to look over some of the high places near at hand. Looking over the northern half of the circle on which you stand, there are miles and miles of sure-enough Rocky Mountains. The line of the Comb [Ridge] shuts off quite a bit of the view to the east, but on beyond is Ute Mountain, the La Platas, the Needles, and Red Mountain.

Looking west from the Hat across the level plain you can see a high promontory, a lookout point much like the one of the Mesa Verde. We headed for that and struck the San Juan [River] about fifteen miles northwest of the Mexican Hat. We could get to the base of the lookout cliff by wagon. There we had to change to pack horses and, further along, to our own backs. In the last stretch, we let the parts down by rope over the lowest cliff to the riverbed at the bottom.

Of course we were on the wrong side of the river, since the main body of water was on the opposite side. Finally, we decided to cross over the river and try a gravel bank and a pile of Chelly formation nearly opposite to where we had been working. The gravel was pretty good, but the Chelly was punk because the gold in it was rusty and would not stick to our copper plate. It was just a dark brown color and might have panned out if it had been free of the rust. This is not usually seen in placer gold or any other sort of gold possibilities. Later on we struck a sort of limey shale and could catch some gold on our pans, but could not get any through the rocker![5] There was a little oil, or something, in the water, or else the grains were too fine. At any rate, it would not stick to the quick at all, even though we cleaned the copper plate quite often.

We had a little rowboat to go back and forth, but one time when the working outfit was on one side of the river, one of the boys and myself were left behind. That did not worry us a bit, since there were a couple of logs right near our camp. So, when we were ready to cross over, we took our saddle ropes and made a raft and started across as the current was running. This was to put us near where we were working.

The current took us down quite a distance while we were sitting quietly on the logs. To make better time, we stood up and were going to dig in with the shovels. The minute we got on our feet, a crosscurrent struck the logs and turned them wrong side up in the icy water. The first thing we knew we were spitting and coughing the muddy water out of eyes, mouth, ears, and nose. Up we both came and were still within reach of the logs, so we grabbed them and looked around to see where we were. We need not have bothered to look, for we could hear the water going over the rocks just a short distance downstream.

I looked at Ben and he looked at me. We had lost our shovels, so [we] could not work the raft out of the current. He did not know if I could swim; I did not know if he could swim and did not know if I was to rescue him or if he was to rescue me. We both decided at the same time to swim to shore, feeling like drowned rats. We did not notice the cold until we shed our clothes to dry them. Then we nearly froze, so we put them back on, went up the cañon to a shoaley place and waded over to

the other side. There we stood around a blazing fire and re-
volved on individual axes until we were dried out and had some
hot coffee for inside warming. We did not catch cold or it did
not catch us, but then we never did when we were outside all
the time. We were just like the Indians who never catch cold
until they get too close to civilization.

When the river got frozen far above where it came into the
cañon, we did fairly well as long as [we] could get to a pool
that had been impossible to work before the freeze-up came.

Once I looked up along the cliff and saw an immense mountain sheep standing there. He did not move and did not mind
my yelling at him. Afterward an old hunter said that mountain
sheep could not hear in the wintertime, because their ears were
stopped up with wax. I did not have a gun along so could not
say yes or no to that question.

One thing I did notice while down there was what I called
onyx but thought that if it was *that* plentiful it could not be
worth much, so [I] did not even bother to bust [break] off a
little sample. It looked like a red quartz bedded in white to
blue limestone. The color was red—like a robin's breast—and
was semitransparent. But this is not a mineralogical story.

The most gold we ever got out in one day was just an ounce
and the price for it was $19 per. Just the same, we cleaned up
a couple of hundred dollars—finally.[6] As it was, we did not even
make our board and if we had not had stock in the country
there, it would not have been anything to stop around for.

Eventually we acquired nearly a thousand acres of fertile
land all in one body. We began to do a little business with Fort
Lewis, too. All the ranges were getting stocked up with cattle
and the ranchers were finding markets for everything they could
raise and this applied to us, too. Often we had officers and men
come out to the Alamo Ranch for a little freedom, as well as
having a stopping place for small scouting expeditions.

Things on the ranch were always the same when springtime
came: the new crop of chickens, colts, and calves; new irrigation furrows to be laid out; more plowing and planting; cattle
working up from their winter range; rounding up horses for
work, gentling others; and so on. And, in the distance, the snowy
La Platas always gave inspiration. As summer advances, the
snowline on the mountains climbs higher and the river takes on
a different gurgle as the melting snow begins to fill up its channel with water.

The La Platas from the Alamo Ranch

As the ranch grew, the stock grew and even the children grew (up). The house grew to a big, rambling place about ninety feet long and forty feet wide, with a porch all of sixty feet long. In front of the house was a big open space and beyond that the corrals. The corrals were for branding stock, breaking horses, and milking cows.

The two rows of cottonwood trees had kept on going up into the air and were nearly fifty feet high, protecting the blue-grass under the spread of their limbs and shading most of the house. Not twenty feet from the front door, between the cottonwoods, was the ditch of clear mountain water. There was an icehouse to the south and east of the house on the other side of the ditch. To the east was a blacksmith shop, a tool house, a workshop, a cow barn fully a hundred feet long, horse barns, and an immense hay barn. We put no limit on size when getting all these houses and barns up and placed.[7] Further [to the south], the road ran out to the open range, with alfalfa fields on one side. The fields for hay and grain reached across a large flat of land nearly to the foot of the Mesa Verde, the section that had been cut off from the mesa by the Mancos River. Closer in was the garden, the fruit trees, and the berry bushes.

Toward the west, Point Lookout of the Mesa Verde hid an early setting sun.

In the course of time, the younger children were able to do housework and field work and we elder ones began to scout around to find out just what sort of a land we had tied onto.

NOTES

1. In a letter written 27 January 1887, Al explained that they were "cowboys, but not the bad kind you read of in the papers. Our valley is between ten and fifteen miles long and is divided into three school districts. Each, of course, had to have a Christmas of some kind. The centre district had a supper and dance, since the majority of the cowboys are in that one, and then had a free fight afterward. There were only three or four crippled, but there was lots of bad blood stirred up."

2. The Alamo Ranch employee records, p. 22, show that George T. Ivins (the Laddy Boy), "Commenced work at $30 per month" 22 June 1887. His employment terminated 27 November 1887, with a two-weeks' absence deducted from the November pay. In 1891, he returned to the Mancos area to figure in the O. C. Olds-Byron McGeoch rustling charge that Frank McNitt records in *Richard Wetherill: Anasazi* (Albuquerque, New Mexico: University of New Mexico Press, 1957), p. 49–50. A *Laddy Boy* of the period was a fancy, meticulously attired individual and, according to the description of Ivins when he returned, his habits had not changed. Al does not record, or else it has been lost, the Olds-McGeoch trial, but the account books contain an account entitled, "Cattle and Horse acct. O. C. Olds fine and expenses in connection therewith," proving that the Wetherills paid the fine for Olds when he was found guilty. The first entry simply states "paid fine—$932." From that time until 16 October 1893 when, "Adv. sale—[$]8.75" is recorded, "expenses in connection therewith" added another $168.45 to the account. The proceeds of the sale amounted to only $672.15, leaving the Wetherills with an unpaid balance of nearly $420. As was typical of many amounts owed the Wetherills, the O. C. Olds account was never balanced.

3. The reference is, without doubt, to the 1879 Mormon migration from Cedar City, Utah, to the mouth of Montezuma Creek, Utah, where a colony was to be established. With the caravan of wagons piled high with supplies and household goods, the Mormons camped all winter at a rock that later became known as Dance Hall Rock, near the junction of the Escalante River on the north side and the San Juan River on the south side, with the Colorado River. During the winter they made a way of descent down to and across the Colorado River at the place they named Hole-in-the-Rock Crossing. The group, weary of the trek, settled at the mouth of Cottonwood Wash and named the townsite Bluff City. A few proceeded upstream on the San Juan River to their original destination, Montezuma Creek; others eventually migrated up the McElmo Cañon from the San Juan River

to the area near Mancos (C. Gregory Crampton, *Standing Up Country* [New York: Alfred A. Knopf, 1964]).

4. The region that so obviously impressed Al was set aside as the Natural Bridges National Monument in 1908. White Cañon drains the major western portion of the Elk Mountains (now called Elk Ridge) to the Colorado River. The eastern side of Elk Ridge below Bears Ears Pass is drained by Mule Cañon and the Comb Wash to the San Juan River. Both areas are included in the National Monument.

5. The formation was probably Moenkopi, but generally known as de Chelly at the time. Herbert E. Gregory (Plate 22, p. 79, *The Navajo Country*, A Geographic and Hydrographic Reconnaissance of Parts of Arizona, New Mexico, and Utah, Water Supply Paper 380 [Washington, D C.: Government Printing Office, 1916]) shows them as one, but separates them by describing the Moenkopi as consisting of thin-bedded sandstone and shale containing lime and gypsum, colored in shades of brown. The formation emerges from beneath the Chinle Valley at Comb Ridge, forms the surface strata from there westward to Moonlight (Oljeto) Creek, and disappears beneath the surface, becoming the Moonlight syncline.

6. To what use the $200 was put is not known. It obviously was not used to pay off the $40 Benjamin Kite Wetherill borrowed from Harry Jackson (the Novelty Carriage Works, Durango, Colorado) to make the trip, for it took the boys sixteen months to repay that money, paying 1% interest per month from date of loan. Dated 18 January 1895, the first payment on the note was made on 27 August 1895 in the amount of $25 and on 13 December 1895 the rest of the original $40 was repaid, leaving the interest on the amount to be settled on 8 May 1896 in the amount of $4.40.

7. Comparison of the Alamo Ranch account books and photographs reveals that a considerable amount of construction occurred during 1886–87, with alterations and additional construction through the winter of 1893–94. Two barns, one large and the other smaller, and a cow shed were built east of the log cabin in the original construction program. A small log cabin occupied by Anna Wetherill and Charles Mason following their marriage was built between the Alamo Ranch house and one of the larger barns and remained in that position until 1890. Parallel to the Alamo Ranch log cabin and about forty feet south of it a building that seems to be a smokehouse appears by 1889. Between the two a chain of rooms progressed southward until, by 1892, the smokehouse became the huge kitchen and milk room of later years.

PART 2

THE MESA VERDE
AND THE ANCIENTS

THE CLIFF DWELLERS OF THE MESA VERDE

Many and many a year ago, in cañons deep and wide,
They built in caves both high and dark and hidden, too, besides.
They had no thought of conquest. All they wished was to be alone,
So in the rocky cañons they built with mud and wood and stone.

They were not brutally minded, but devoted to arts of peace.
Yet the law that keeps the fittest ruled that the race should cease.
The buzzard and the eagle have claimed all rights around,
'Til the coming of the white man those wondrous structures found.

The stately towers and frescoed halls all speak of life of a former day
And silence now on each one falls who treads those aisles of clay.
'Tis not the mentally superior who win out at the last,
But the race that's nearest Nature sees the weakness of the past.

Benjamin Alfred Wetherill

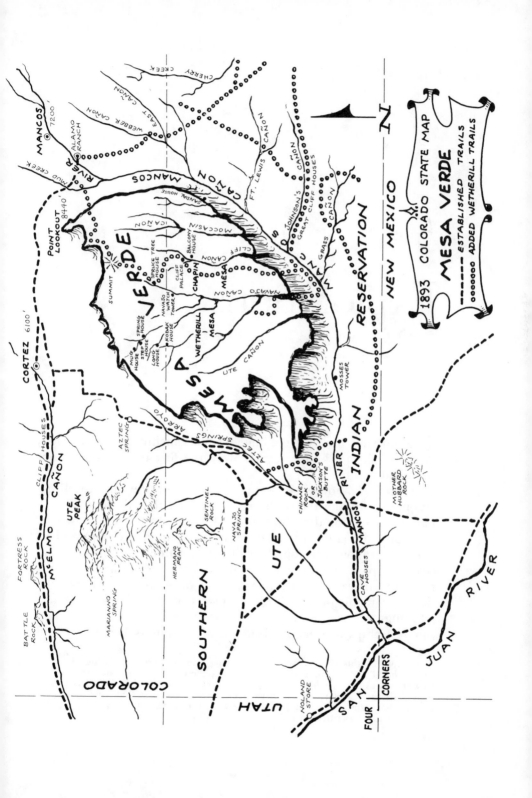

5
Explorations

I cannot tell how we graduated from ranching to archaeology and I do not know why we were the first to annex it as our principal work.

Our first knowledge of the existence of the cliff dwellings was not in finding the buildings all at once, but through a gradual step-up from the abundance of ruins scattered everywhere. In almost the entire distance through the Mancos Cañon and its tributary cañons are found evidence of ruined dwellings of ancient peoples. All over the Mancos Valley and the cliffs surrounding it was evidence of what was once an immense population. Fragments of oddly colored pieces of crockery with strange markings, often of fine geometical designs of angles and squares; chips of flint or obsidian; arrow points, some tiny and

---

Portions of this chapter and the following one (Collections) include parts of Al Wetherill's 1948 summary of their Mesa Verde years that he sent to the Department of the Interior, Washington, D.C., at the request of C. Girard Davidson, then Assistant Secretary of the department. Those passages that appear only in the summary and are not a part of the earlier records, yet provide an integral contribution, are written in italics.

others larger; and stone axes were found everywhere. In plowing, we were always turning up broken crockery and stones of not ordinary shapes and sizes in the fields. Occasionally, too, we came upon large flat stones hollowed on one side and decided they were made to pound [grind] corn or seeds on. They are the same as modern Indians use and are called *metates*.

Our curiosity grew and grew as we dug into the mounds on the ranch, trying to find entire vessels of the unknown people. We were unsuccessful, but we did not give up, for we knew we had evidence of a very different people and had a desire to see where they were in history. I do not remember when we found our first piece of pottery, or if it was given to us. If we asked any of the old timers what the mounds and pottery represented, they would say it was just some old Aztec stuff and could be found almost anywhere in the Southwest. We received pamphlets and books along these lines, but all the knowledge we gained by them was nil. The mounds, or buildings, when spoken of, were passed by as Aztec ruins, although it was hard to see where there was any connecting link whatever, although it probably came from an Aztec superstition saying that they came from the north.[1] Other claims were that they were just the ancient villages of the Moquis, or the Zunis, whose villages are to the south of the Mesa Verde. But all of those village Indians were always village people and never scattered out in little patches of individual houses such as were found in the valley and on the mesas everywhere.

So, we kept on with the job of looking for anything that could help us explain to ourselves the job we had undertaken.

From 1882 to about 1892, we (the Wetherills of the Alamo Ranch on the Mancos [River]) had cattle running on the high plateaus and cañons of the Mesa Verde, because our range became limited at the ranch. The cattle became like wild animals and it was necessary to hunt constantly and [to look] everywhere for strays so as not to overlook the hiding places of a wandering bunch of the piñon splitters. After the younger boys had grown up, we were all, at different times, scouting around through the mesas and cañons of the Mancos River.

Miners, freighters, and stockmen usually came down from the mountains to winter their stock in the warmer valleys and sunny slopes of the Main [Mancos] cañon. It was an economical place to winter stock. There was game for the taking and beaver and other fur-bearing animals just longing to be trapped. One spring, shortly after we established the ranch, a freighter who had wintered his work stock in the cañon told us of a ruin a few miles down the valley, a ruin that had some strange markings on the walls.

I guess I had a greater bump of curiosity than the rest of the boys, for I caught a small pony and, without blankets or grub, or telling anyone, just followed the cañon on the mere chance of seeing the ruins and collecting an unbroken piece of pottery or some arrow points.

Finally, when I thought I had gone about ten or twelve miles (the distance he had told us) and had not found any evidence of a thing but rocks, ridges, and perpendicular cliffs, my mind was beginning to call a halt as the sun was getting low. I had just turned the pony's head for the backtrack when, just above me where the slide rock and dirt bumped into the cliff, I saw the top rim of an eroded cave. It was only about seventy-five feet off the trail and only about a hundred feet up to it, but it would never be noticed just riding along the Indian trail.

I made a hurry-up-quick scramble to get up to it. It was not a difficult job at all, but the standing walls of rooms and heaps of dirt and rock covering other rooms fully repaid me for the trip, although I found only fragments of pottery and chips of flint. But, there were the broad, white stripes on the walls, just as the freighter had said.[2]

Like any tenderfoot, I did not know how to take care of myself at night and just spread the saddle blanket on a nice flat rock and tried to sleep. At that altitude, the night brings cold waves down from the mountains. Between the rock and the cold, there was little sleep. (I soon learned to dig a little hole in the ground, fill it with dead grass or piñon needles, build a fire on the windward side, and then the cold dropping down does not bother.)

But, at the ranch, my report of the ruin did not seem to register, so that was the last of archaeological investigations for the time being.[3]

As early as 1883, officers from the military post at Fort Lewis and many people from as far as Durango began to be interested in what the Mancos Cañon's ancient people had left for our scientific world to puzzle over. They quite often came to the Alamo Ranch for our assistance.[4]

Soon after locating that first ruin (which we later named Sandal House), one of the officers from Fort Lewis was scouting

Sandal House: The Origin of Wetherill Archaeology
"I had just turned the pony's head for the backtrack when, just above
me where the slide rock and dirt bumped into the cliff, I saw the top
rim of an eroded cave. . . . There were the broad, white stripes on
the walls, just as the freighter had said," Al wrote in triumph after
locating the ruin. Following the directions given him by a man who
had wintered in the Mancos Cañon, Al, who "had a greater bump of
curiosity than the rest of the boys," made an exploratory trip down
the cañon in 1882 and almost missed the location. A few years later
when they made excavations at the site they found so many sandals
in the debris that they named it "Sandal House."

around the country, became interested in the caves, and wanted
to see them. I remember Captain Baker well, for we did not
take a camp outfit with us; just a couple of blankets and a medi-
um-sized one-man lunch. He was very much pleased with what
he saw, but, not having a shovel along, we did not dig in any of
the rooms.[5] He at least took mental pictures and, so far, was well
pleased and glad that he had been one of the first men from the
post to know about what had never been pictured before.
     It was late in the day when we decided to move out, so we
went back down to the trail, unsaddled our horses, hoppled
them, and put them down the cañon to level ground and good
feed. Then we built a little smudge of a fire, divided our scanty
lunch, and sat around for awhile before going to bed on the

trail with only our two blankets for bedding. The reason for sleeping on the trail was to keep the horses from backtracking on us during the night.

I do not know if the Captain slept any, but all my worries were over as soon as I laid down. Some time in the night, one dickens of a rain began to pour down and we tried to snuggle up close to each other to keep the rain from soaking us. But, the way the mountain storms just drop down and empty the largest clouds almost in one shot, we were wet through in a minute or so. We hopped up and worked our way back up to the over-hanging cliffs where the building was, soon had a swell fire of trash going, and were steaming away [as if] it was hog-killing time. We did not try any more sleeping but just nursed the fire along until day.

Since our horses stayed below us, it did not take long to get them and beat it out of there and so [we] got to the ranch safe and sound, even if hungry as hound pups.

Then we got a copy of Hayden's Geological Reports of 1874–76 in which was mentioned some ruined buildings of an ancient race in the Mancos Cañon, which was the first record of them being in the Mesa Verde.[6] According to the Report, the earliest record of cliff dwellings was by Escalante in 1776 when they saw them along the Dolores [River]. (But they must have been insignificant affairs of only a few rooms.) The Dolores River is just a few miles north of the Mesa Verde tableland. Escalante's route, when he went through the region searching for a short route to California, took him right through the Mesa Verde region and up along the base of the La Plata Mountains, on across the Grand [Colorado] and the Green Rivers and back across the Colorado River below the mouth of the San Juan River, covering all the country formerly inhabited by the ancient races.

Hayden's Report said that the next official notice [of pueblo-type ruins] was by the military expedition of the United States from 1846–48 by Lieutenant Emory, Lieutenant Simpson, and then later by Powell's Geological Survey.

We learned much from the survey. To be exact, the Mesa Verde is 108°–30′ west and 37°–15′ north, lines that strike in the center of the mesa. The Mesa Verde is in the shape of an arc, around ten miles by fifty miles in area, with the north and west rims going up as high as eighteen hundred feet above the valley. The mesa, as a name, is slightly misleading, because it is cut up with such a labyrinth of cañons that it consists entirely of cañons with just a few ridges of soil to hold them together. The east and south of the Mesa Verde are marked by the Mancos River, which drains the entire mesa as well. Most of the tableland east of the Mancos is drained off into the La Plata River, although there are a few cañons tributary to the Mancos [River] that extend back for quite a distance and are of considerable interest to scientists. On the west of the Mesa Verde is the broad Montezuma Valley. It [the Mesa Verde] may have received the name Mesa Verde (or green tableland) from the members of the Geological Survey.[7]

The mesa formation is mostly of sandstone, heavy with iron. Under the sandstone formation comes a little shale and then a body of coal and also some fire clay (kaolin). In places, iron with more shale, or slate, and sandstone covers the entire distance from the top to the bottom of the cañon. In the different levels are found many plant and marine fossils.

Cutting through the mesa country, generally from northeast to southwest, are dikes and blow-outs of volcanic action. Alongside one of the blow-outs, the one on the east side of the main [Mancos] cañon between Moccasin and Cliff [Cañons], I picked up pieces of a clearlike substance. It was a curiosity on account of its double refraction. It turned out to be Iceland Spar, which is not supposed to be there at all.

Near by is a streak of red paint that the Utes use for special ceremonies.

The high country has great coal beds near the top of the ground, while the deep valleys have nothing of the sort underneath. Toward the lower end [of the whole mesa], where the Mancos River gets through the cañon, there are many square miles of coal; burned out or still burning. The body of coal is exposed for miles at the south end of the mesa. The rock indicates that the coal has all burned out, with the broken and tumbled appearance of the upper stratum telling the same story. Just on top, and on the south side of Grass Cañon on the east side of the river, smoke is coming out of fissures and holes and is called locally "The Volcanos."

It seems that in ages past there were no valleys—just high tablelands. Then came along a mighty upheavel and all the ranges seen from the summit of the Mesa Verde pushed themselves up from the center of the earth and tore all the high plains into gorges, valleys, and cañons. The Mesa Verde is not an uplift, but was, and is now, part of the gradual slope of land from the La Plata Mountains. The torrential rains and the snows from the peaks cut their way through, across, and around the impassable volcanic peaks, seeking an outlet. The waters took great bodies of land with them and left low, flat lands. The valleys surrounding the Mesa Verde have all been cut out by the water and are gradually filling up, or had been up to the time of the cattle and sheep men.

The soil is called *adobe;* some black, some white. The white is worthless, but the black is rich and has no underlying clay, or hardpan, between it and the rock on which it rests. The land of these valleys looks like ground-up shale and where it got the fertile composition of plant food is a question.

The top of the mesa is covered with a heavy growth of cedar and piñon, with some spruce in the gulches and hillsides. Occasional patches of sagebrush, greasewood, and rabbitbrush are the small stuff, In early summer, the fragrance and beauty of the flowers is more than impressive.

Under the upper stratum of rock, a seepage of fairly good water runs through the greater part of the mesa country. It is this seepage that has hollowed out the caves and caverns, with their overhanging cliffs forming arched roofs, making ideal places for the homes of animals and, later, of mankind. Very little evidence of the very first signs of man have been positively identified, but there is all kinds of evidence of the Cliff Dwellers as we know them.

As soon as we could, after we read the Reports, we commenced checking up on the tales told us by prospectors, freighters, and trappers. They told of buildings, still standing, with perfectly made walls with roofs still on them and great rubbish heaps covering many others.

One man even told of finding a piece of cloth in a loom in one of the buildings, [a piece] which he said he cut out of the loom itself. We thoroughly investigated the place and found that it was pretty well cleaned out of whatever it may have contained. The room was one of the lower rooms where water is nearly always standing. We doubted that the piece of cloth ever existed, because there was so little in the way of woven fabrics that could have weathered the attacks of trader rats or the moisture there.

That ruin is located in the main part of Cliff Cañon and is easily reached by climbing the jagged rocks in front of the main building.[8] The people themselves had used notched poles to climb up by. It was pretty well cleaned out of what it contained before the coming of any of our party, perhaps by hunters, trappers, prospectors, or even by the surveyors. Still, it was not mentioned in either the 1874 or 1876 Hayden Reports.

The lower part of the wall along the south part of the cavern connects with a leaning rock and makes a narrow tunnel. The hole to crawl through is only about eighteen inches wide by maybe two feet high. The picture of myself crawling through the opening shows that it was a tight fit for me and we had to come through almost sideways.[9]

Balcony House
Of this ruin Al recorded that it was easily reached by climbing the jagged rocks in front of the main building, although the people themselves had used notched poles as ladders. He considered pothunters and government surveyors as equals, for either would wreck an entire ruin to get one bowl they neither appreciated nor really cared for.

The Wetherill Brothers
All appearing stiff and weary, the Wetherill brothers pose for this
glass plate negative picture in the yard at the Alamo Ranch. Winslow
(left) and Clayton (right) stand behind (left to right) Benjamin Alfred, Richard, and John. Missing is Charles C. Mason, for years an
equal member of the rancher-explorer-archaeologist team.

Charles Christopher Mason

Al Wetherill included Charles as part of the Wetherill family, always writing of themselves as six, not the five brothers alone, who worked together as a team, not only in the Mesa Verde but also on the ranch as well. The Mason family had supplied spring water to the Wetherills in Joplin, Missouri, but had moved away before the Wetherills left that town.

Because it had a most pronounced balcony and the guarding wall along the edge of the cliff in front of the building, we called it *Balcony House*. Across the cañon was another probable prospect called *BrownStone Front*. Like the other houses, the pothunters had removed whatever was loose in the rooms of the two large buildings, as well as every small ruin in Cliff Cañon. It was discouraging to find not one scrap of anything to show who had lived there or why they had left. (Later, with good equipment, we were able to clean out and repair much of the damage done.)

Fortunately, pothunters usually take only what is in sight, because their ambition does not prod them into excavating below the surface. Since miners and all the others had wintered in the main cañon for years and knew of some of the buildings, they might have been the original pothunters themselves. They and the government surveyors came under the category of pothunters who would wreck an entire ruin to get one bowl they neither appreciated nor really cared for.[10]

In the main [Mancos] cañon, a great deal of digging had been done and smaller ruins had been demolished at an early date, probably having been worked by Hayden's crew. The Spaniards also could have been the ones who wrecked the houses in seeking buried treasure that they thought the ancient people had hidden there.

But the native Indian: never! They are too superstitious.

Thus began an eighteen-year self-imposed assignment of excavation and research among the ruins of the Mesa Verde. Ranching, unfortunately, took a secondary place in our interests and we gave time, material, and labor we could ill afford to cleaning out the ruins and giving the necessary care to the articles that we excavated in order to preserve them. Six of us worked at it and we, as did other ranchers of that region, had somewhat heavy responsibilities, one of which was an immense mortgage. [11]

It all reverts back, of course, to the fact that no one told us to do it. Any hardships were our own responsibility. But, we could not shake off the feeling that we were possibly predestined to take over the job, knowing what depredations had been committed by transients who neither revered nor cared for the ruins as symbols of the past.

Mostly we worked during the winters, carrying supplies and equipment up cliffs, across cañons, over ridges and mesa tops; through mud and in snow. (Summers we had to work on the farm from early to late just to keep the home fires burning and the inner man fit.) Because there were no roads and very poor trails, everything taken in or out was, by necessity, carried by pack horses. They had to be left in the cañons miles away while we scouted with a mighty few provisions and our equipment rolled up in compact form to make back packs. Many a day we went over and around slippery cliffs, always looking for the places of the ancient people. When a likely place showed up, we camped and brought up the pack animals and horses. Even then there was much carrying on foot and swinging around by ropes to reach certain points. Sometimes we came down on ropes from above; sometimes we roped a projecting piece of timber; sometimes we made high tripods and extended them even higher with timbers. In camp, it was necessary at times to dig shallow holes in the ground, fill them with piñon branches, put the blankets over, and then crowd the dirt close around the edges so as to be able to get warm enough to sleep.

In the Hayden Reports, the Mancos Cañon ruins were [stated to be] all small buildings, with one exception, and no ruins of importance in the main [Mancos] cañon except a round tower ten or twelve miles below the first ruin. Any further exploration of the cañons were not considered worthwhile at the time. (In fact, it was taking a chance, even now, because sometimes the Utes are quite ugly customers to have dealings with. Trappers occasionally went through the main cañon, for it is well stocked with beaver; but a trapper goes anywhere there is good trapping and considers the risk when he gets out.) No excavations or restorations were made by the survey members, so said the Report, and observes that it is unknown whether the ruins were destroyed by invaders or simply crumbled. We noticed the results of destructive hands; the buildings were too well protected to have crumbled.

One of the members of the Hayden surveying party said that the people in the Mancos Cañon must have been Sun Worshippers, because they always built in the cliffs on the western sides of the cañons so as to get the first rays of the morning sun. Such is the case in the main cañon, but for the reason that there were no caverns worthy any other place, so facts do not bear out that theory. We soon found that there were more and larger buildings on the opposite sides of the cliffs, since more and bigger caves are there. The Report entirely overlooked the greater ones in almost inaccessible places at the heads of box cañons tributary

to the Mancos Cañon. In those places, none of the great buildings face the east. Nearly all face the west and south, which
leaves the Sun Worshipper theory improbable.

At times, we were so short on supplies that we tried to get a
snowbound deer, but they were so poor that deciding to eat
them or go hungry stood about fifty-fifty. Once, though, we did
get a fat deer up a side cañon from our camp. Long after dark
we were on our way back to camp. I think now that the wind
was blowing up the cañon, for a bear met me face on, not over
fifteen feet away. The horse I was leading (with the deer across
its back) snorted and tried to pull away. The bear went "woof,
woof," and went tearing off up the cañon through the brush.
The boy with me shot him dead in his tracks, but said later that
if the bear had been a little closer he probably would have shot
up a tree instead of [shooting] at the bear.

In scouting around the country for a short time, we seldom
took a cooking outfit; only a frypan, coffee pot, and tin cup, or
even just a tin can hung onto the saddle. We would mix our
baking powder and salt in the flour before leaving the ranch
and all that was necessary to mix what we wanted was to add
water right in the top of the sack until we had enough dough
mixed to pick up. If we had a frypan that was not doing anything we would stand it on edge right next to the fire (with the
dough thick enough so it would not run out). We would let it
cook on one side and then turn the pone over to cook on the
other side awhile. If we had to, we would hunt a flat rock and
cook on that.

In a permanent-camp outfit, our equipment consisted of tin
plates, coffee pot, Dutch oven, frying pans, knives, forks, spoons,
and tin cups. We could cook beans and meat overnight in the
Dutch oven after digging a good-sized hole in the ground and
getting a good bed of coals under and over the oven and it
would work out its own salvation by morning. (At the home
ranch whenever we would kill a calf, we would take its head,
smear it all over with mud and chuck it in a similar way and by
morning it was ace-high. The Indians cook prairie dogs the same
way, only they would not take out the insides and that did not
look a bit appetizing. We liked prairie dogs pretty well until we
saw how they cooked them.)

Every man you saw could cook 'most anything that you could
eat—prospectors, ranchers, mule skinners, bull whackers, cow
punchers, desert rats, burro punchers, and even cattle rustlers.
The main diet was meat and more meat, with coffee, hot bis-

cuits, and dried fruit sometimes. Dried fruit, tea, cocoa, and rice were an unnecessary luxury, though.

In camp it is the rule that if anyone made a kick about the grub, it was his turn to do the cooking. Here is one tale that was going the rounds:

> The fellow who was doing the cooking was getting tired of his job and thought it about time that someone else should carry on for a spell. So, the next meal he fired a whole handful of salt into the stew. Nobody said a word for awhile, but finally the fellow at the foot of the row yelled out, "Great Scott! The salt!" Before they could call his hand, though, he added, "But I sure like it that way."

During our scouting around we had a camp miles down in the main [Mancos] cañon. Once a Ute with his family came along and, because he was out of flour, we traded him a small sack for a pretty good-looking pony. He then went on about his business and we with ours.

We hoppled out the pony and put him with our bunch of horses and supposed he would stay with them, so gave it no more thought until morning when we wanted to move camp. After we got our horses rounded up, there was no pony and we could not pick out his tracks with so many just like his around. We searched the hillsides and up the cañon, but no pony was to be had. We took it for granted that the Ute had just put one over on us.

Since it was still quite early in the morning, we saddled up a couple of top horses and intended to make a sneak on the Ute and go through his bunch before they began to move out. There was a dim trail going up the cañon sides, near a big volcanic blow-out. It took some time to make the top; about twelve hundred feet above the river.

From there on we put our horses in a hurry-up-quick order and went through their horses before they even knew we were around, but saw no sign of the pony we had traded for. The Ute wanted to know how we got there so we told him of the trail and about the loss of the pony. He then wanted to know if we thought he had taken it and we told him we thought he had. Then he said he was "heap mad" and just what were we going to do about that? I had a new knife handy, so handed it out to him and told him that it should settle the bill. He was perfectly satisfied then.

We got back to camp in an hour or so and scouted every hillside and backtrack and at last spotted Mr. Pony 'way up the hill-side just under the rimrock, where he was having the time of his life in the high bunches of grass all around him.

As for clothes in the searching, we finally had overalls made from tents. We seldom wore boots. There was too much grunting and cussing when they were wet and, too, they were such beastly things to climb around over the cliff and cañons afoot. In the winter in the snow, we did just like everyone else—used three-cornered pieces of gunny sacks. To half-sole our shoes, we made tacks from parts of broken axe handles.... We had our own bellows and anvil [at the ranch] and shod the horses and sharpened the tools. We made tallow candles, our own soap, and even pewter buttons and spoons. But everybody was in the same position, so all that made little difference to us. Everyone just took things as they came and no one was ever far from happiness.

It seems strange that it should have taken us so long to explore the cañons until we found the ruin that has ever been our pride and joy—Cliff Palace. But, we knew there must be many ruins that we had not discovered.

It may have been the year 1885, or it may have been a year or so later, or even before, when we had Dr. Comfort from Fort Lewis at the ranch. Since we had been scouting down through the cañons quite a bit and had a few things of interest from the cliff dwellings, he wanted to go down there and see for himself what they were all about. Although we had been interested in the ancient buildings for several years, we were still making a home worth living for and so could not give our attention to much outside work.

Brother Richard and I took him to the same ruin [Sandal House] that Captain Baker and I went to, but this time we had a pack horse and stayed over the night at the ruin, camping just below it in a little grove. We took in all the then-known ruins along the Mancos [River] as well as the side cañons.

In the morning we decided to look around a bit. Each did our own scouting independent of the others and they rode off up Johnson Cañon, which comes into the Mancos Cañon from the east. I skipped out on foot and headed down the river to the mouth of Cliff Cañon. I wanted to cross over the top of the mesa and could not take a horse along, for he could not climb the perpendicular cliffs. I wanted, also, to see how many of the buildings were worthwhile.

I took in every cliff house in sight up Cliff Cañon. I thought I could follow the cliffs around without climbing up and down to get to the next group of ruins. It was impossible, though, to follow the ledges and so I had to go to the bottom of the cañon and climb back up again to each ruin. One large ruin on the south cliff was thoroughly demolished, showing how unthoughtful a pothunter could be. Where the floor had been, the pothunters had almost completely excavated the cavern in an attempt to get "old Indian relics."[12] There was nothing to be found except fragments of pottery and scraps of material woven from yucca fibre.

A person who has not been over the route has little conception of the amount of physical force that was necessary to visit all the ruins in sight, none of them being less than twelve hundred and some as much as fifteen hundred feet above the bed of the cañon. A short distance up Cliff Cañon, there was a small gulch on the left hand that had been formed by the breaking away of a part of the immense cliff, leaving scattered rocks below the break. It was an almost impossible job to climb up through the break, but I managed it and noticed a small branch cañon coming into the main cañon. I passed it up because it did not look favorable from a cliff-dweller's point of view. That first left-hand branch of Cliff Cañon was not known to the surveyors of 1874 or 1876, because they did not mention, nor have any views of it, and [it] shows on the map as only a stub.[13]

As long as I was that far up, I thought it would be well to cross over the top of the mesa and come back down that small branch cañon.

The next ruin of any importance was Balcony House (the name tells why) perhaps two miles further up the cañon.[14] Across the cañon and at the same level was another good prospect, BrownStone Front. But, as usual, it was a total wreck. I took them both in, but, without tools to work with, I could not see if there was anything below the surface.

I came back across the cañon and went up the stub, or gulch, just above Balcony House and, through a small gap broken through the top ledges, got on top. Well, when on top of the mesa, it was just a short walk over to the cañon I had seen earlier in the day; maybe only three-quarters of a mile. As the day was getting far spent, as well as my energy and interest, I was losing the propelling force necessary to follow around the upper ledge. When I could find a place to get down over the edge, I just slid down into the cañon and was not looking for cliff dwellings any more.

The sides of the slopes were covered with small trees and

brush so as to almost cover the view of the top ledges. Great rock slides and jump-offs were hard to get around and over. Getting around and through the stunted-growth trees and brush wore me out completely. By this time I was just about dragging my tracks out, but I did occasionally look up to see what the upper cliffs were like.

Half-a-mile or so from where I came into the cañon, I looked up and saw, under an overhanging cliff, a great cavernlike place in which was situated what seemed like a small ruined city. In the dusk and the silence, the great blue vault hung above me like a mirage. The solemn grandeur of the outlines was breathtaking. My mind wanted to go up to it, but my legs refused to cooperate. At the time I was so tired that I thought later would be the time for closer investigation. Keeping on down the cañon was easy, but if I could have realized the extent of the find I had nearly made, I would not have been the least bit tired any more. My strength had waned to such an extent that I passed it by, not knowing what a great thing of archaeological value I was overlooking.

The cañon was short, perhaps only two or three miles from its beginning to where it reached the main Cliff Cañon. Soon after getting back into the main [Cliff or Mancos] cañon, I met Richard and Dr. Comfort trailing me up to see what had become of me, supposing that I might have fallen off a cliff or some other accident that would have held me up. I told them of the ruin, but was unable to impress them at the time and, as time went on, it was just about forgotten.

Now when Cliff Palace is mentioned it always makes me feel like the nations that discovered America must feel when America is mentioned. My own discovery has become completely clouded over for not following up the lead that was offered to me.[15]

Some time after I sighted the Cliff Palace, Richard and Charles [Mason] were riding the mesa top to locate water holes and cattle signs and came into view of the great ruin from across the cañon. Remembering what I had told them, they were half-prepared for the immensity of the vision but then, as later, the feeling struck them that the eerie sight could not be a reality. The cattle got away, but the amazement at seeing a miniature city spread out before them never did.

When they excitedly brought the story home, we all returned immediately to begin on this new project.[16] For a number of years after that, everything else was of minor importance to us.

The ruin was quite accessible, not much over one hundred fifty feet from the top of the mesa to the ground floor of the ruin. A hundred yards up the cañon, there was a stone stairway, through a crevice in the rocks, which led down to the level of the cave, and it was easy to follow the cliff around right into the house.

Things were arranged in the rooms as if the people might just have been out visiting somewhere. Perfect specimens of pottery sat on the floors and other convenient locations; stone implements and household equipment were where the housewives had last used the articles; evidence of children playing house even as children do now; estufas where the men congregated, leaving the ancient ashes of altar fires long dead.[17] There was no indication of violence toward the people themselves, but the greater part of the immense buildings had been pulled apart and the timbers in the roofs and floor removed.

We wondered about the possibility of the Spaniards, in their constant search for hidden gold, being responsible for the depredations. It had not been done by pothunters because the things that would have interested them were untouched. Nor were they destroyed by fire, for the walls still standing were not smoked up. The timbers had plainly been taken out and carried away, leaving the walls standing. Neither was there any evidence of battle, for the "mummies" indicated death occurred in the routine manner. They were not really mummies, but just the dried-up remains of a people without a name.

Looking over the magnificence of the ruins, Richard titled it the Cliff Palace.[18]

To know that you are the first to set foot in homes that had been deserted for centuries is a strange feeling. It is as though unseen eyes watched, wondering what aliens were invading their sanctuaries and why. To complete the absolute isolation of the dwelling, there was a buzzard's nest on the small ledge in the cliff back of the buildings. According to ancient mythology, anyone finding a buzzard's nest is in luck forever after. But, to our deep disappointment, they quit the nest and were not seen again.

Cliff Palace is the grandest structure in all that country and the most noticeable feature its two towers. The C.P. [Cliff Palace] is built under an arched roof ninety feet high, ninety feet deep, and had perhaps four hundred feet of front originally. In back of the series of rooms was an open space the entire length

Cliff Palace

"History" has not given Al credit for discovering Cliff Palace. On 8 December 1888, Richard Wetherill and Charles Mason exploring on the top of the mesa had their first view of the same ruin. "To me," Charles wrote later, "this is the grandest view of all among the ancient ruins of the Southwest. . . . A year or more before this Al had seen Cliff Palace but did not enter it . . . [for he] was very tired . . . and so it remained for Richard and I to be the first to explore the building." Charles said, in awe, "It looks just like a palace." Richard immediately dubbed the ruin "The Cliff Palace."

The Palace

Cliff Palace was often referred to simply as The Palace by the Wetherills. To make their pictures, they had to transport materials via horse or mule back from the Alamo Ranch down the Mancos Canyon a distance of forty-five miles to the various canyons and then up them to a base camp. Leaving the pack animals, the equipment then had to be carried by back pack up to the mesa top. Even then there were places where it was necessary to swing by ropes to reach certain points from which to photograph the ruins.

of the cavern that was filled with all sorts of trash, as well as burials and hidden pottery (which perhaps contained seeds originally).

There is no regularity in the plan of construction of this or any of the buildings scattered around in the desirable locations of the Mesa Verde. The unusually good work in the dressing of the building stones and the construction of the walls are the most distinguishing characteristics of Cliff Palace. The rooms go up three to four stories tall and each room was an average of eight feet square.

Three rooms are especially noticeable. At the west part of the building, the walls of one room are decorated in red. Another room is circular, six to eight feet in diameter, and is carefully constructed of dressed stone. It is about ten feet high, but unfinished. How these old timers could possibly build a wall so symmetrical with such a limited number of tools as they must have had is beyond comprehension. Adjoining the unfinished circular room, on the smooth plastered walls of an interior is a brightly colored figure, or drawing, in red and brown. It looks like an open book, about eighteen inches each way, with zigzag lines running up and down. Near the center of the ruin is an unfinished, oblong-shaped room; unusually large in comparison with cliff-dwelling rooms in general.

A large open-space well out toward the front of the building, yet under the protection of the overhanging cliff, was a sort of milling ground. There were quite a number of their grinding stones bedded in mud and kept in place with other flat stones, which formed a sort of box.

On the cliff opposite Cliff Palace is a comparatively small, circular, reservoir-appearing structure, with a long wall reaching back from the circular room for some distance, as if it might have constituted a guide for falling rain. That way the people would be supplied with water without having to go down over the cliff to the spring in the cañon below.

And when we rode into Navajo Cañon and found the ruins there, we rolled our world back unknown centuries. Everything was just as the original dwellers left it. None of the groups had been incorporated in the Hayden Reports nor the Jackson photographs, probably because of the inaccessible location or because of hostile Indians. We have no record of others but ourselves knowing first of the immense buildings in the branches of Cliff and Navajo Cañons, as well as many other small buildings in other branches.[19]

We went prepared to blaze trails and took care of the Indian situation by feeding them when they came around camp. Not many called, however, because of their superstitious fear of the dead, regardless of the era of interment. White people did not call either, because it was too hard a proposition to get through the labyrinth of cañons and ridges and [to get by] the Indians, who were not at all friendly to them.

There was only one ruin we failed to get into. It was along the main cañon of the Mancos [River]. The main part of the ruin had been below and perhaps [had been] built up to the upper ledge, which was about seventy-five feet high, but the lower part was all destroyed and we did not consider the risk would justify the attempt to reach it. The only means of reaching it was by coming over the cliff from above on a rope, an almost impossible feat for the reason that it would require more than one hundred feet of rope. Then, when on a level with the ledge you would be out from the ruin thirty or forty feet. To make a swing that distance would mean that much more [additional] distance to swing out into space beyond the perpendicular. We all had cold feet at the time we were working the lower part but, at another time, I believe Charley made an attempt.

As preliminary surveys and excavations were made, the dust of centuries filled the rooms and rose in thick clouds at every movement. We swallowed dirt and dust and dried-up Cliff Dwellers until we could almost read their hieroglyphics on the walls of the caverns and mud-smeared rooms and estufas.

As the work went along we could let our imaginations run riot, thinking of the people who had been there and were now gone. With the proper spirit of romance, you can gradually allow the mood of the Mesa Verde to take possession and let the silence speak and the mind's eye bring back to life and being the people whose book of life is forever closed. We could almost see them around us. We could watch them at work in the fields, with the dogs barking and the turkeys calling; the men coming in from work; women busy at their looms or grinding corn for the midday meal; the children playing near. The mothers loved them the same as moderns do and the effort to bring them up right was a full duty, too. She made them toys and baskets and things and she looked after them both day and night until they were big enough and strong enough to handle bow or stone knife or axe. To be sure, the children were human things and got their usual spankings when impressions of their little hands were

Baby Mummy
To this baby mummy Al composed the following ode:
Greetings, child of an ancient race.
How little is told by thy baby face
Of children's joys and a mother's tears
All lost now for a thousand years.

Thy once bright. eyes beheld great things.
Thou hope of parents that childhood brings.
Yet thou, with others of thy race,
Were doomed to pass; leave but a trace.

None there are who can thy story tell.
All are gone where thou didst dwell.
All voices stilled; all lips are sealed,
Forever closed and unrevealed.
Benjamin Alfred Wetherill

pressed in the mortar or for the mud balls they threw on the ceiling of the cave. Many are stuck there, even now. With so much just as the people left it, it is almost impossible to reconcile ourselves to the mental awakening of finding nothing but silent walls before us.

It was so much like treading "holy ground" to go into those peaceful-looking homes of a vanished people. It is something you have to experience to appreciate. It recurred again and again as we found new houses, untouched through all those long years. We knew that if we did not break into that charmed world someone else would, sometime—someone who might not love and respect those emblems of antiquity as we did. It was a strange feeling: perhaps all this had been given into our keeping until someone else might do it more capably than we.

In Navajo Cañon we found Square Tower House and in it ashes from coal. Directly across the canon was the Navajo Cañon Watch Tower. In a little stub of a cañon, just up from Square Tower House, was Spruce Tree House, the most perfect in condition of any of the buildings. It had a balcony, many good floors

Navajo Cañon Tower

and roofs, emblematic figures, and a corner fireplace. In a branch cañon was Spring House, all evidently under the supervising guardianship of the watch tower that overlooked the territory for miles around.

It [the Navajo Cañon Watch Tower] is the most conspicuous in all the Mesa Verde, situated on a section of the cliff that jutted out from the main cliff and could be approached only by a very narrow and dangerous ridge of rock. It was fully fifteen hundred feet above the bed of the cañon and fifty or more feet out from the cliff, although it was still a part of the rough cliff front itself. It was perhaps twelve feet across and the walls that were still standing were not over eight or ten feet high. It must have been a thing of beauty when at its best, with its smooth rock walls

Spruce Tree House
If this picture is compared with recent pictures of the same site, the ravages of time and nature will be strikingly evident. Several trees grow from oasis-like spots in the rock cap above the ruin in this picture while recent photographs will show a near-barren surface. The height of a spruce tree in the foreground toward the right makes a comparison standard for estimating the date of subsequent photographs taken by those the Wetherills escorted to the sites.

plastered both inside and out. It could have been only for a watch tower, since there were no rooms on the mesa back of it and none near. From it the view down the miles of cañon toward the river was exceptional, with the points of the Mesa Verde jutting in and out while the morning fogs from along the river rose from below.

There is also a large ruin of a round tower in the main [Mancos] cañon and, just above it on the rock walls, are pictographs of ancient ideas of art or history.

The watch towers (or Torreones, as the Mexicans call them) are little-known points of interest in the Mesa Verde region. The builders of those strongholds gave evidence of just plain preparedness. It certainly proved to us, the modern people, that, under the conditions of their time, they were no mean class to be imposed upon. The towers show care and ability in their construction and upkeep. Some towers were round, some square, and some were decorated in colors. But all were well protected from enemy arrows or whatever class of weapon was used. Almost anywhere you go in that ruin-infected district there are scattered towers in the piñons and no one ever thought of them except as store houses or for protection. We found the "watch tower" buildings scattered in southwestern Colorado near the Utah line. In one of the small branches of McElmo [Cañon], where it meets the Yellow Jacket [Cañon], there was at one time an immense ancient village. There are several of the square towers at that site. A number of towers are reported to be in the piñon country twenty to thirty miles east of Pueblo Bonito [in Chaco Cañon, New Mexico].

The watch towers were not by any means the only observation points. The high terminal points of the Mesa Verde afforded them, too. The Summit and the long, narrow, extended portion of the mesa we called *Point Lookout,* looked out to the north, the east, and the south. These were all that a besieged nation would need. The enemy would have to attack from all sides at the same time to get any satisfactory results.

In the course of a few years we had explored nearly all the cañons and mesa tops, naming every ruin, waterhole, and cañon, except Moccasin Cañon (which was already named for the trappers).[20] They all became almost as familiar to us as the walls of our own ranch house. All were named for persons or work done in the cañons—such as Ute, Navajo, Johnson, Grass, and so forth. The Cliff Palace was named for its impressive appearance; Balcony House because of the balcony (it was a picture sitting there upon an upper ledge) from which to scan the country for miles up and down the cañon; Long House because it was the longest (it may have surpassed Cliff Palace at one time but much of it lacks protection and so suffered from the elements—all the outer rooms not under the overhanging cliffs are now merely a mass of upturned rocks) ; Step House for the steps coming down the cliff front; Spring House for where it is located; and Spruce Tree House from the immense spruce tree, eighty feet tall and three feet in diameter, which was growing out of the center of an exposed estufa. Broken Arm House, where we found a mummy that had a broken arm that had never been put in place and had knit with one part of the bone overlapping the other; and Mug House, for all the mugs, were examples.

Then there were the reminder names such as Kodak House, where we hid the cameras, Jackson's Cliff House, Fortified House, Crevice House, Figured Rock House, Metate House, and Mountain Sheep Cañon. Other descriptive names were High House in North Cañon, Peter the Great's House, and the like, and that is the way we easily described them when referring to work done in any special place. We worked them all, with a miscellaneous assortment of lesser ruins, estufas, towers, and burial mounds thrown in for good measure.

The cliff-dwelling work was much more exciting than hunting gold (and I have done both), because we never knew what we might find next. We had started in as just ordinary pothunters, but, as work progressed along that sort of questionable business, we developed quite a bit of scientific knowledge by careful work and comparisons. Then, pottery was just pottery, but later on we noticed variety and quality. The beautiful, fragile pieces had to be carefully wrapped and carried down to the main cañons where our horses were. We always trusted brother John to this special class of work because he seemed to have a knack of packing and of dodging trees and rocks in the trails.

NOTES

1. At that period of time, it was impossible to completely discount the story that the ancient pueblo-building peoples of the Southwest were Aztecs. F. H. Chapin relates (*The Land of the Cliff Dwellers,* p. 170f) part of the Aztec-Montezuma legend as being "generally conceded facts of history" even while quoting Bandelier's report that discounted the legend completely. Belief in the Aztec legend spread from the theory that the builders of the disintegrating pueblos of the Southwest

must have been related to the Aztecs of Mexico. The native Indians of New Mexico obligingly adopted the theories as their own history and even found a suitable locale for the legend of Montezuma and the Aztec people. (*See* E. D. Cope, "Report on the Remains of Population Observed in Northwestern New Mexico, 1874," *Report Upon United States Geographical Surveys West of One Hundredth Meridian* [Washington, D.C.: Government Printing Office, 1879], p. 320f.)

2. In later years, this incident caused Al some anguish. When an article, "How I Found the Mesa Verde Ruins, as told by Benjamin A. Wetherill" (John Edwin Hogg) appeared in *Touring Topics* 23 (February 1931 [Beverly Hills, California: Automobile Club of California, 1931] p. 30f), it contained so much error that Al bitterly wrote in one of his notebooks: "Fact and truth in story writing are unnecessary. A supposed interview with me of the finding of the Mesa Verde ruins [shows that] a strong imagination and a liberal supply of adjectives does the job." The story stated that he had ridden a horse named Danté, when in truth the horse's name was "of a descriptive nature to match his unusually large stomach." Al attempted to record the other errors but gave up, wrote "rotten B. A. W." across the page and threw away the magazine. Unknown to him, Martha rescued it.

3. Al's exploration of and relationship to the ruins has never been recognized outside the family. Charles Christopher Mason, who married Anna Wetherill, gave a short account of their activities in the Mesa Verde cliff dwellings in later years. As Al stated, the Utes permitted the Wetherills to use the cañons of the mesa, but, Charles noted, to other settlers "they were not friendly and made it unpleasant for all who came into their country, so no one had thought it worthwhile to explore the side cañons." The Wetherills spent some time at their winter camp in the Mancos Cañon with "Al spending more time there than anyone else. . . . [We] learned that up the cañon were several cliff houses much larger than any yet discovered and Al more than anyone else explored them" (C. C. Mason, "The Story of the Discovery and Early Exploration of the Cliff Houses at the Mesa Verde," The Denver [Colorado] *Post,* 1 July 1917, section 2, p. 6.)

4. On 24 January 1887, Al wrote a friend that they had "had quite a fine time lately. Some of the officers from Ft. Lewis and a number of young ladies from Durango have been visiting us and we made an excursion down the Mancos Cañon to the cliff houses. We found quite a lot of interesting relics, among which were a number of sandals such as the ancients wore, great big pieces of woven material, and some perfect crockery, which was very nicely marked."

5. Captain Baker and others later became enthusiastic users of the shovel, according to Nordenskiöld's *The Cliff Dwellers of the Mesa Verde* (trans. D. Lloyd Morgan [Stockholm, Sweden: P. A. Norstedt and Söner, 1893] p. 46). At least once, Baker and his men registered at the Alamo Ranch on 16 October, 1889. They were: Capt. S. Baker, 6th Infantry; Geo. McK. Williamson, 2Lt. 6th Cavalry; F. H. Beach, 2 Lt, 6th Cavalry; and A. B. Shattuck, 2nd Lt., 6th Infantry.

6. The copies used by the Wetherills are no longer in the Wetherill library so it is not certain whether the Surveys or Reports referred to are several or only one. Several publications carried almost identical material: *Annual Report of the U.S. Geological and Geographical Survey of the Territories, 1874; Ninth Annual Report of the U.S. Geological and Geographical Survey of the Territories, 1875; Bulletin of the U.S. Geological and Geographical Survey of the Territories, 1876, Vol. 2; Tenth Annual Report of the U.S. Geological and Geographical Survey of the Territories, 1876,* all published as the reports of Dr. F. V. Hayden, U.S. Geologist in Charge (Washington, D.C.: Government Printing Office, various dates).

7. F. H. Chapin gave Dr. J. S. Newberry credit for naming the Mesa Verde during an 1859 expedition (*The Land of the Cliff Dwellers*, p. 174). Newberry's use of the term, however, indicates that it was a known place name even then ("Geology of the Banks of the San Juan," *Exploring Expedition from Santa Fe to Junction of Grand and Green Rivers, 1859* [Washington, D.C.: Government Printing Office, 1876]). Herbert E. Bolton (Pageant In the Wilderness, p. 6) is not able to definitely place the date of the origin of the Spanish names in southwest Colorado, but does record expeditions out of the northern capitol of New Mexico as early as 1765. Probably before and certainly after that date came traders who made the region east of the Colorado River nearly to the Gunnison River a fairly well-known area, complete with roads and named physical features by 1775. Escalante's diary refers to known place names as well as those they named themselves during the 1776 expedition, names which are, for the most part, still in use today. "Mesa Verde" is not mentioned in the diary, but Bolton feels their route was laid out along the old trapper's trail past the Mesa Verde, well known by that name before 1776 (p. 14).

8. The Cliff Cañon named here is not the short cañon known as Cliff Cañon today, although the ruin described is Balcony House. The text of the official Mesa Verde National Park brochures originally located Balcony House in Cliff Cañon and Cliff Palace in "the left branch of Cliff Cañon." This location was carried in the text from 1912 to 1917, although Cliff Cañon, in the list of major cañons, had been renamed "Ruin" Cañon by 1914. The 1917 map included in the brochure (U.S. Geological Survey, *Mesa Verde National Park*, Administrative Map, 1916 [Washington, D.C.: Government Printing Office, 1917]) replaced the name "Ruin" with "Soda" for the major cañon east of Navajo Cañon, but the text still continued to locate Balcony House in Ruin Cañon until 1923.

9. The sketch drawn in the margin of Al's notes at this point matches the picture on page 68 of Nordenskiöld's *The Cliff Dwellers of the Mesa Verde*.

10. One member of the Hayden Survey, W. H. Holmes, admitted his part in obtaining one whole piece of pottery and the pieces of another. He had been so "diverted by the fascinating relics" encountered in the Mancos Cañon during the 1876 Survey that he "made it a point to camp for the night directly below" one of the cliff houses on a return trip. While he was investigating the cliff house (probably Sandal House), one of his workmen, digging about in the debris of the ruin, uncovered the rim of a large, buried vessel and excitedly called for assistance. With the aid of sticks and a geologic hammer, Holmes and the workman, who was "fairly breathless from the anticipation of [finding] 'piles of [gold] moons,'" dug out a four-gallon capacity coiled-ware jar. Holmes, determined to take it with him, managed to wrap it in a blanket and to fasten it across his back with straps, carrying it in that manner for days. (W. H. Holmes, "Pottery of the Ancient Pueblos," *Fourth Annual Report of the Bureau of Ethnology, 1882–83* [Washington, D.C.: Government Printing Office, 1886], pp. 285, 315).

11. The six were the Wetherill brothers (Richard, Alfred, John, Clayton, and Winslow), and their brother-in-law, Charles C. Mason. In addition to the immense mortgage on the ranch, they constantly had to borrow operating money and to charge food supplies. Between 1889 and 1893 (the period of time when later publications claimed they were selling artifacts for fabulous sums), they were paying interest rates of 1% per month on food supplies to run the ranch and to feed "guests." Even small accounts that amounted to less than $50 required as much as three years to pay off.

12. The pothunter activity was denounced in precise terms by Dr. Prudden: "For any one who chooses now to gather them, the ancient pottery and other utensils . . . have considerable value for purposes of sale. . . . It is the practice of the settlers, on Sundays or other holidays, to organize picnics to the ruins. And the rustic swain is wont to signalize his regard for his Dulcinea by digging for her out of the desolate graves what articles the chances of the hour may bring. She cozily seated amid piles of broken pottery, darting lizards, and dead men's bones smiles complacently . . ." T. Mitchell Prudden, "A Summer Among the Cliff Dwellers," *Harper's Magazine*, September 1896, p. 552.)

13. The *Bulletin of the U.S. Geological and Geographical Survey of the Territories, 1876* substantiates Al's claim that the cañon was not named or positively mapped at the time. The map (p. 46) shows the entire northern side of the Rio Mancos as a, "Plateau cut by the Gulches into deep cañons and covered with Piñons and Cedars."

14. In 1930, Virginia McClurg claimed credit ("The Making of Mesa Verde into a National Park," *Colorado Magazine* 14 [November 1930]: 218) for discovering Balcony House in 1886 during an exploring expedition led by her into the cañons of the Mesa Verde. She did not, however, state whether she named the ruin herself, or whether it was named later, nor did she explain how the name was chosen.

15. Al's reference is to the garbled stories of the discovery of Cliff Palace. The official Mesa Verde National Park brochures gave Al and Richard credit for the discovery in the early years after the park was established. Later pamphlets changed the credit to "cowboys" Richard Wetherill and Charles Mason (often identified as a Wetherill cousin) ; others credited the discovery to "local cowboys," omitting the names entirely, while others carried only "1888. Discovery of Cliff Palace" in the Mesa Verde chronology. Excluded completely were two published accounts of the discovery. First was Charles Mason's account that he and Richard "rode out to the point of the mesa . . . and . . . from the rim . . . had our first view of Cliff Palace. . . . A year or more before this, Al had seen Cliff Palace but did not enter it. . . ." (C. C. Mason, The Denver *Post*.) The second was Louisa Wade Wetherill's record (with Frances Gillmor) in *Traders to the Navajos* (Cambridge, Mass.: Riverside Press; Boston and New York: Houghton, Mifflin and Co., 1934, when she related (p. 30) that during the winter of 1888 Al had seen a great cliff house in a branch of Cliff Cañon, but had been too tired to climb the cliff to observe it at close hand.

16. Of the publications since the second discovery of Cliff Palace, only F. H. Chapin and Charles Mason agree with Al's statement that Richard and Charles immediately returned to the ranch with the news: "Returning to the ranch he [Richard] met a party of hunters, among whom was Mr. Charles McLoyd, of Durango" (F. H. Chapin, "Cliff Dwellings of the Mancos Canons," *American Antiquarian* 12, no. 4 [July 1890]:195) . "On our way home, we came across the camp of some old friends, Charles McLoyd, Howard Graham, and L. C. Patrick (C. C. Mason, The Denver *Post*) .

17. The words *estufa* and *kiva* have been used interchangeably to describe the sacred, round rooms of the Pueblo Indians of the Southwest with little definition of the origin of the terms in much of the written material of the region. Herbert E. Bolton (*Coronado, Knight of Pueblos and Plains* [Albuquerque, New Mexico: University of New Mexico Press, 1949, 1964, and 1971], p. 417) explains that

Coronado and those following him called the round ceremonial rooms of the Cibola [Zuni] Indians by the Spanish term of *estufas*, meaning heated or hot rooms, for to them they appeared to be sweat houses. Frank H. Cushing ("A Study of Pueblo Pottery as Illustrative of Zuni Culture Growth," [Fourth Annual Report of the *Bureau of Ethnology* to the Secretary of the Smithsonian Institution 1882–83, Washington, D.C.: Government Printing Office, 1886], p. 476) defines the word *estufa* as being the same as the Zuni word *ki wi tsi we*, for the circular semisubterranean room, thus establishing the valid use of one or the other term. When the identical or nearly identical style room was found in the abandoned and deteriorating dwellings of the ancient peoples, the terms were applied to identify those recessed chambers.

18. Richard is credited with naming the ruin but Luella Mason Dunkelberger adds more detail to the actual naming process. She related that when Charles Christopher Mason, her father, looked at the ruin through the mist of sifting snow, he said in awe, "It looks just like a palace." From this, Richard phrased the title "The Cliff Palace." Several conflicting dates have been given for the discovery. Only F. H. Chapin (*American Antiquarian*, p. 195) matches Al's date of "Dec[ember] 8, 1888 Cliff Palace" in the Alamo Ranch books.

19. Al repeatedly draws attention to his search for a record of the discovery of any ruins in the cañons tributary to the Mancos Cañon previous to their discoveries. G. Nordenskiöld states flatly (*The Cliff Dwellers of the Mesa Verde*, p. 12): "The researches of Holmes and Jackson were until recently the main sources of our information as to the ruins of Southwestern Colorado. The cliff-dwellings which they saw and described are, however, small and insignificant in comparison with those discovered in recent times. If they had only left Mancos Cañon . . . they would have found ruins so magnificent that they surpass anything of the kind known in the United States. The honour of the discovery of these remarkable ruins belongs to Richard and Alfred Wetherill. . . ." In addition, Clarence S. Jackson, son of William H. Jackson, lamented (*Picture Maker of the Old West: William H. Jackson* [New York: Scribner's Sons, 1947], p. 214) that if Jackson and Holmes *had* gone up the side cañons, they and *not* the Wetherills would have discovered the magnificent ruins of the Mesa Verde.

20. At some period of time there must have been some controversy about who named the ruins, for a marginal note of Al's bluntly states: "The Department of the Interior had no word to say about the naming of them. Our 2,100 words to them gives the most correct names and the names have stuck." Nordenskiöld, however, claims credit (*The Cliff Dwellers of the Mesa Verde*, p. 49) for naming several of the ruins and the section of the mesa between Navajo and Cliff Cañons for F. H. Chapin, who was the first to publish any description of the more important ruins of the Mesa Verde.

6

Collections

IN making long trips down the cañons we met up with some miners, McLoyd and Graham, who wintered there, trapping along the river as it runs through the Mancos Cañon. They had named the large cañon known as Moccasin Cañon for the reason that at the mouth of it they had their camp and worked their buckskin for moccasins. They had been digging around a bit in some of the ruins of the cliff dwellings and had quite a number of articles such as pottery, woven material, and implements, which all looked good to us. Finally, we made an arrangement with them to go it on a larger scale, since we had the necessary equipment of tools and, the most important, horsepower. We grubstaked them and we were to see to getting the stuff out of the cañons.

The men went to work among the buildings with a will, working in all the cliff dwellings along the main [Mancos] cañon and a short distance up side cañons, mostly in the main part of Cliff Cañon. They did not, however, keep a record of which house, room, or cañon [where] they found the material. Neither were there any photographs of the articles found, nor room positions in the building given.[1] They did no destruction to any standing walls, but they threw the dirt and broken walls of one room into another that had already been worked. They pretty well dusted out the lower parts of Cliff Cañon. To them, all was just so much stuff to get out to market.

Brother John brought out of the cañon the stuff that they dug. It was a matter of packing it down there for carrying out by hand, practically a piece at a time. It was some long, hard job. When he got it to the ranch, it was repacked and boxed for shipping.

The grubstake men (McLoyd, Patrick, and Graham) considered the work well done and came out and took the collection on to Denver. McLoyd made contact with the Denver Historical Society, who bought the collection in 1889.[2] After that winter's work, they went out on their own and eventually became authorities on the Basket Maker People, working the region of southeast Utah.

With the sale to the Denver Historical Society as encouragement, Father and I decided that it was time to acquaint the general public with the archaeology of the Southwest. Spurred by his encouragement (he was never well enough to give more than moral support and a deep interest in the proceedings), we went at the second collection, during the winter of 1889–90, with fresh enthusiasm.[3] We commenced cleaning out the debris and collecting pieces of baskets, grains and seeds, pottery, weaving, implements, and even what remained of the people themselves. During the winter we were able to duplicate and add a little to what the previous collection had been. In this second collection were the living and burial customs. We worked over the same buildings as the first, as well as many others in the strangest and [most] remote spots. We tried to bring to light everything that might later be taken by the regular army of pothunters and so be scattered to the four winds.[4]

When the exhibit was ready, we catalogued the articles, packed it, and shipped it to Durango—all ready to educate the public [in the winter of 1890–91]. We opened with a, "Hip, hip, hurray, boys! Come and see what your country produces besides 'taters, corn, and grains."

To our complete dismay, the public did not particularly care about being educated. We decided Durango was too small to be interested in anything but civic-betterment activities. We did have fairly good results, at that, for we at least did not go in the hole.

We went on to Pueblo and lived through a short session there, meeting indifference verging on ridicule. We did make enough to buy our eats, but that was all. We simply could not believe it. We were too young and inexperienced to know when we were licked.

And we were so sure that our mission was worthwhile!

Through the kindness of the management of the Denver and Rio Grande Railroad, we shipped the whole works and ourselves on north. With heads bloody but unbowed, we decided to take Denver by storm, sure that there we would find enthusiastic audiences. I shudder to think of Denver, even now. We needed a smart agent and advance booking, I guess. It was a decided letdown to find that others did not share our enthusiasm and that, for the main part, people in the outside world cared not a thing about our ruins or their treasures. To us, it seemed that people have to be educated up to being interested in archaeological work, especially the historical and scientific classes.

We suffered for a couple of months and then the whole thing blew up. Just before leaving Denver via poverty row, we met up with the art director of the Minneapolis Industrial Exposition. He decided that we had just what he needed to fill out his part of that exhibit. He paid us well for our stuff, for which we were truly grateful, because we had no margin to go on and it was beginning to look as though we just might have to "ditch" our treasures and hobo it back home.[5]

Later, the collection was exhibited by them at the Columbian Exposition [Chicago, 1893], with a fairly good representation of a cliff and a cliff dwelling, with everything placed in the building as near as possible [to the way] they would have been used by the original people who made and used the pottery, baskets, cloth, and bone and stone implements. It even had a rough and rugged trail leading up to it. I did not go to the Exposition, but brother Richard did and had something to do with the placing and management of the things that were as familiar to him as our own household stuff. It [the collection] eventually went to the University of Pennsylvania.

Those first collections were a good sample of the others taken out of the Mesa Verde or adjacent territory, with the exception of the beautiful red pottery that was so plentiful over in Utah and Arizona. We could pick up fragments of the red pottery almost anywhere in any of the Colorado ruins, but the people there did not make it, probably for the lack of proper coloring matter, or the clay.

As work progressed, we developed quite a bit of scientific knowledge. Before then, nothing worthwhile considering the region had been written or photographed. We supplied both. All this, though, is in a separate account and will be attached. We did not, however, keep any records other than that which went with the collections.[6]

The third collection was by Gustaf Nordenskiöld, the first scientific and the only famous one made by us at the Mesa Verde. We were all proud of that collection. In coordination with amassing the collection, he wrote *The Cliff Dwellers of the Mesa Verde*, which was published in English in 1893.

But even before his coming, we had worked over the entire mesa and the cañons and furnished historical societies and individuals with enough material to keep scientists busy for years trying to place the people who once lived, fought, and died there, or simply drifted away.

During the spring of 1892, the state of Colorado made an appropriation for the Historical Department of the World's Fair Board to display a representative collection at the same Columbian Exposition as the Minneapolis Industrial Exposition and we did all we could to see that it was supplied. Making that fourth collection meant another summer's work in heat and dust.[7] But, we girded up our loins and, under the care of a could-be capable man, we attacked the dust heaps again with the plan to sift things clean this time. In all, we left the rooms intact, except for the great quantities of soil that we took into our own systems. It was so bad at times that we even tried to avoid breathing because the dust from the ancient, dried-up people was something awful.

We did get an immense amount of material. We all worked hard, since we did not know any better, but the collection was something to give the world an idea of who was who in Colorado in prehistoric times.

But, our boss did not know a thing about science, archaeology, or even photography, and did not last long in our midst.[8] So, we went merrily along, each one the boss of his own style of dirt slinging.

Everything brought in to where we were working, as well as material found or excavated where we were working, was transported out to the railroad via pack horse. It was some job to get so much of the fragile stuff into breakproof packages in the alforjas (saddle panniers) and, too, the entire route was through thick growths of cedar, piñon, and willow. We had to make our own trails and broaden any of the Indian trails. The Indians did not bother us at all. Of course, we did give them a hand-out occasionally when we passed their camps.

Richard was a sort of a representative for the state when the Exposition opened and he could make a pretty good spiel about the Cliff Dwellers. He was the most fluent talker and, being the oldest, always represented the rest of us. At the same time he, in a way, was represented as an authority on the previous collection.

The immensity of the undertaking commenced to worry us so we appealed to the government to 'take over.' We felt ourselves against a blank wall. There is no money to be made at archaeology, either as a scientific worker or a pothunter, and no future to one's efforts. There was never any money to do things the way we wanted and, unless an appropriation was made, no way to do anything. We contacted Smithsonian to see if that body would be interested in the project.[9] The reply was that they could do nothing themselves, but, if we cared to assemble a collection for them, they would be glad to accept it. Unfortunately we lacked financial backing to assemble a col-

Alamo Ranch Museum

Charles Mason at Grand Gulch
Whether the conditions that existed were snow or sand is difficult to
determine in the indistinct picture. The picture was supplied by
Luella Mason Dunkelberger from the Anna Wetherill Mason mem-
orabilia.

lection to meet museum requirements for that worthwhile organization, or any organization.

During 1893, we completed our own museum at Alamo
Ranch, in a building made purposely for the accumulation of
both the ancient and the modern work that had been piling up
on us for years. All the exhibits were properly classified and
catalogued.[10] The bulk of this collection we gave to the Colorado
Historical Society in 1901.

Also in 1893, we were all included in the work done for the
Hyde Exploring Expedition. The Hydes, backed up by several
million dollars as soap manufacturers, decided to make some
scientific donations for museums. The district [from which the
collections were taken] covered the Mesa Verde, as well as
southeast Utah and northeastern Arizona, and the Ruin Cañon,
or Hovenweep district, [which is] a branch of McElmo Cañon
in Colorado. This was followed up by several years at Chaco
Cañon; more particularly, the Pueblo Bonito cluster. In cooperation with Fred Hyde and brother Richard, the collections
were made under the supervision of Professor Putnam and
George H. Pepper.[11] Once again we were all together when our
own affairs permitted.

And, in all those years, the only backing we had at any time was when some hombre of Montezuma County had us all taken away from the ruins. I do not know to this day what it was all about. When the sheriff reached us, we were all just sitting in camp in idleness. When we reached Cortez, we had a friend there who stood by us; a Mormon we had known for years. We were turned loose, but it cost us sixty-nine dollars for the trouble *they* caused *us*. We went right back to the cliff and found that we were three miles out of the county and on the Ute Reservation.

Just a few years later, all pothunters were put out of commission and only scientific societies could vandalize the ancient monuments of the prehistoric races. Sure-enough hostile Indians had roamed the country when we were first in the Mesa Verde and they were followed by sure-enough hostile whites!

Many of the people we met and worked with were willing and able to see that we received proper credit with the powers that make fame and fortune, but the original discoverers of anything in this world of ours seldom get far in the hall of fame. It is unnecessary to quote instances: hunters, trappers, explorers, cattlemen, and even farmers.

Over the long period of years, John, Richard and I did most of the actual work. Charles [Mason] helped, as did Clayt and Win at various times, but we three felt that, somehow, the ruins were our personal responsibility. We derived much satisfaction from it all and felt that by our interest we helped to preserve treasures that otherwise might have been destroyed by vandals. If we accomplished anything at all toward giving Southwestern archaeology its rightful place in scientific interest—and I feel that we have—then it was more than worth all the hard labor, all the mummy dust we ate while we dug through those hot summer days, and [all] the unfriendly attitude[s] we often had to cope with from many who could have cooperated.

Those who followed us in working the ruins thought of us as vandals. It has been a sore spot with all of us every time we have heard ourselves referred to in that category. We never destroyed, nor permitted destruction, of any of the buildings nor their contents, feeling that we were the custodians of a priceless heritage. Those who came as tourists were aware that we would allow no damage nor wanton pilfering, and not many of them were the type who would. It was a difficult trip and there had to be a deeper interest than casual curiosity for any-

one to take it. Also, we had worked the ruins too long and put too much of our hearts and our sweat into careful excavations prior to the tourist years to let anyone treat them roughly.[12]

The collection of the Denver Historical Society was a great advertising boom for us and the Mesa Verde. It was the Society that brought before the public the discovery of the Cliff Dwellers. From then on, it was open season for the tenderfoot and the scientific people. We met them all with the best hospitality we could hand out. We were prepared to show the traveling public through the most interesting sights of our Southwest country. The business grew until the Alamo Ranch developed into an archaeological museum headquarters.[13]

NOTES

1. Criticizing the working methods of the McLoyd party indicates that the Wetherills were developing excavating methods that later became standard archaeological techniques and led Kidder (*An Introduction to the Study of Southwestern Archaeology* [New Haven, Connecticut, and London: Yale University Press, 1924 and 1962], p. 161) to credit them with being the first to use the principle of stratigraphy in the Southwest. But the criticism set a precedent in the Mesa Verde, for each archaeologist working there follows the pattern (J. Walter Fewkes, "Antiquities of the Mesa Verde National Park: Cliff Palace," *Bureau of American Ethnology,* Bulletin 51 [Washington, D.C.: Government Printing Office, 1911] p. 11) and Don Watson, et al., *Archeological Excavations in Mesa Verde National Park* [Washington, D.C.: U.S. Department of the Interior, 1954], p. 1) of criticizing his predecessor or predecessors.

2. Despite Don Watson's assertion (*Indians of the Mesa Verde* [Mesa Verde: Mesa Verde Museum Assoc.: Ann Arbor, Michigan: Cushing-Malloy, Inc. 1953], p. 26) that the Wetherills sold the collection for $3,000, no records or signatures have been located at the State Historical Society of Colorado building in Denver. In fact, the Society's "Major Archaeological Collections" tract compiled 29 November 1962 states that the purchase price is still not known, but that the collection was made specifically for the Colorado State Museum. Watson inserts the statement when referring to the article written by Charles C. Mason for the Denver [Colorado] *Post* (1 July 1917) and implies that the Wetherill brothers signed a statement that they received the amount for the collection. A search of Mason's statement shows that there is no mention of any amount of money, although he does corroborate Al's notes by stating that "McLoyd, being in charge" took the collection to Denver where "it was soon sold to the State Historical Society." No amount is entered in the Alamo Ranch cashbook, nor for any part of the amount, for the sale of the collection.

3. With obvious admiration for their enthusiasm and endurance, F. H. Chapin wrote of this second collection that was "secured under difficulties. It took ten pack animals to do the winter's work. . . . On one trip the snow was belly-deep

to the horses and mules. The corrugated jars, swung in sacks, were 'packed out' on the shoulders of the explorers—a difficult task considering the distance . . . forty-five miles from the ranch." (*The Land of the Cliff Dwellers*, p. 156f) .

4. Al clearly states their purpose in excavating with thorough intent, for he was well aware that indiscriminate collecting provided no record. He may have been aware that W. H. Holmes had made a comment ("Pottery of the Ancient Pueblos," *Fourth Annual Report of the Bureau of Ethnology*, 1882–83, p. 316) about removal of artifacts: "The collections from the valley of the Rio de Chelly, one of the richest sections of this district, are very badly scattered and the vessels can not be identified. Many fine things have been carried away . . . without a proper record of the locality. This . . . makes it impossible to study the shades of distinction between the wares of neighboring localities." Al was also aware of the then current custom of selling artifacts. No publications ever named those who supplied the material for Hildebrand and Bauer, a Mancos firm that advertized "Aztec relics" for sale as early as 1890 (McNitt, *Richard Wetherill: Anasazi*, p. 35) . Nor did the article, "Cliff Dwellers of Colorado" (Littel's *Living Age* [Boston, Mass.: Littel & Co. 1890], 2 August 1890, no. 6, p. 319) identify the individuals who returned to Durango [Colorado], "having collected . . . many relics . . . [from] one cañon . . . honeycombed for a hundred miles with cliff dwellings." The article was a reprint from *The Spectator* (A Weekly Review of Literature, Politics, Theology and Art [London, England: John Campbell, 1 Wellington Street Strand] 64 (26 April 1890) : 583) and carried no identification as to the author of the article.

5. The purchaser was H. Jay Smith, since "Art Director Minneapolis Industrial Exposition" in his handwriting follows his signature in the Alamo Ranch guest register on 5 March 1892. Further proof is found in "Exposition Art," *The Minneapolis Industrial Exposition Annual*, 1891, which carried an article (p. 20) about Smith's acquisition of the "famous Wetherell [sic] collection of Cliff-dweller relics" and its display just under one of the balconies in the Sculpture Hall. Although some have thought that the purchase occurred at the Alamo Ranch in December 1892, it is obvious that Smith was already in possession of the artifacts long before that date. Smith, instead, purchased a collection from C. M. Viets of Cortez, Colorado, at that time (F. W. Sharrock, "The Hazzard Collection," *Archives of Archeology*, no. 23 microcards [Madison, Wisconsin: University of Wisconsin Press, 1963]) .

6. The "separate account" has disappeared and, unfortunately, the records that "went with the collections" have not always been kept with the artifacts, leading to the presumption that the Wetherills were remiss in their manner of collecting. Dr. Prudden denied Wetherill omission as follows: "The excavations controlled by them were conducted with the utmost care and conservatism, careful records and descriptions being made. The learned men of the day seemed to care nothing for the pots or the ruins and no funds were forthcoming then from the government or from other sources to make investigations" (*Biographical Sketches and Letters of T. Mitchell Prudden, M.D.*, Yale University Press [New Haven, Connecticut: Yale University Press, 1927] p. 140) .

7. This collection, termed the *State Collection* by the Wetherills, is exhibited by the Historical Society of Colorado in Denver as the Wilmarth [sic] Collection. According to the Society's tract "Major Archaeological Collections," Jesse Nusbaum provided their information (p. 4) that the material was purchased from the

Wetherills for $3,000, with The Denver *Republican* (22 January 1893) cited as reference. That particular article makes an entirely different statement, reading instead (p. 7) that the state appropriation "allowed only $3,000 for the *entire historical department,* of which the archaeology of the cliff dwellers *is but a branch*" [italics added]. The name Wetherill is not even mentioned, but "four men" were reportedly "employed by Mr. A. F. Willmarth in making his collection for the state." If the Wetherills were the "four men" employed (and it is agreed that they did make the collection), the Alamo Ranch cashbook does not record that they were even paid for their labor. Under no circumstances could they have "sold" the collection to the state. Search into the records of the World's Columbian Exposition, 1893, reveals no mention of the Wetherills and only one sentence that even remotely pertained to the cliff-dweller relics when Governor Davis H. Waite reported that the historical department, which included ethnology and cliff-dweller relics, had received five awards at the World's Fair (p. 36 of a pamphlet entitled *Biennial Message of Governor Davis H. Waite and Inaugural Address of Governor Albert W. McIntire Delivered Before the 10th General Assembly, State of Colorado, 1895* [Denver, Colorado: Public Records, State Archives and Records Service, Records of the Office of the Governor: Albert W. McIntire, 1895–1897; *Executive Records,* 1895]. Combing through the warrants issued for the World's Fair produced none that included the name Wetherill (Denver, Colorado: Public Records, State Archives and Records Service, Register of Warrants Issued from the Auditor's Office, Book C, pp. 276–82, 23 November–10 December 1892; pp. 289–99 February through March 1893. Book D, pp. 10–31, March through May 1893.)

8. The "boss" could have been either D. W. Ayres or Arthur F. Willmarth, for both signed the guest register as representing the state for the historical exhibit. Ayres signed the register on 19 April 1892 and probably brought the news that the state historical exhibit would include cliff-dweller artifacts, for the date matches the, "4-19-1892, State Appropriation," recorded in the ranch records. The news was a year old, however, for Senate Bill 120 (1891) had been passed on 18 April of the previous year and had provided for a total appropriation not to exceed $100,000 for the cost of the entire state participation in the Fair of 1893 (Denver, Colorado: Public Records, State Archives and Records Service, Sessions Laws of Colorado, 1891, "World's Columbian Exposition," pp. 406–409.)

9. Proof of contact has been elusive, although Willa Cather used such a situation in *The Professor's House* (New York: Alfred A. Knopf, 1925) to describe the government indifference to the discovery of the cliff dwellings. Miss Agnes Cowing voluntarily provides a valuable contribution by recalling that she listened to Julia Cowing and Richard Wetherill discuss the "Hyde Indian Museum and efforts to get Congress interested in the Mesa Verde as a National Park" when Richard was visiting in their Brooklyn, New York, home in 1893. In addition, Dr. Prudden wrote (*Harper's Magazine,* September 1896, p. 552) that "it is one of our numerous national disgraces that the United States government does not realize the importance of the immediate occupancy of this wonderful field of archaeological research."

10. The museum contents were insured in 1894 for just $75 less than the contents of the by then ten-room Alamo Ranch house, giving evidence of the value the Wetherills placed on the museum artifacts. The insurance company—Prewitt, Pickerell, and Kephart—evidently did not hold the contents in such high esteem, for the insurance policy listed the collection as being "relics consisting chiefly of

pottery, mummies, and aztec and indian curios." A letter from Richard Wetherill written in the summer of 1897 (Appendix E, (McNitt, *Richard Wetherill: Anasazi*, p. 332) mentioned that the Alamo Ranch Museum contained hundreds of sandal specimens and several sandal-shaped stones. Interviews with members of the Wetherill family established the collection as still being intact during the summer of 1899, once more verifying the fact that the Alamo Ranch collection did not become the Smith-Hazzard Collection.

11. Although Frank McNitt (*Richard Wetherill: Anasazi*, p. 172) was convinced that Richard Wetherill and George H. Pepper became enemies during 1898, the Alamo Ranch records do not appear to bear out that theory. Pepper was at the Alamo from April to June of that year and some of the entries in the cashbook appear to be in his handwriting. Until May, Richard and his family were also there, following the birth of Richard's first child. If discord developed, it was not extended to the rest of the family, since autographed copies of Pepper's later publications were given to Al.

12. This entire paragraph, taken from Al's 1948 summary, displays a meditative perspective on the Wetherill role in Mesa Verde history and notes the derogatory references to themselves that occurred long after every Wetherill was gone from the area. In their defense, T. Mitchell Prudden wrote that the Wetherills "were early impressed with the scientific aspects of the matter and while they have been often identified by ignorant critics with the earlier devastations, they were in fact most eager and persistent in preserving from harm the great ruins of the Mesa Verde, as well as others, through a series of years in which they were neglected by the archaeologists, ignored by the government authorities, and sorely threatened by the tourists— (Yale University *T. Mitchell Prudden*, p. 141.)

13. McNeil Camp of Durango contributed much pertinent history concerning the Alamo Ranch as archaeology headquarters in an interview conducted by Ralph Bennett of the *Durango* (Colorado) *Herald* (31 August 1952, p. 8). Excerpts from Camp's quotes revealed that when news of the Wetherill discoveries of the major ruins of the Mesa Verde was

"flashed to the four corners of the world in 1888, . . . correspondents were sent down post-haste. . . . Following them came the world's greatest archaeologists, ethnologists, and geographers. . . . The archaeologists and explorers . . . lodged at the Alamo, the roomy, ever-hospitable hacienda of the Wetherill clan. . . . The correspondents and scholars were pretty dependent upon the Wetherills. In turn, the Wetherill boys, keen of intellect as they were, received as it were a free university education in archaeology and kindred subjects, from the world's best minds of the time. Already the best guides in the Southwest, they quickly became the Southwest's best-informed amateur archaeologists, as well."

CHILDREN OF THE ANCIENTS

Little sandals in the trash heap just beside the door,
The welcome little patter of the feet upon the floor.
We hear their voices echo on the cliffs across the way.
Little children playing grown-up in what they do and say.

The laughter of the children and the pounding of the loom,
We imagine we can hear them in the quiet of the gloom.

Mud balls on the arching roof still show where children played.
Hand prints in plaster soft, a thousand years have stayed.
Mother catches soon the youngster. We can almost hear him squall
As she paddles with her sandal where there are no pants at all.

Benjamin Alfred Wetherill

7

Basket Makers

W E have come a long way since we found a few pottery
shards and broken points in the small mounds on the
ranch and tried fruitlessly to excavate in the vicinity where we
unearthed the pieces. When we learned that the inhabitants of
our country were not Mound Builders, as was first thought by
many, our progress has been steady.[1]

The Cliff Dwellers did not occupy the vast region in which
they lived without having predecessors, neighbors, and succes-
sors. The country had been well populated before them and has
been a center of population since then.

We advanced the theory that the Cliff Dwellers had been
preceded by a more primitive culture, which we originally referred to among ourselves as "those wild fellows," and were, in
turn, followed by yet another group, the Village (or Valley
Land) Dwellers, or so-called Aztecs. We class as Cliff Dwellers
proper the group who were a superior race for their time and
whose skulls were flattened in a perpendicular manner.

Although the ancients of these valleys and caverns have never been the object of any research expedition, we feel we have
made careful study and enough comparisons to say that now we

know our southwest archaeology.[2] The ancient peoples left indisputable history of their manner of living and the dangers that surrounded them. Wood, bone, stone, shell, copper, bronze, and iron follow each other in the different ages. Stone, bone, shell, and wooden implements tend to show the age in which the Cliff Dweller lived. The crania of the people themselves throws a great deal of light on the several steps of advancement toward civilization. A single skull does not tell much, but where a dozen or more similar to the first one occurs, it does tell much, twenty such skulls considered sufficient to make a decision as to the type specimen.

Perhaps some day the different tribes, races, and people will be classified and tagged as to the age of the existence and the time, as well as the cause, of their disappearance from this once thickly populated region.

We owe the preservation of all the ancient dwellings to the superstition of the native Indian, however. All the abundant supplies of articles of archaeological interest, the untouched decorations on the walls, and the near-perfect condition of so many of the houses are all due to the fear of the places of the dead.[3]

And, of course, the lack of moisture in the air results in the preservation of many perishable articles.

For some reason, never explained, all Anasausies [Anasazi] have been classed as "Aztecs," but there is no similarity between the races, or their dwellings, in Old Mexico and these scattered villages and individual wrecked houses, and only a trace of resemblance in either handiwork or decorations. Nor can the ruins in the Mancos Valley be compared to the immense structures that formed the population centers of the Southwest. There is so much to get at when trying to state the date of when a race of people lived and how long they were the masters of a certain section as told by their implements of war and chase, their pottery, baskets, weaving, and so forth, and even the tree rings in the logs of their houses. It seems odd that the positive date of their occupation can not be placed.

When we were with G. Nordenskiöld during his research in the cliff dwellings of the Mesa Verde, we had our suspicions confirmed about the "wild fellows" we felt must have also been in the mesa. At the building known as *Step House*, we had just about finished work when we came upon a little mud-and-stick wall. In probing around in it, we came across some strange and unusual pieces of pottery. The largest was nearly fourteen inches

in diameter and perhaps three inches deep and was all in fragments. It had been made in a basket, because the marks of the
basket were pressed on the outside surface. It was uncolored and
heavy, coarse in quality, and had been dried, or maybe burned
a little, in the basket until hard enough to use. On the inside,
there was a figure made by indentations with a sharp implement
while the clay was still soft. G. N. [Gustaf Nordenskiöld] has a
picture of it in his book. One piece seemed to be just a chunk of
mud beaten into shape on the inside of a basket. Three other
pieces represented cups or drinking vessels. In shape, they were
like a cocoanut with the top cut off. These were similar in quality to the bowls and none could have been baked. This class was
just beginning pottery making and had but few baskets, either.

We felt there was no relationship between them and the
Cliff Dwellers, because there was evidently too long an interval
between their wild, nomadic ways and the almost civilized state
of the Cliff Dwellers. We felt these early people buried, and perhaps lived, in the large potholes under the overhanging cliffs.
But, finding the pieces that were so different attracted no special
attention, not even to Nordenskiöld, even though the little mud-
and-stick room was a number of feet below the walls of the later
people and was so different in construction.

After G. N., we found another curious structure there [Step
House]. It had been burned, but it was like the houses the Navajos have today, and with it was some mica pottery, all crude and
coarse like the ones in the little mud-and-stick room.

A few years later, we found out what an important find it had
been, for, with the Hyde Exploring Expedition, we soon discovered where our strange pottery belonged.

In looking for new worlds to conquer, we had scouted over
southeast Utah and on south of there into Arizona; country containing deep, dark cañons, gorges, and cliffs. We hoped to find,
in the out-of-the-way places, ruins and archaeological specimens
that would link together our rapidly growing record of the ancient civilizations who had lived in the Southwestern deserts in
the lost ages.

Thousands of square miles of the Southwest, with the Four
Corners as a center, are supposed to be composed only of sand
dunes, lava flows, and barren rock. Yet here, since the beginning
of time, Nature has been busy smoothing out the heights and
filling in the valleys, only to tear it all apart again to cut the cañons. The vegetation is considered to be only cacti and yucca

and the land the home only of horny toads, lizards, and rattle-snakes. Yet in all that wild country, one is seldom out of sight of some evidence of the human race. The archaeological possibilities of this region are unlimited and perhaps untold ages have slipped by since the first of the human races hunted, fought, and passed on, leaving what little we now find. All through that country, in almost every recess, cavern, or overhanging-rock shelter is found evidence of both the ancient and modern life.[4]

The first people to occupy any of these retreats did not understand the art of building places for comfort, other than some sort of windbreak of brush or animal skins. Later, a few mud walls or rock was piled up. In the out-of-the-way places, under the cliffs, and in the protected caves, yet beneath where the Cliff Dweller and Pah Ute had lived in the dirt and trash of centuries, we found potholes and burials of the same nomadic people as the early ones we found in the Mesa Verde and in the cañons and gulches along the lower San Juan [River] district.

The lower San Juan seemed to be the main territory of that race. They were probably just hunters, because the evidence shows that they did not have pottery then, but acquired the art later. Even when they did learn pottery making, the pottery was negligible—just rough daubs worked into crude vessels. The class of pottery was the same as that strange pottery of the Mesa Verde, yet the fur and feather robes were of the finest grade and the baskets the largest sizes and greatest number ever brought to light.

The basketware was so plentiful and of such sizes and shapes as to make them a distinctive people. The basketry was of all descriptions and for nearly every use conceivable. It was an art with the people that has not been improved on in the long period of time since their existence. Split willow and willow twigs were used and some were made into mats for the floors and were also used as one of the coverings of the dead.

Where the three races (the modern Pah Ute, the Cliff Dweller, and the earliest people) had lived for centuries, it was hard to determine what belonged to which people. As the drawings, the pottery, and the baskets of each and all were found in the middens (trash heaps), it was necessary to find some term to keep all the peoples separate. Richard gave them the name *Basket Makers*, not only on account of the great number and variety of baskets, but [also] to distinguish the material of their time. The name of *Basket Maker* has been generally accepted, although there has been some objection to it. At any rate, it is distinctive.[5]

The Basket Maker graves were dug in the dirt of the caves, mudded all around, and a number of bodies put in the same pit. (The same manner of pothole was used as storage pits or safety deposits to keep their contents away from the rats or prowling animals.) Beautifully figured burial robes of feather cloth or of heavy cloth made from yucca fibre were used as the inside wrappings for the bodies. The sandals were yucca and were shaped rather square at the toe. Always, a large basket was used as a covering for the dead, as well as many smaller ones placed with the body.

These "wild fellows" (and they certainly looked the part) were larger people than the later ones—about the size of some of the modern Navajos. Their crania were natural in shape, rather long from front to rear and short from top of head to chin, the forehead being rather narrow, but with plenty of brain capacity. There was no unnatural flattening of the back part of the head, which was common with nearly all the later people, so perhaps their method of carrying their youngsters was different.

One man in particular had a near seventy-inch brain capacity and another large man, upwards of six feet in height, was probably some fighter. He had met up with a bear and had never had a chance to climb out on a limb. He was on the little end of the fight in which both met their death. A major operation was given by the professional members of his clan, because he had been cut almost in half about his waistline. A bear claw was inside of him and the place sewed up with a string of yucca fibre the size of heavy wrapping cord. The operation was not successful, since there was no evidence of the incision having started to heal.

Another body was that of a very large woman who was, without doubt, an albino, having the regulation red hair and light red skin. Albinos are found in a number of the Village Indian [Hopi] tribes at the present day. There were numbers of other large people, but it is so with all races—they do happen occasionally.

The hair of these folks was not always the heavy, coarse, black color, but a dark brown, and their skin was inclined to be of a finer texture than one would expect to find with people who were out in all sorts of weather and climates.

Broken bones were not doctored, but left to the tender mercies of Nature. The teeth of these people were nothing to call perfect, but rather was just the opposite. I guess the reason of it was the quantity of strongly acid wild fruit with no sweetening of soda compounds to offset it. They had the fruit of the yucca for food, but it has a sickeningly sweet taste. Still, the Indians of today make a sort of bread out of the stuff, not unlike ginger-bread without ginger.

They must have lived almost entirely by the fruit of the chase, although they may have raised a little corn in some favorable spot near their open-air homes.

What may have originally brought these people together socially and for the mutual benefit of all, may have been the disappearance of game sufficient to supply the population. Also, starvation is a great civilizer and it compels people to adapt themselves to altering conditions. So, a lack of easily procured game would drive a race to the pursuit of agricultural methods and the cooperation brought about by a group would lessen each one's individual tasks.

We found no bows. The atlatl and the stone axe seemed to be the weapons of offense and defense. In a cave near Bluff City [Utah], we dug out a body with the dart of an atlatl in the skull, the dart having gone into the head under the chin with sufficient force for the tip of the dart to penetrate half-an-inch beyond the top of the skull. There were other bodies with just dart-point wounds.

The atlatl is strictly an American Indian development and numerous ones were found in the ruins of the Four Corners district. It was not common among the early peoples, although the Aztecs in Old Mexico had them in quantities. The make and method of using this harmless looking thing is as follows: A stick nearly three feet long and an inch in diameter is hollowed at one end and loops for fingerholds made about ten inches from the end. The shaft holding the flint point—about six inches over-all—fits into the hollowed end of the longer stick for a depth of perhaps two inches. When in use, the section with the point on it would be put loosely into the longer shaft, the fingers put through the loops, and then the whole thing drawn back over the shoulder and brought forward with all the force the arm could give. It must have gone like a bullet, as the points in the skulls show.

They also used a boomerang, a distinctly Australian weapon —or could the Australians have copied them from our people?

The drawings on the walls of the caves are so mixed up with

those of the Pah Utes and the Cliff Dwellers, that it would be hard to separate the various graphs from those of the Basket Maker. Pottery would be the usual route in comparing similar makes and designs in decorations, but there would not be much to decipher from the decorations on Basket Maker pottery.

Just what became of the Basket Maker is a question. Were they run out by the incoming Cliff Dwellers, or had they already vacated all that high land for the more hospitable country of the lower San Juan before that time? Who can tell or enlighten?

For all that, where did they come from? Always, too many words and too many so-called proofs are offered that place the ancient Americans as drifters from Europe and Asia. But just consider what we find here in the U.S. right now. Would ethnologists in a few thousand years from the present classify *all the races in this country as one people?* Or would they take up twenty crania from the region of New York City, Philadelphia, or Boston and pronounce them as being the same race as some of the folk we hear about in the hidden mountain districts of the backwoods? In comparing the highly developed head of anyone having access to the advantages of the scientific devices at present, with the man whose only ambition is to hunt and fish, the former would be classed as a highly developed race and the other just out of the Stone Age.

NOTES

1. Probably the evaluation material used was "The Great Serpent and Other Effigies" article by S. D. Peet in the July 1890 *The American Antiquarian and Oriental Journal* 12:211, for the Wetherill library contained a worn-out copy. Peet included in his discourse sufficient information for the Wetherills to determine that there could be no relationship between that culture and the one they were familiar with. They may also have had access to the *Houses and House-Life of the American Aborigines* (Washington, D.C.: Government Printing Office, 1881) by Lewis H. Morgan who presented an argument that the Village Indian ruins of Mc Elmo Cañon and Ute Mountain were possibly related to the Mound Builders (p. 188–201) and the Mound Builders of Ohio explained as a natural spread of Village Indians from the valley of the Rio Grande or San Juan Rivers. If so, the Wetherills rejected the theory.

2. Al does not claim to know Southwestern archaeology around the turn of the century without just cause. George H. Pepper gave them such credit: "The Wetherill family of Mancos, Colorado, have been closely associated with the archaeology of the Southwest for nearly a quarter of a century and they have had the honor of bringing before the public the great Cliff Dweller region of Colorado and Utah. They have been untiring in their efforts as collectors and are keen

observers. . . . It is from . . . the statements of the Wetherill brothers, whom I consider authorities on this subject, that I shall draw many of my facts ("The Ancient Basket Makers of Southwestern Utah," *American Museum of Natural History,* Supplement to *American Museum Journal* 2, no. 4 (April 1902) , Guide Leaflet no. 6, page 3f) .

3. Reluctance to enter the cliff houses did not last long, for Dr. Prudden regretfully recorded that "the Indian has learned his lesson from the white brother and learned it well. A few years ago the Indian stood in superstitious dread of these ruins. . . . Now all is changed. The Indian has learned that no harm seems to come to the white man . . . so, at last, they too have begun to dig and devastate on their own account, destroying great amounts of valuable relics" (*On the Great American Plateau* [New York and London: G. P. Putnam's Sons and The Knickerbocker Press, 1906] p. 173.)

4. Evidence of Al's close observation of the area is revealed through his photographic file. One such cavern that contained "evidence of both the ancient and modern life" was rediscovered and named Promontory Ruin in Tse-a-chong (Ugly Rocks) Cañon of the Carriso Mountains in the northeast corner of Arizona (Charles L. Bernheimer, *Rainbow Bridge* [Garden City, New York: Doubleday-Page, 1924], p. 151) that Al had photographed some time in the 1890s. According to Martha, Al was known as a "loner" in the family and any time that he could get away from the duties on the Alamo Ranch he saddled up, often with a camera, and took off for a search in the Four Corners area. Seldom, though, did he carve his initials in a ruin, for he felt such action desecrated the memory of the ancient peoples. Thus, he left no proof, except through his photographs, that he had been there. In later years as he learned of "new discoveries," Martha reports that he would chuckle and say, "I have been there. There is not one dwelling in the whole area that I have not seen."

5. Frank McNitt described the development of the term *Basket Maker* in *Richard Wetherill: Anasazi* (p. 64f.) . In his progress reports to the Hyde Exploring Expedition (H.E.E.) , Richard's original term was *Basket "People,"* but left the choice of naming the people to Talbot Hyde. Hyde altered the title to *Basket "Maker,"* a term that Richard accepted, according to the H.E.E. records, with reservation. In the collection of family letters, however, John, writing to Al, commented about a group then excavating in the Kayenta, Arizona area and added that "they did not know we named the B.Ms. [Basket Makers] because of the huge carrying basket we found over the burial and because they had no pottery." This would indicate that the Wetherills had either used the term *Basket "Maker,"* or had considered using it, from the inception of their discoveries of the early race.

8
Cliff Dwellers

THE subject of the cliff dwellings and the people who built and occupied the buildings and then finally disappeared is like taking a page or two out of a book of interesting mysteries—mysteries without beginning or end—the only key being what we see of the buildings and their contents. Perhaps it was ages and ages after the Basket Makers before the Cliff Dwellers ever developed into their homemaking, house-building habits. In between, we find evidence of a people occupying the same protected places; the people who were just beginning to come up a step into pottery and basketmaking. We could not, at the time, see any immediate connection between the long-lost Cliff Dweller and any of the neighboring semicivilized tribes.

The Cliff Dwellers occupied not only the Mesa Verde, but [also] a large area of the Southwest, for the ruins of their buildings are to be found far out into Utah and Arizona (scarcely any north or west of the Colorado River, [although] Dellenbaugh took a view of a small house at Green River Crossing, near where Escalante crossed in 1776, and I believe that it is the most northern cliff dwelling of any we know), south down into New Mexico, and farther south well down into the state of Sonora, Mexico. The Mesa Verde was, without doubt, the center of the population of that people. The eastern Arizona Cliff Dwellers were, however, a superior lot of builders and workers. They, the Kitseil [Keet Seel] and Cañon du Chelle [de Chelly] people seem to show more kinship to the last Mesa Verde people than to any other. There was another group along the lower San Juan River region who seem to have been, if one is to judge by the buildings, a degenerating race of Cliff Dwellers.

It would seem that the Mesa Verde Cliff Dwellers had an eye for the beautiful in the selection of locations. So much there is to testify to such a feat. The deep-wooded cañons stretch miles away to the southward to meet the river and the view from the northern rim can not receive adequate justice from any author of descriptive articles. It all fills one with a feeling of the greatness of all of Nature's work and the mere insignificance of man and his work. (It is easy to see how I feel and how I love the scenes of this description, but a person can not help but imagine themselves living in such conditions of freedom, happiness, and contentment.) The immense, arched locations clearly illustrate "a thousand years are but a day," for it has taken countless ages for the seepage of the water and the whirling of the winds to waste away and scoop out enough rock to make the caverns.

Many would class the wonderful monuments of this once-great people as merely dark holes in the rocks, but they are really well-lighted recesses in the sandstone formation. To describe them makes it almost necessary to see them and that requires at least three days of constant jog-jog-jogging on horseback, climbing knifelike ridges and crossing the cañons between, leaving few in a mood to appreciate the exquisite views from the heights. It is a great misfortune that the Cliff Dwellers could not have built their entire dwellings completely under the protection of the caves, for so much of their work is lost and gone wherever it has been exposed to the devastating hand of the elements.

Almost all of the buildings of the Mesa Verde are under the upper ledges of the cliffs, perhaps one thousand feet above the bed of the cañon. Without exception, all the locations can be approached only along narrow ledges or by a stone stairway through some crevice to the top of the cliff. Rarely, if ever, was there a direct route that could not be easily guarded. Also, all the buildings had an abundant supply of water.

Our [Mesa Verde] Cliff Dwellers apparently came equipped

with everything in the way of utensils for household use and had the art of house building, potterymaking and decoration, spinning, weaving, the making of baskets, and the growing of agricultural products. There does not appear to have been any evidence of progression, or regression, in any of their works during the tenancy of the cavern strongholds. And they apparently left without adding a thing to their manner of living, their construction ability, or their art in the making of useful articles. Unless, of course, they were the forerunners of the builders of the mesa and valley dwellings, which have the same building plan, the same implements and pottery, but not the same treatment of the skull formation.[1]

By far the most important work in pottery, baskets, weapons, weaving, agricultural products, and implements were found in the accumulation of rubbish behind the buildings, places that looked as our own back yards would look if the scavenger did not make his periodic visits. The Cliff Dwellers did all in their power, not knowing it, to give us the means of fitting them into history.

CONSTRUCTION OF DWELLINGS

Generally, the plan of building was to construct high outer walls and to leave open spaces the entire length of the cavern close to the inside cavern wall, the open space between often used as refuse heaps, for burials, and for storing containers of seed, and so on. None of the buildings used for living purposes or for storage were built with any plan or system, for the rooms were stuck on one or two at a time wherever convenient, much like the honeycomb of a beehive. To save time and work, each Cliff Dweller just attached his building onto the side or the end of a neighbor's claim. As the population increased, there was a demand for more and larger rooms, both for living quarters and storerooms. Eventually, this process resulted in a good-sized village, or house. Comparatively few of the houses were capable of housing more than a few hundred people. Many modest one-to-two-room houses were stuck around in available crevices outside the caves.

The masonry was good, bad, and even indifferent, ranging from structures [made] of rough, jagged stone, to finely dressed stone eight to ten inches square. Some walls were of thinner rock, broken to an even surface.

The Cliff Dweller did not know the meaning of breaking joints, but did know the system of stretching willow, or some other kind of sticks, along the cracks between the stones to keep the mortar from washing or crumbling away. In all the walls, the idea of reinforced concrete seems the prevailing plan; a limey clay used for the concrete, and the willow and cedar sticks used for iron rods. In any case, mud plaster covered all defects. All the floors and walls were plastered with a hard, thoroughly worked mud which, on drying, left a fine, smooth finish that afterward was colored brown, red, or white. Often, figures of birds, animals, or other objects were then drawn on the walls to represent what they may have attempted to tell of exploits in war and chase. In numbers of rooms, the coating of plaster can be peeled off in thin sheets, which shows that, as the walls became smoked, or whenever there were any important ceremonies, it was necessary to give their houses a thorough cleaning.

The children had to be spanked occasionally, or should have been, for when their elders were putting the finishing touches on the mud plaster of a room, little hands made impressions in the wet surface. The children also threw mud balls on the ceiling of the caves and many are still stuck there even now.

While many buildings have floors or ceilings still in place, the greater number have but few to show the material used in the making. For an ordinary room, there are a number of poles across the top, then willow sticks; after which cedar bark and cedar strips split from white or red cedar are added. On top of all this is a heavy mud coating, which answers as floor or roof, as the case may be.

Usually, the entrances to rooms were small and narrow, most being no higher than two feet nor wider than sixteen inches, more like windows than doors. These were easily secured by outside fastenings across a thin slab of rock. In ancient masonry, the arch, or a substitute, is always looked for. Where not found, the stonework is merely in the amateur class. Some doorways are in the shape of the letter T, which must have meant a great deal to the people of the house, or possibly, to the entire race, for the T was of frequent occurrence all over the Cliff Dweller district. The Indians of today say that the T-shaped doors were used only by the chiefs of the different clans. Folks also say that they [the Cliff Dweller] were a little people to have such small doors, but we found them to be average-sized, with an occasional oversize.[2] But, anyone can see that the T-shaped openings were not used to get through the opening with a back pack. The rooms were too small to make comfortable living quarters, so most of the time must have been spent out in the open spaces toward the front of the caves.

Places like Cliff Palace may have been a sort of general headquarters because there are so many little one-to-two-room buildings and a shortage of large ones. What could have been the cause of the comparatively wrecked condition would be hard to surmise, and nobody seems to be able to advance a reasonable theory for the removal of all the wooden parts of the floors and ceilings. It would have been impossible to have used the timbers for fuel, because the life of the wood is gone and it could be consumed only by having enough other wood with it to do the burning. Not many of the buildings appear to have been burned, which would destroy the roofs and ceilings. Not many people were killed in the buildings, either. So, anyone's opinion about the abandoned places would be good if properly expressed.

But all the dismantling process brought into distinct view all the wall decorations. We do not know with what superstitious dread, or religious awe, the later generations beheld the symbols pictured there, some of the symbols dating back almost to the beginning of time.

Spruce Tree House was a model that other buildings would have done well to copy, having its floors and roofs and balconies all in the best of order and having the corner fireplaces, too. All was in the best of order and even the markings on the walls were more conspicuous, probably because it was so very hidden even from the elements.

ESTUFAS

To be thoroughly fashionable, a house required at least one circular room (*estufa*, or *kiva*, as they are called). Generally, this room was built at a lower level than the main rooms of the buildings. Some of the ruins show as many as twenty of these, and they probably represented as many different clans, clubs, or ceremonial orders. In trying to determine why the estufas were developed, we thought about the likes and dislikes of people, some perhaps preferring to lay around and do nothing, perhaps some wanting only to hunt small game, while others had more adventurous ambitions. In the long winter evenings, some of the men did not want to mix with those who were not so brave, and so evolved the plan for the estufa, the room that was to accommodate those who wanted to hunt big game or an enemy's scalp. At any rate, the estufa provided private rooms where they could go and talk freely to the other members of their clans, or to perform any rites or ceremonies not the common property of the whole village.

The estufas were the only part of the buildings that even started to be made after a preconceived plan. They all average twelve to fourteen feet across at the floor and not much more than seven feet from floor to roof, having an offset in the walls about halfway up. This leaves a shelf about fourteen inches deep and made the upper part of the room nearly three feet greater in diameter than the lower half. Six pillars, evenly spaced, reached from this recess to the top of the wall, and may have meant nothing more than just providing support for the roof logs.

An opening in the wall, perhaps ten inches square, starting at the floor and running outward and upward, was probably for ventilation, because it usually has some sticks crosswise in it. In front of this and a couple of feet distant is always an altar nearly three feet long, eight inches thick, and eighteen inches high.[3] Near by, in line with the airshaft, but further out toward the center of the room, is a pit about two feet across. So far as we know, they were used as fireplaces, but may have been where the perpetual fire of the ancients was kept burning. Further back of the altar was a small hole in the floor, probably covered up and smoothed over except for ceremonial purposes. The same similar hole in use by present-day Indians in their kivas is the route they say the first of the human race used to get into this world.

The way of entering the kiva, or estufa, was through the center of the top. The walls were often decorated with drawings in groups of three, and may have actually represented pyramids. Other designs were also used (occasionally that of an animal), but most were of symbolic intent, the T being the most common.

BURIALS

The burials were often found in the trash heaps back of the buildings, along with other refuse and vessels of stored grain. Sometimes they were in tightly sealed rooms. A convenient hole under a rock, or an overhanging ledge would answer, too, but most often a regular burial mound could be found a short distance from the house. These were easily found by the heavy growth of black sage over the spot. Always, pottery was put in the grave near the head of the body, with a small chip broken off the edge to release the spirit so that it could accompany its owner to the spirit land. The pieces usually consisted of a bowl and a spoon and sometimes a cup or mug. Not always, but often, many other objects were found in the grave, and a basket near, or over, the head generally found. If the person was of note, he had all his bows, arrows, and other equipment along with him. There was no such thing as having them facing the east or any other direction. The bodies were simply doubled up and placed in position after being wrapped, generally, in a feather robe. Over this was a mantle of cotton cloth or yucca fibre and all was then covered with a mat woven of rushes or willow. If in a room, the room was closely sealed up. If not in a room, then a rough wall of rock was used instead, a large basket and willow matting covered the grave, and a large, flat rock finished the job.

Some of the little fellows who did not make the grade looked so lifelike, all buried away in their little wicker cradles, their quiet little bodies carefully wrapped and bound in cotton and feather cloth. Their features were not shrunken at all—they looked like they were lying there peacefully sleeping, with their small pottery toys alongside of them.

The people as a race were just average-sized humans but were a superior class of people, even if living in the Stone Age. Their heads were round and short, caused by a perpendicular flattening on the back part of the skull. The bones of the arms averaged 28 cm. [11.02 inches] and the femurs of the leg near 40 cm. [15.72 inches]. The hair was short and usually dark brown in color, although some had red hair, and was not black and coarse.[4] We found at least one albino. Teeth were generally pretty good, but there were some badly decayed ones and, among the older folks, often no teeth at all.

Surgical attempts were seldom indulged in. The case of a broken arm that had knitted together with the bone overlapped more than an inch was found at the ruin we named Broken Arm House.

POTTERY

When we were first working the mounds and buildings, pottery was just pottery, but later on we noticed variety and quality.[5] Various kinds and sizes were made for all the uses and convenience of that early day housewife, ranging from the tiny play dishes and infant-sized containers, to large coiled-ware vessels of four- to five-gallon capacity. Other waterproof, glazed vessels were of unlimited variety and shapes to accommodate the people's needs, [that is] jars, mugs, cups, bowls, spoons, ladles, cooking vessels, pipes, sifters, storage vessels, and many odd-shaped containers that must have been used to carry lights around in the pitch dark rooms, [for] the cotton wicks were still in them. These were quite numerous and some of them had the small T-shaped openings in them. From the same clay was made toys, ornaments, bird or animal figures, pipes, and the like.

From the blackened and smoked appearance, some of the corrugated, or coiled-ware, pieces were used for cooking purposes. They were also used for keeping a supply of water always on hand and, not having the waterproof glaze, there would be enough evaporation to keep the water cool. The coiled-ware jars were also used for storing foods and seeds and many were buried in the floors of the rooms. We have found them sealed and buried in a row along the walls. The only decorations on these jars were a few raised spirals near the tops of the ollas and indentations on the coils on the sides. In the process of building up a jar, the indentations were added to hold the coils of clay together and to make a decoration. In all, the sizes ranged from jars only two inches across the top to the four- and five-gallon capacity, but were not always of the same clay.

The decorated pottery has a waterproof glaze on the outside and also the inside. The decorations were put on and burned in with the glaze (either white or red) and are as permanent as the pottery itself. All the higher grades in quality are generally black on a white background, mostly of geometrical design. Perhaps the skill in pottery marking was the result of ages of practice. No doubt the decoration came along gradually, with straight lines at first and then, as the quality improved and the surface became smooth, lines and squares, and then variations of lines and squares were developed. Finally, perhaps some came to represent an individual family, or the clan, and the race at the time of the making. The Navajos have a system in blanketmaking that permits each family to have a design that is strictly their own, representing, as it were, their family coat-of-arms. (All that is passing now, though, since the Indian trader usually marks out a design that he thinks will be a good seller.) Perhaps the Cliff Dweller had a similar system in their pottery.

The use of circles, or coiled figures, all came at a later date than the squares and angles. Few animals, trees, or birds are pictured on the pottery. At that art, the C. D. [Cliff Dweller] was a dismal failure, although decorative art was highly developed on the vessels made for daily household use.

A word or two about children is never out of place. Judging from the number of toys they made for the children, they did as much as they could for the little folks, to keep them contented and happy. The children had small pottery toys and clay dishes and some animal and bird figures. Their make-believe houses are found in and around all the buildings and [they] seem to take away the many hundred years that have slipped by since their happy voices and calls filled the cañons with their presence.[6]

Very few complete pieces of colored pottery have ever been found in the Mesa Verde cliff dwellings, although there are thousands of fragments scattered everywhere, along with the fragments of the black-and-white kind. Further west, though, we find the red pottery, but the C. D. of the Mesa Verde did not seem to make any red, although there was the streak of natural red paint near the blow-out in the Mancos Cañon. (Iceland Spar at that same blow-out had not ever been used by the Cliff Dwellers or anyone else.) The red vessels may have been made from a superior kind of clay, or where the red pigment was not so scarce, for whole pieces of the color and kind were common in the ruins òf northern Arizona and over in Utah.

Often, the glazed vessels had an opening in the shape of the letter T, the same as the door openings. The frequency with which the T is used, as well as the Maltese Cross, the swastica, the serpent coils, and probably numerous other well-known symbols of these ancient people could be a stepping stone toward solving the history and habits of the Cliff Dwellers.

One thing is sure, the pottery is far superior to anything the modern Indians make and they admit it, not verbally, but through their method of pounding up the ancient fragments of the C. D. ware and mixing it with the clay and sand to make their own pottery.

BASKETS

Articles of this class are not as perishable as would be supposed, for articles of rush and grass matting were found in a good state of preservation. Baskets were made from willow and the inner bark of pine trees, the designs the same as used on the pottery, and often were made watertight.

FABRICS AND WEAVING

The largest pieces of woven goods were used in wrapping the bodies of the dead for burial. For everyday use, buckskin was just as serviceable and much more easily obtained. We have found caps, jackets, moccasins, belts, and other items made from the buckskin and, for winter use, different kinds of skins with the hair or fur left on. Moccasins, snowshoes, and feather or fur cloth, were combinations of yucca, buckskin, corn husks, feathers, and fur.

Yucca

Yucca was the most common material used, it being the most easily obtained, but other materials, not so coarse, were also used in combination with yucca fibre.[7] Finer fibres of yucca, or soapweed, were used for baskets, papoose boards, snowshoes, and sandals, but coarser classes of things were just the heavy blades of the plant, braided, or sewn together any old way, to give service.

The yucca fibre was spun into threads and used as a foundation for the feather cloth and fur wrappings, a practice that was in general use with the other Ancients. The yucca, being the most durable material, was used in both fine spinning and heavier spinning. Thread, strings, or ropes were spun in two cords for the finer, and three cords for the heavier, but not in six or more [like] our machine-made kinds. The Egyptian cord was only two-cord, so in that industry they were not advanced beyond the Stone Age Cliff Dwellers. The C. D. spinning was done in the same manner as that done by the modern Indian, with just a light stick eighteen-to-twenty inches long with a disc about the middle of it that was rapidly whirled about by hand. This we know because we have found the spindle whorls in the ruins.

Feather wraps were made by fastening the downy part of feathers around the heavier yucca threads, binding it with fine fibres split from yucca leaves, and then worked into a loosely woven yucca cord base, generally being worked in colors. The fur robes were made the same way, only long strips of the skin with the fur left on were wrapped around the yucca cords. Both the feather cloth and fur wrappings were in general use with the other races up to the time of the Aztec conquest, or subjugation.

The finer yucca fibre was spun and woven into patterns and colored fabrics, the designs and colors being the same as that of the pottery and basket work. The colors were usually dark brown, red, black, yellow, and the natural colors of the yucca. Some papoose boards, baskets, snow shoes, and sandals were of the finer fibres of yucca.

Sandals were knitted, woven, braided, or plaited of yucca using both fine and heavy fibres from it, as well as just the heavy blades themselves. They must have had an unlimited number, for we still find so many of them in the trash heaps. Some of the sandals were similar in construction to those of the ancient Egyptians, but most far surpassed anything the Egyptians made, so sandals may have been a specialty with our ancient Americans.

We found no sashes such as those used at present by most of the native people of the Southwest, but *cinchas* for carrying loads were common. The *cincha* is a long strip, usually woven of yucca, that goes around the forehead to carry a load on the back. In this manner, the hands were left free for climbing or moving about.

Cotton

The cotton cloth was uncolored and may have been the same grade and class as that spoken of by the Cortez historian at Montezuma's capital. The size seemed to be a standard eighteen inches wide by about twenty inches long. The threads are spun down to about the size used in flour sacking. We have been unable to find anything even remotely connected with cotton-loom work, but they most certainly did their own spinning and weaving because we find so much cottonseed cast out with the rubbish.[8] The cotton they may have obtained from their more southern neighbors, yet they seem to have had no commercial intercourse with the Aztecs. Fine cotton-fibre spinning and weaving among the Cliff Dwellers is just a closed book so far as we are concerned.

OTHER WOVEN FABRICS

Quite often we find stockings or leggings knitted of human

hair and the long, pointed wooden needles that were used [to do the knitting]. This might explain why the Cliff Dwellers nearly always had short hair, to judge from our own observations. Perhaps it was all used up in the making of hair goods. Or, long hair could have come from captured enemy heads, but still, the supply does not seem sufficient to make all the hair goods we found in stockings and other articles.[9]

Indian hemp was also used for the knitting, but where it came from, we do not know.

Willow mats were common and, in addition to being used as coverings for the dead, were used as floor rugs. In this class, rush mats were also used.[10]

Most of the snowshoes were shaped of twigs and were of the webbed Canadian sort, usually with cedar bast added. The Cliff Dweller would have had to have [had] some sort of snowshoes in order to travel around in the brush and over the mesa tops in winter.

STONE WEAPONS AND TOOLS

It was certainly a long and hard road to travel from the rough beginning of using stones to the date of heavy stone axes and many an age after that before the bow and arrow, such as the Cliff Dweller used. No doubt the atlatl and the bow and arrow were developed after the stone axe was found to be lacking in power to get game or enemies at a distance. The bow has not been improved upon in the many years since they [the Cliff Dweller], as a race, ranged the hills and valleys.

Onyx, jasper, agate, flint, and obsidian were the materials used and some were often quite ornamental in manufacture and in the quality of the stone, there being so many combinations of silica in the rock formations from which they were constructed. Some of the tips, [those] scarcely an inch long, were exceptionally beautiful, [when] made of agate or colored quartz. Occasionally, a flint piece was T-shaped, evidently a symbol stone. Larger points of flint or obsidian were used as atlatl points, for we occasionally found an atlatl in the Cliff Dweller ruins.

Some points, fully five inches in length, we classified as spear points, although we failed to find anything that passed as a shaft for a spear. Many of these larger points were used as knives, being set in a handle at an angle, stuck in place with pitch, and then bound tightly.

Stone axes also show an advance in class, being made more with a view to weight and shape. Nearly all those found are rounded and ground down to quite symmetrical proportions. Some were made from the river-washed cobblestones and included quartzite, trachyte, granite, porphyry, and even sandstone. Such stones were abundant and were used for many purposes, both in civil and in military life. Immense trees were cut down with such tools and stone for building was broken out and dressed—deeds that would be almost an impossibility in this age. The sizes of the axes ranged from little ones weighing one-fourth of a pound to the great chunks weighing as much as ten pounds. The handles were of a pliable wood that was wrapped once around a groove in the stone and then securely bound with tough bark strips, or willow switches, once close to the stone itself and once further up the handle.

IMPLEMENTS

The method of starting fires with a couple of sticks must have originated with the first members of the human race. The firesticks of the Cliff Dwellers were the same as the other primitive races, consisting of a hardwood stick whirled rapidly on the edge of a softer one (like willow) with some cedar bast to catch the sparks.

The drills for making holes in hard substances were very much like the firemaking sticks, with the exception that a harder point was used and a cross stick was attached. This worked up and down, winding and unwinding a string attached to the top of the perpendicular shaft. Present-day Indians still use the same implement.

The boomerang we also find with the C. D. and it is probably for the same purpose that it is used among the Village Indians [Hopis] of Arizona today: to kill small game such as rabbits and birds.

Bone knives, awls, and wooden tools were used for all classes of cutting, sewing, and weaving, as well as in sandalmaking, and were common finds. The use of many wooden implements, large and small, we could never determine. Some we know were used in weaving, from the similarity of the loom sticks now used by the Navajos and Hopis. Some might have been for war or protection and some must have been for agricultural work. Yet, with all the agriculture production indicated, we have never been able to identify any farming implements for sure.

A papoose board, too, was a necessity in daily life, because the women had to have their hands free to move around. Then [when arriving at a destination] she could hook the little chap up on the limb of a tree and let the breeze rock the baby while the songs of the birds and the voice of the wind acted as a lullaby.

Although stone, wood, and bone weapons and implements were plentiful, *no metal of any sort has ever been found.*

FOODS

If, as it has been frequently stated, the Cliff Dwellers were driven out of their strongholds, they certainly lived high, both in altitude and foods, when in the undisputed possession of the territory they occupied, as the results of our work and observations show. Unless the climate has changed in the past few hundred years, they had over three hundred days of sunshine yearly. They also must have had soil free from the weeds and insects that we have today, insects that have been imported from the four corners of the earth. They possibly developed a high class of products from their gardens and most certainly had quick-maturing seeds, due to the limitations of the altitude of the Mesa Verde.

For meat, they had the usual wild game of all kinds—sage hens, grouse, ducks, prairie dogs, squirrels, beaver, rabbit, deer, and the like, as well as the ferocious animals such as bear, mountain lion, wolves, and cats. The mountain streams abound in trout, so that could be used for meat, although they could have had the same superstitions regarding the fish tribes that the Navajos have. There is every evidence that the turkey was domesticated. Perhaps the children had dogs trained to go with them in protecting and rounding up the droves, the same as the Navajo now handles his sheep and goats. We know they had dogs because dog bones are scattered around in the buildings and are easily distinguished from wolf or coyote. Possibly, too, the dogs were used to carry light burdens, the way the Apaches formerly used the family curs. It would be natural for them to have dogs, for in all history the dog has been associated with man and his works.

Wild fruits were plentiful. The buffalo berry (*Shepherdia Canadensis*) is about the size of a small pea and is red or yellow in color; the service berry (*Alnifolia*) has fruit that looks and tastes like the huckleberry, but it grows as large as small hazel nuts; several varieties of cactus grow on the mesa; wild gooseberries; raspberries; currants; thimble berries; and, to complete a large selection, the fruit of the yucca plant, which grows in plenty.[11]

Piñon trees (*Pinus edulis Piñon,* if you want to look them up) grow in abundance all over the entire Southwest country. The nuts supplied a great deal of oil, or fatty material, and could have been used for lighting purposes in the lamps and also as a cooking substance in preparing foods. Maybe they even had piñon-nut butter from the pounded up nuts.

Wild potatoes (*Solanaceae Jamesii,* Nightshade family), it would be well to suppose, were an article of diet, since the whole country is overrun with them where the conditions are favorable.

The Cliff Dweller had pipes and all smoked, either for general use or for ceremonies. Smoking seems always to have been an American habit. Wild potatoes, wild tobacco, and the Jimson weed (*Datura meteloides*) are all of a kin, the tops poisonous and the flowers not much for beauty or fragrance.[12] We eat the potatoes; bugs eat the tops; worms and men chew the tobacco; and we make poultices from the Jimson weed.

Packages of herbs we find in abundance, some for food, some for medicinal purposes, and some for coloring matter. (The mountain sage is rather an insignificant plant only about six inches high, but nothing in all medical science has anything to compare with it as a remedy for mountain, or intermittent, fever. The black, and also the white, sage also have their uses, but this is not a medical paper, so we shall pass over them.)

Cultivated foods were plentiful, too. Two kinds of beans were noted, white and brown. Squash and pumpkins were grown, and the shells used for storing [items], some of the dried shells being over a foot in diameter. The most important food was the worldwide necessity, corn. There must have been a few Luther Burbanks at the time, for we have found corn of a size and quality that would be difficult to put in the background at any present-day agricultural display. It was very unlike the small, rounded sort that the present native people grow. There were several varieties, some with the round, colored kernels similar to the present Indian corn, and intermediate sizes of both types.

Often we have been asked if we ever tried to grow any of the seeds of squash, corn, and beans. We did try, just to be able to say that we had, not because we did not know any better. It is well known that the life germ of different seeds is limited to the kind. Corn is good for about twelve years and wheat from twenty to sixty. We often hear that wheat from the Egyptian pyramids has been planted and grown, but there is nothing to it. Just plant some old seeds and see.

The grinding of corn and the crushing of seeds was carried on in community rooms or in the open spaces of the caverns, the grinding being done on stones the same as the Indians use today. The grinding stones were placed in walled enclosures approximately fourteen inches by twenty-four inches and fixed at an angle of about 25°. Often, a dozen or more of these primitive mills were joined together at the ends and sides, so that an enormous lot of corn could be worked at the same time. Smaller stones, hollowed out, were for crushing seeds, and an eight-inch cube was used for the pounding.

I have been told that long ago the Village Indians [Hopis] kept a three-year supply of provisions on hand to tide them over the dry years or when a siege compelled them to stay close in. The Cliff Dwellers must have had the same storing habit, because we found many vessels filled with corn or beans, sealed and hidden in the trash heaps, and as many as thirteen of the large coil-ware jars buried in one row along the walls on the inside of rooms. With such an abundance of food and seeds found safely stored for future use within the walls, there seems to have been no reason for leaving. They certainly were not starved out by another race.

TERRACING AND IRRIGATION

To what extent these high tablelands and fertile valleys were cultivated is shown everywhere. Intensive farming must have, of necessity, been a high art with all the inhabitants of this Southwestern country. It has always been a problem why the Cliff Dweller found it necessary to terrace the hillsides for agricultural purposes when there was so much level and moist valley land. Unless, that is, they had been crowded off the lower lands by another people and the population was so great that they had to resort to the use of every available foot of land on the mesa top and [to] utilize every drop of moisture.

I do not know where the system originated, but the flooding of land in small lots was in use by the Ancients, a method that built up the land without any danger of ditches breaking and carrying off any of the topsoil. The most primitive method is just to flood the land, regardless of the slope. The next step was to divide the land into small squares, with a low embankment surrounding each one, and then to turn the water in, possibly burying the small plots with mud.

The Ancients of the Mesa Verde had stone dams across every little wash. At one place in Navajo Cañon, terrace walls still stand a couple of feet high and about twenty feet apart and can be easily traced a half-mile or more along the hillsides. In addition to these, all over the mesa tops, wherever a little wash led away toward the main cañons, small masonry walls were extended across the flow at intervals of a few feet to a number of yards. Here the fertile washings would accumulate and the retaining wall hold the moisture, resulting in family gardens innumerable from but little expenditure of labor. There must have been a very fertile section of ground on the slope that drops down from Step House, which still bears the evidence of much terracing. And, too, there are so many storehouses located there, which makes it appear that it was a fertile section. Probably, in addition, this section was subirrigated by seepage of water through the soil, much like the Philippinos use their sloping mountain sides.

Anyone who has been along any of the little washes in the sand-rock could not fail to see how little rock dams were put in every few feet apart to take advantage of the little moisture, yet the hurry-up-quick tourists never notice the terracing walls and some of the scientific parties overlook them also.[13]

There are still what we call "tanks" formed in the soft parts of the sand-rock by whirling water and grinding of stones in every sloping grade where the late summer rains and winter snows find their way toward the main channels. Every house has at least one to depend on.[14] Across from Cliff Palace was the ruined walls of what seemed to be a reservoir, with the long row of stones reaching back from the circular enclosure as if it constituted a guide for falling rain.

Two reservoirs on the Mesa Verde, over one hundred feet in diameter, are still used at times by present-day Indians and cattlemen. There is no doubt but what the Cliff Dweller understood the art of irrigation. The supply ditches can be traced from them to smaller watercourses, supplying irrigation waters for the Cliff Dweller farming. Ditches going over hills looked like an impossibility, but———.[15]

In numbers of places in New Mexico and Arizona, old irrigating ditches can be traced. Maybe the furrow system originated in some of the ancient Egyptian or Persian countries in
dry seasons, with large water wheels used to raise the water
from the well, or stream, to let it flow along the ditches. Over
in the Eagle River country (or some nearby stream), there was
a small patch of ground in the curve of the river [that had been
irrigated] from a water wheel that looked like it was between
twenty or thirty feet in diameter. It must have been used to
raise water from the river channel before it could be applied
to irrigation. Probably, there was not a chance to work a ditch,
to do away with the water wheel.

It is reported that there is evidence of irrigating ditches
around this district [the Mesa Verde or Four Corners area] on
the more level land, but I have never happened to find any of
them.

To those who have lived in irrigation regions, the treatment
of the land is no mystery. Where the land is level, the small pens
to hold the irrigating water has to be adopted, but, wherever
there is sloping land, the water is led from the lateral ditch
across the headland and regulated so as to run through small
furrows about thirty inches apart. A man has to be on watch
all the time until the water reaches the end of the land. Too
much water, and his land goes on with the water. Or, if a couple
of the small furrows run together, it is more grief, because the
water will be going at such a rate that gulleys soon form.

ORNAMENTS

Queer as it may seem, no finger rings, no earrings, nor
bracelets have been found on the bodies or in the buildings of
the C. D. The lack of ornaments (jewelry) is very noticeable
in a country where turquois, opal, garnets, and all precious metals are so bountiful. No metal is ever found. Neither did they
use jet, contenting themselves with beads of dried cedar berries,
a few bone pieces, and some shells (which they must have traded for).[16] Little pear-shaped pendants of clay were probably
ornaments, along with small hollow balls, made like a sleighbell,
which had a small pebble inside to rattle around. We did find
one small piece of galena (lead ore) and a small disc of jet with
four or five small turquois, but that was all.

It is so easy to confuse the Cliff Dweller with the builders
of the great works at Aztec and Pueblo Bonito, but the subject

of the ornaments show that, as a race, they were entirely a distinct class from the C. D. The Cliff Dwellers, being the practical sort of people they were, would certainly have traded back and forth with any of their neighboring tribes who utilized metals and turquois *if there had been any during their era.*

GAMES AND OTHER ITEMS

Small blocks of wood that looked like dice, and other blocks very much like dominos are puzzling if they are not for games. The Navajos have a game using blocks, very much like domino blocks, and if the ones that looked like dice were used like the same class of articles of the present-day seven and eleven, there is no way to tell. We also have found a number of flutelike instruments about fourteen to sixteen inches in length and about one inch in diameter, with holes in the side. They surely were musical instruments of some sort. So far as their conditions and knowledge permitted, the Cliff Dwellers seem to have been a happy and contented lot.

SYMBOLS

Unfortunately, our Cliff Dwellers do not seem to have left any regular form, or set, of hieroglyphics or pictographs. Pictographs on rocks and cliffs might have meant more than just hunting expeditions or warring raids, but to our uneducated eyes, there is little else shown. A few spiral drawings do not prove they were snake worshipers, however, yet they seem to compare with nothing but Stone Age characters. Of course, the walls of many rooms had drawings, but they could have represented only individual effort with but very little idea of trying to record events.

The best preserved emblems, or pictures, are in Spruce Tree House, where the figure of the Maltese Cross and the T, or "tau," of the ancient European continent is depicted. There is scarcely a building in the Mesa Verde without a doorway, or opening of some sort, made after the T and numbers of pottery vessels show the same design, along with flint ornaments occasionally made in the same shape. With the Egyptians, the T was supposed to speak of the Eternal Life. With the Aztecs, it was a message to the White God who was to come sometime and be with them forever. We can not tell, and may never know, what all these signs really mean, or what day and age of the world they were first developed and passed on from generation to generation. Evolution of man and the development of his symbols do not go hand in hand. Probably, the symbols mean much in the unfolding of their early migrations, but what they meant to the people, or how they came by them, we are not to know.

What the Maltese Cross meant to the Cliff Dwellers, or what connecting link it may have been to the ancient peoples of other continents, we do not know. We must not overlook, however, that, to the scientific mind, these symbols may in time help in the solution of this continent's people.

The swastica is a common symbol found in the works of the Ancients, but who can really tell what it symbolizes? We can read pages of explanation and still get nowhere, yet one of the most reasonable is that all nations started from a common center and scattered to the four directions. Even modern Indians have a hazy idea of the ancient significance of the swastica, in their mode of smoking first to the north, then to the south, then to the east and, finally, the west. It could be the reminder of the migrating movements of man to the final peopling of the entire earth. There is also the theory that the swastica represents the movements of the Big Dipper and the Little Dipper at different times in twenty-four hours, and also the yearly movements. This was recognized as such by ancient races all over the world in all probability, but most certainly by the ancients of Mexico, Greece, and Egypt.

It is surprising to know that the apparently ignorant Indian knows so much about the starry heavens and movements of the planets, but it is just the result of ordinary observations of anyone who spends night after night in the open. The cowboy at night tells the time by the relative position of the Big Dipper to the North Star.

RELIGION

What may have been their religion we care not, neither whether polygamists or monogamists, but, if we were as sure of a final reward for merit as these aboriginal people were, we could feel perfectly at ease in regard to final reckonings. It is all a matter of living up to one's belief, anyway. For example, the bloody wars of our Christian and civilized days far exceed anything of the ancient, uncivilized, un-Christian days before Bible times and leaves us with a great big question mark as an answer to just what is improvement and advancement!

Also, what form of government they had, or to whom they paid tribute, we can only imagine.

DISAPPEARANCE OF CLIFF DWELLERS

It would seem to me that the people of the cliff dwellings pioneered the same way as all others since the coming of man into this world. On account of the shortage of game, or crops, or [because] of pestilence, a family or two would drift out and locate at some distant place. In the new location they would acquire habits and customs better fitted to their new locality and, unless they were in communication with their original homes, their language would be lost and they would develop new words and expressions to suit their work and surroundings. In addition, they would pick up words and expressions from their new neighbors.

No one knows with any degree of certainty when the Cliff Dweller lived in the region bounded on the north and west by the Colorado River, on the east by the Rio Grande, and on the south by Mexico. There is no reason to believe that the cliff buildings were occupied continuously for untold ages, but, rather, it is likely that in time the houses were deserted for some unknown cause or else they were driven out. But even that is uncertain, for there is very little [evidence] to show bloodshed or starvation.

Are the present Village Indians their descendants? They certainly have some customs the Cliff Dweller might have had. Comparisons and differences are to be found between any two tribes, or races, of people, so it is best to let things rest and not try to say they were the same as the present races of Pueblos, or Aztecs of Mexico, or an improved stock of any Indians existing now.

Even the weapons and implements help to mystify, for there is so much similarity between so many races. The boomerang is a weapon of the present Village Indians, but also was used by the Cliff Dweller; yet it is also an Australian weapon, as well as being used in the Aleutians. The atlatl is both that of the C. D. and the Basket Maker, but also belongs to the Aztecs, although it was going into disuse in Mexico about the time of Columbus. Woven matting and wickerware of the Cliff Dweller is identical with that of the ancient Lake Dwellers of Switzerland. Grades of cloth from the cliff dwellings resemble the cloth of Egypt. Much of the pottery resembles that of the ancient Caledonians, yet drawings resemble those of ancient Greece. In time, it may be that the buildings still unexplored in the rough and rugged region of Navajo Mountain may yield up an answer to the great mysteries of the Southwest country.

To have our Cliff Dwellers come to this country via the Atlantis route is reasonable. It is reported that there are ruins similar to the Cliff Dwellings in Morocco on the coast of Africa. The drawings in Yucatan of both white and Negro people seems proof there was a connection between the two continents. Also, the Aztec tradition of the flood is the same as our Christian history.

Equally plausible is the Bering Sea route, for the reason that both the Navajo and Aztec traditions say their people came from the far north, although it would seem very difficult to carry rations and equipment across that way. Even at the present time it would be difficult to carry rations and implements across the Bering Sea and that part of the country for any great number of people.

No doubt there were occasional castaways drifting across the Pacific, as well as the Atlantic, and perhaps some of their habits and arts were adopted by the people they met up with on their arrival. Aztec drawings and ornaments would indicate that such things could happen.

It has been proved that man existed as one of the earliest mammals, along with the mastodons and mammoths, for the drawings of both are found on ivory, bone, and in caves [in France], proving that they must have lived at the same time. Man was on this continent during the Glacial Age 150,000 years ago when the ice sheet extended as far south as 37°. Stone Age man [of that period of time] had for company the elephant and the mammoth, as well as being well fitted to hold his own against encroaching strangers. Everyone knows of the fossil remains of fish and mammals and sea monsters in the Bad Lands of northern New Mexico and southwestern Colorado. If scientific research were made, surely stone implements and human bone could be found with them in this country, too.

We have frequently heard that there are ruins of ancient

habitation under the lava flow of the Zuni Mountain. How many ages ago that volcanic action could have taken place, the Indian tradition does not state, but their traditions usually go back several thousand years. In all, we see the great number of unanswered questions we have. Too great a cloak of myth and superstition exists without an unraveling process.

Is America actually the New World, or is it really the Old World rediscovered? It seems that all our ancient American history was destroyed by Cortez the same as that of the European world was destroyed by Caesar.

The appearance of the Cliff Dweller is as difficult to solve as their disappearance. But once, there was a lost tribe of Israel, wandering into oblivion. And once, there was a continent, Atlantis, which connected the mainlands. Is it too fantastic [to think] that these children of Israel might have crossed and, in the land of exile, lost their identity and finally emerged as a new race?

Where did they go? Famine, war, or altar fodder for Montezuma? The Cliff Dweller may have been absorbed by other races; besieged and slain; exterminated by disease; or still exist as a race now living within our range of vision.[17]

But from the bloody altars of the Aztec gods in Mexico comes the sacrificial chant as helpless thousands of the vanquished tribes who walked the paths of peace are slaughtered to pacify greedy deities. So much must be only conjecture, but in the wailing songs of the Village Indians [there] echoes a forgotten memory carried through the centuries by the pitiful remnant of a lost race. One of the chief rewards of work of this sort are the dreams that touch it with an aura of the unreal. Each of us is permitted his own theory because none can deny it.

NOTES

1. Al could not determine, during his time at the Mesa Verde, whether the mesa dwellers came before or after the cliff-dwelling peoples, but does note the differences in the various skull types. A picture in the Wetherill photographic collection of three types of skulls found in the region were classified, in Richard's handwriting, as "Nomad—the natural skull of the Grand Gulch, Utah people" [later named the *Basket Makers*]; "Cliff Dweller—perpendicular flattening of the Mesa Verde Indian"; and "Mound Builder—oblique flattening of the Montezuma Valley, Colo. people." Nordenskiöld wrote (*The Cliff Dwellers of the Mesa Verde*, p. 76) that "Richard Wetherill states that the mesa dwellers were a different people,

for the artificial depression of the posterior parts of the cranium has been applied obliquely from above, so that it principally affects the parieto-occipital region; the skulls from the cliff dwellings have been flattened straight from behind, the occipital region being the most affected." Alice Eastwood considered that the mesa-top dwellers were the ancestors of the cliff dwellers, for she wrote in "Notes on the Cliff Dwellers," (*Zoe* 3 [January 1893]:375) that on the mesa top "are ruins of houses and towers which were probably occupied before defense became necessary and the people fled to the cliffs. The mesa ruins have usually become mounds overgrown with vegetation, but the cliff houses . . . are in a good state of preservation."

2. "Average" is a relative term. If Al considered the Wetherills of average size, the comparison would be nearly correct. He was much taller than his parents, yet was only 5' 7" in height. Dr. Ales Hrdlicka, a well-known anthropologist, had carefully measured Al on one of his visits to the Alamo Ranch and had pronounced him physically perfect except that his arms were too long, his legs too short, and his mouth too wide. How this examination contributed to Al's concept of "average" was not clarified.

3. Most archaeologists now use the word *deflector* instead of *altar* to describe the stone slab or earthen bar, but the term *altar* is still partially retained as correct. Jesse Walter Fewkes, an archaeologist at the Mest Verde, used both terms. In "Antiquities of the Mesa Verde National Park: Spruce Tree House" (*Smithsonian Bureau of American Ethnology Bulletin 41* [Washington, D.C.: Government Printing Office, 1909] page 18,) he states that "an upright slab of rock or narrow thin wall of masonry . . . , sometimes called an *altar,* serves as a deflector. . . ." In a companion publication dealing with Cliff Palace (*Smithsonian Bureau of American Ethnology Bulletin 51* [Washington, D.C.: Government Printing Office, 1911] p. 50) , he wrote that "there rises from the floor a device called the *deflector* (sometimes called an *altar*) . . . ." As late as 1949, Bolton in *Coronado, Knight of Pueblos and Plains,* Appendix, page 418, appears to continue to use the term *altar* in the same connotation.

4. H. C. Hovey also considered that the hair was not as coarse as might be expected, adding ("Homes and Remains of the Cliff Dwellers," *Scientific American,* 28 October 1893, p. 279) that it was "soft and abundant, varying in color from a light brown to jet black, and occasionally to gray."

5. Although the Wetherills recognized the differences in pottery, they evidently did not accept subsequent classifications. John, in one of his letters to Al in the 1930s, gave the latest development on pottery divisions, but added that he did not know whether "you want me to muddle you up with a lot of new ideas or not. . . . We did not know how to sepperate [sic] them until Clate [Clayton Wetherill] and Sam Guernsey began to see the difference around 1915. . . . The pottery classifications [are] so numerous that they only confuse the student. . . . I have tried to tell them there is only one Basket Maker and if they want to use the name that they should say pre-BM and post-BM. The Basket Maker 3 should be Pueblo I."

6. In her memoirs, Alice Eastwood recalled a circumstance concerning the children who had lived at Sandal House. "I picked up what was to me more interesting. It was a slender curving stick with a string at one end. The other end had a loop which when fitted into the other end of the stick formed a bow. It was undoubtedly a child's bow made by itself [the child]. It brought to me more vividly than any relic the life of the people."

7. F. H. Chapin recorded (*The Land of the Cliff Dwellers*, p. 165) that his microscopic examination of a combination-of-fibres fabric revealed that the fabric was actually a combination of yucca and milkweed fibre, although it appeared to be yucca and wool.

8. The cotton goods impressed all writers. Alice Eastwood observed that they found cotton in three different forms in 1889: "on the pod, spun into thread, and woven into cloth (*Zoe* 3: 375). (Alice) Palmer Henderson wrote ("The Cliff Dwellers," *Literary Northwest* [May 1893]: 84) that the cliff dwellers raised "sea island cotton . . . by irrigation on the mesas above" their cavern homes. H. C. Hovey emphatically claimed that, "I saw the cotton seeds, the carded cotton, cotton in the spindle, in the ball and skein, cotton wicks in the lamps, and as many as a hundred pieces of cotton cloth . . . [at the] H. Jay Smith and C. D. Hazard [sic]" exhibit at the World's Fair (*Scientific American*, p. 279).

9. Both Nordenskiöld (*The Cliff Dwellers of the Mesa Verde*, p. 104) and Chapin (*The Land of the Cliff Dwellers*, p. 161) comment upon finding red and auburn hair in the hair collected for the purpose of making some sort of fabric. Nordenskiöld adds a footnote that the hair fabric was quite similar to that of the hair fabric found in ancient graves on Santa Cruz Island off the coast of California.

10. Alice Eastwood supplied the term *Phragmites communis* for the type rush used. She also noted that they found "many bunches of *Oryzopsis cuspidata*, a coarse grass with stiff stems, tied into bunches to make brushes, probably for the hair" (*Zoe* 3:376.)

11. When Alice Eastwood made her botanical collection from the Mesa Verde, she noted (ibid) that "in the cañons where their [the cliff dweller] houses stand like statues in their rocky niches, the wild fruits are more abundant than elsewhere, leading to the belief that to some extent they were cultivated. The most valuable plant was *Yucca baccata*, the fruit [of] which most likely served as food. The Utes at the present time dry large quantities cut into strips for winter use."

12. Although Jimson weed may have been classified as *Datura meteloides* at the time, it is now termed *Datura stramonium*. In "General Notes of a Trip Through Southeastern Utah," Alice Eastwood wrote that she and Al found, in McElmo Canyon, "*Datura meteloides* [that] was rather startling. It is not supposed to grow so far north, but here it was abundant. . . . The seed pods are often found in the ruins of the ancient people who once filled this land. . . ." Of tobacco plants found on the Mesa Verde, she noted (*Zoe* 3:376) that "*Nicotiana attenuata* is common near their [cliff dweller] homes," which would seem to imply that it was cultivated.

13. Placing a positive date on the period of time Al made the first drafts of his autobiography is difficult, but this passage indicates that some of his observations were recorded before 1900, since he used the present tense.

14. Chapin called the "tanks" of special interest, from the fact that they were used by the cliff dwellers. In some cases they were walled up to increase their capacity and . . . steps . . . cut in the rock to enable the carriers to descend and bail out the water (*The Land of the Cliff Dwellers*, p 176). Dr. Prudden enlarged the observation (*Harper's Magazine*, September 1896, p. 552) to say, "The earthen ladles or dippers not infrequently found in the ruins or in the graves are often much worn and beveled on the edges, an indication they were used to ladle up water from hollows in the rocks, such as abound on the plateaus above and about the cliffs."

15. Nearly every article written about the Mesa Verde in the years immediately

following the Wetherill discoveries of the major ruins drew attention to the irrigation system on the mesa top. An article in *Living Age* (2 August 1890, p. 320) pointed out the "many reservoirs of stone, evidently intended for irrigation. One, . . . some fifty yards across, still has water in it." The Denver *Republican* called the cliff dweller ("The Cliff Dweller, 22 January 1893, p. 7) a distinctly agricultural people who practiced irrigation, for "remains of large reservoirs, here and there" could be seen and "channels of irrigating ditches are to be plainly traced." That same month, Alice Eastwood used similar wording in *Zoe* (3:375) : "The relics found in their houses indicate that they were an agricultural people, and to strengthen this belief remains of ancient reservoirs and aqueducts exist on the mesas above." G. Nordenskiöld not only noted the reservoir near the summit of Chapin Mesa, but also added (*The Cliff Dwellers of the Mesa Verde*, p. 74) that "traces of a ditch which formed the connexion have been observed north of the reservoir by Richard Wetherill" and "quite near the reservoir we find the ruins of a considerable village. . . ." By 1919, the *Bureau of American Ethnology, Bulletin 70* (Fewkes) publication metaphorically called the by then dried-up reservoir "Mummy Lake" and named the site of the ruined village "Far View House." Mesa Verde National Park brochures of the 1920s repeated the earlier observations concerning irrigation.

16. Alice Eastwood formed the same conclusion concerning trade, for she had noted (*Zoe* 3:375) that they found seashells entwined in the "hair of the dead, salt carefully preserved in balls, and for their arrow points, stones not found near by."

17. The date this passage was recorded had to be pre-1922, for that was the year Al left the Southwest. In all probability it was recorded between 1917 and 1919, for at that time he was living on the Navajo Reservation where cliff dweller descendants could have been the race living within his range of vision.

9

Village Dwellers

ERRORS we all make without a thought is that all the ancient people of the Southwest states of Colorado, Utah, New Mexico, and Arizona were Cliff Dwellers, regardless of the difference of the buildings (if any). There may have been many hundreds of years between the time of the Basket Makers and the coming of the Cliff Dwellers, also an equally lengthy period from the Cliff Dwellers to the time of the builders of the outside ruins, the Village Dwellers [Pueblo builders]. We came to the conclusion that the Cliff Dwellers antedated all other races occupying the Mesa Verde, or any part of the region, except the Basket Makers. The proof of this is rather hard to make convincing unless one is familiar with the pueblo buildings. The ground plans or masonry styles of the Cliff Dweller can not be compared with the ruined buildings of the Aztec or other Plains People, or with the buildings at Pueblo Bonito.

This third group of people, the Village Dwellers, were probably the most numerous. They built the immense community houses in Hovenweep (in the lower McElmo Cañon), Yellow Jacket Springs, and Aztec Springs in Colorado and [also those

170

of] Chaco Cañon and Aztec, New Mexico—in fact, all over the country that had previously been occupied by the other two races during their respective periods.[1]

The argument in favor of relationship between the community-house builders and the Cliff Dwellers, is the circular underground room (club room, ceremonial chamber, or whatnot). The kivas or estufas would be one of the similarities: those of both peoples having the altars, the firepit in the floor, and the small hole in the floor near the center of the room. But the general plan of the main buildings is not the same. The room constructions of the buildings in the lowlands and on the mesa tops of the Mesa Verde were similar as far as possible. Also the designs and the quality of the pottery and baskets were very much alike. But, it must have been many years between the last of the cliff-house people and these more advanced folk of the outside world, *but still no metal.* Perhaps they were about as much related to each other as the Mayas were to the Aztecs.

A difference in the people themselves shows in the skulls. The people of the so-called mounds, or villages, away from the cliffs had their babies' carrying boards at nearly a 45° angle, which caused the little skulls to grow with a flattening from the top, while the Cliff Dweller skulls were flattened straight up and down.

One more point, and it is rather hard to reconcile the objector to this view, is that among the outside people [Pueblo builders] there were found great quantities of turquois ornaments. The people of Pueblo Bonito were just almost buried in turquois, yet the Cliff Dwellers gave no indication of their meeting up with any precious stones of any sort except the one small disc of jet with a few spots of turquois. Had the Cliff Dwellers lived in the cliffs at the time when Pueblo Bonito was the metropolis of that Southwest country, there would surely have been some exchange of handicraft or produce between the two, the Cliff Dwellers being the practical sort of people they were.

The most noteworthy village dwelling is the ruin of Pueblo Bonito in Chaco Cañon. The name is hardly appropriate, for it signifies beauty or grace, and the description should refer to its impressive or inspiring appearance. To give a clear understanding of Pueblo Bonito and the tributary villages, all within sight of it, would be impossible in a limited space or time. The merest descriptive outline will give one an idea of the vastness of the ancient works and people.

The group of villages is located about sixty miles northeast of Gallup [New Mexico] in a wide, sandy valley and on the cliffs surrounding the valley. Compared with any buildings of prehistoric structures in North America (except those in Yucatan, Honduras, and Mexico) Pueblo Bonito is the most impressive and extensive, having been built on the ruins of more ancient dwellings ten to fifteen feet below the surrounding surface of the country. Until quite recently, the lower stories of Pueblo Bonito itself were buried under ten to twenty feet of drifted sand. This preserved, in almost their original condition, the rooms containing great quantities of the most valuable material from an archaeological point of view.

Pueblo Bonito is near one side of the valley and is semicircular in shape. The straight line of the front faces a broad valley, while the rear walls have a protecting cliff two hundred feet high, less than one hundred feet from them. An open amphitheatre is in the center, perhaps two hundred-fifty to three hundred feet across. The rooms seem to have been built in terraces all around the inside of the outer walls. From these flat roofs all ceremonies, either religious or otherwise, could be reviewed. There were comparatively few doors or openings in the outer wall and the approach to the town was through a narrow opening in the straight line facing the valley. The buildings, which required years of patient toil to construct, show the peaceful organization of a multitude of people. The ability to oversee the supplying of food, clothing, and protection against enemies deserve the respect of any municipal body of the present day.

To look at the walls, one could scarcely imagine the long years that have elapsed since their construction or desertion. The walls were made of not very large stones and but few of them were dressed smooth. Over all, a smooth coat of mud plaster was put on and often this was colored and an occasional figure was scratched or worked into it. It will soon be discovered that, in an attempt to shake a wall down, the mud mortar, mixed with small fragments of rock to keep the mortar from washing, has hardened almost like the rock [itself]. Where high walls were necessary, they were built heavy enough at the bottom to hold the required weight above. Some especially noticeable in this respect were fifty or more feet in height. Casa Grande, near Florence, Arizona, an old adobe ruin with walls six feet thick, was put up in exactly the same manner that modern concrete houses are put up—the walls appear to have been run in forms similar to modern concrete.

The rooms were generally small, seldom any of them as much as ten feet across, except in the case of the circular rooms—estufas, or kivas, so-called—that often have a diameter of more than twenty feet. These rooms, council room, club rooms, or the like, are to be found in all the ancient and modern ruins of the Southwest.

Probably a thousand rooms would be a small estimate for Pueblo Bonito and a comparison with the modern pueblos would give an idea of the population—eight or ten thousand would not be out of reason for Pueblo Bonito and its nearby villages. From all evidence, the very small, square rooms in it were for storing food and seed, and the like; the larger ones being used for ordinary domestic life.

In the construction of this village, great numbers of large timbers of spruce and pine were used for roof poles (numbers of them being twenty feet in length and twelve to fourteen inches in diameter). Since timber does not grow in such sandy soil or at that altitude, it would have been necessary to have brought them from the higher country forty or fifty miles distant. The mode of transportation of timbers weighing from five hundred to a thousand pounds each must have been a problem that was, without doubt, solved by brute force and the pleasure of the elements. It would seem that the only possible method would have been to drag them in the winter over an occasional snow or to have floated them down the cañon during one of the rare cloudbursts.

It would be folly to try to put a date on the habitation or desertion of the original structures, or even on the present visible ruins, for the reason that the time could be proven or contradicted, depending entirely upon what position one wished to take in the matter. Argument favoring a very remote age would be in the lack of any gold or copper ornament so plentiful with the Aztecs. There is no doubt but that the great Aztec race before the [Spanish] conquest had scouting and trading parties all through this country, bartering for whatever they might fancy, making alliances, taking hostages, or securing by force whatever they might fancy or the occasion demand. As nothing of the sort has been found, one would naturally place them [the Pueblo Bonito people] many years beyond the age of gold and silver discoveries. One might get a hazy estimate of the date of occupation from the knowledge that, when these people lived there, all the timber or fuel material surely must have been used up. After they left, all the ridges have been recovered with the slow-growing piñon and cedar.

One thing we do know: the ancient people are not there now, not even the dead ones, except in rare cases.

The question of the water and food supply naturally arises when it is brought before the mind that the population of the several villages must have numbered several thousand. The water supply is easily accounted for because no deep arroyas cut the valleys with their drainage systems—no sheep, cattle, or horse trails crossed the lands to cause them. There was sufficient grass everywhere to hold the soil in place and to keep the underground shadowed and free from the evaporating effects of the burning sun. Even at the present day it is possible to get water within a few feet by digging in the cañon bed, so ages ago the valley was just long meadows and garden spots. It would have been possible to have farmed for miles along what are now apparently dry wastes by subirrigation, the water naturally rising to any level not cut out by deep ditches or cattle trails.

Large tanks, both natural and artificial, are cut in the soft sandstone in the cliffs above the valley. If necessary, that helped out in the water supply, perhaps being used for a change from the alkaline waters of the valleys below. A series of steps, thirty feet wide, come down the solid rock slope on one side of the cañon and are to be seen [going up] on the opposite side.

Their food supply must have been largely agricultural products because game undoubtedly was rather scarce for many miles distant from the villages. It is possible that the turkey was a domestic fowl with these people, the same as with the Cliff Dwellers. Otherwise, their meat diet must have been rather limited, even though they may have made hunting trips into some far-distant and better game-stocked country.

To enumerate all the articles representing the work and daily life found among the habitations of this interesting people would be out of the question. They had pottery, baskets, woven material, and ornaments of turquois and jet, but to what extent these things were their own work, we have very uncertain ways of determining. The Moquis [Hopis] make pottery and baskets, but do very little in the way of weaving blankets. The Navajo weaves blankets, but does very little work in baskets or pottery.

The Ute supplies the most serviceable baskets for all purposes, also the finest of beadwork. So, by trading around, each tribe gets from some of the others what they themselves do not make and would not have otherwise. So it was with the people of Pueblo Bonito.

We found great quantities of turquois, however. Even in the projecting timbers of an estufa, there were hollowed out places containing turquois. One room contained a body wrapped in some of their finest specimens of weaving. With the body were hundreds of specimens of carved turquois and an unusual number of pieces of pottery and a variety of baskets. The most common article found in the ruins was what the Navajos call "Doclisy clin-cleshy," meaning "blue bugs," which were tiny carved turquois figurines. One of these was a life-sized frog of jet with turquois eyes. An Indian working for the [Hyde] Exploring Expedition sneaked it out and sold it for $50.

Because of the resemblance between these trinkets and the Egyptian scarabs, we could not help but wonder if there was a connecting link somewhere. Many other similarities between things we found and those of the old-world culture gave us reason to think. One room contained hundreds of dried-up bodies of small Mexican parrots, which may have been held sacred to them, the same as the messenger hawks of the Egyptians.

Another room could have been an armory, because it contained nothing but the war and hunting implements of that time.

It is surprising that a people as far advanced toward civilization as they were would have no regular system of hieroglyphics, pictographs, or characters for keeping records. Yet in all this Southwest country we find only crude figures that may or may not have been intended to represent in some way the work or history of that period; a period that might be termed the Dark Ages of our world.

We would like very much to classify these ancient people with one of the thirty-odd so-called pueblo or Village Indians [Hopi] presently living in a narrow zone in this part of the country. All have similar customs and rites and superstitions, but, of the thirty or more different dialects or languages, which village could show that theirs was the original one?

The same questions could be advanced in reference to weaving, pottery, or basketwork, as well as tools or weapons. The better grades of weaving and pottery work are somewhat of a lost art with the present races and what is made now will not stand in the same class with the finer and more serviceable articles the ancients made.

The work of the archaeologist is as full of interest and as exciting as that of the gold miner when he is working on a lead and expects to break into a pocket. Of course, Pueblo Bonito is the subject to be considered at this time, but it does not lessen the interest yet to be awakened when the scientific world realizes that there are other sections just as important in their way as these in our immediate vicinity. The Hovenweep, Yellow Jacket, Ruin Cañon, Grand Gulch, and dozens of other ancient villages, as yet undisturbed, will teach us the proof of our own insignificance.

NOTES

1. Aztec Springs, Colorado, is located south of Cortez, just a few miles from the western base of the Mesa Verde, and is known now as Yucca House National Monument. In the 1929 issue of the U.S. Department of the Interior's *Glimpses of Our National Monuments* (Washington, D.C.: Government Printing Office, 1929), Al had annotated the text on page 70: "It is really Aztec Springs and was the cowboys' winter camp. There were two groups of ruins and the cowboys tried to get a greater supply of water at one of them by blasting, but the spring stopped. Since there was water at the other ruin, it made no difference to them."

PART 3

TOURIST YEARS

WESTERN PARADOX

There's everything to look for in the wild and wooly West.
The brightest men you'll ever see might be the poorest dressed.
You can not pass your judgment on anything you see
For looks are still deceitful and always bound to be.
A mountain looks ten miles away, yet you can travel days
And still it seems same as the first, the air's so free from haze.
If you drink the water that looks so nice you'll be burned with alkali;
Yet to take the bath you think you need you'll catch a cold and die.
You must always take a second look at everything you find
For there's lots of gold you'd not expect in places never mined.

                    Benjamin Alfred Wetherill

10
Vignettes

THE railroad had now climbed over the range [from Durango], circled the La Plata Mountains, and had gone on through Mancos and Dolores up past Rico to Telluride, where it made connections with the through line from Denver to Salt Lake City. The railroad brought supplies, mining and smelter material, people, and last, but not least, the money to develop the resources of the country.

We had thoroughly explored the entire region, mapped it, named the cañons, ruins, and waterholes—perhaps not to the satisfaction of anyone else—to meet our own requirements. So, managing for a limited amount of publicity, we commenced catering to the tourist trade.[1]

Gradually, then, we slipped out of being dirt farmers, except by proxy, and let Mexicans and other help handle that part of the game, while devoting most of our time to cattle and to guiding the tourists to the cliff dwellings.

All the wide-open spaces were reeking with globe trotters of every sort and we bagged our just proportion, both foreign and domestic. Some who came were ordinary sight-seers, some were teachers, some were scientific men, and some were world travel-

179

The Cliff Dwellings

At Mancos Canon, in southern Colorado, are the prehistoric cliff dwellings, homes of an extinct race, the oldest and most wonderful ruins in America. Do not fail to visit them. It can be done with ease and comfort.

Richard Wetherill, who has explored the ruins for years, will act as your guide, and will furnish all necessaries for the trip. His home, the Alamo Ranch, has the finest collection of Mesa ruins and Cliff Dweller relics in the State and furnishes excellent accommodations For full information address R. Wetherill, Alamo Ranch, Mancos, Colo., or call at 15 Gazette building, Colorado Springs.

Colorado Springs Gazette *Advertisement*
"*Managing for a limited amount of publicity, we commenced catering to the tourist trade*," *Al recorded. The cashbook showed sums paid to Colorado newspapers. The 5 September 1895 issue of the* Gazette *carried the advertisement that used one of the first pictures taken of Cliff Palace. The clipping was contributed by Alys Freeze, Western History Department, Denver Public Library.*

ers, but all a likable bunch. There came friends and friends of friends. Some wanted to know about the C.D. [Cliff Dwellers] and others could talk over our heads. But, any and all were ready to believe the most improbable and impossible tales in exchange for the same sort of stuff he hands out from his own unlimited supply of hooey.

The tourists wanted to go places and see things and to camp out. To the cliff dwellings and back was a three-day trip and to where the four states corner was' four days or more of a tiresome jog-jog-jog-along on horses. Indians and Indian traders were always an interesting part of that Four Corners trip, however.

We had all sorts of gentle saddle horses, but they were all classed as cow ponies even if some of them weighed upwards of a thousand pounds. To transfer people from civilized beings to the stone age we had twenty or more saddles, but only one old-fashioned sidesaddle. The women had to rig themselves up to make the trip up and over the top of the Mesa Verde to get to the cliff dwellings. They rode the same as Indian women do— and no questions asked. They all came back sore, lame, and sick, but none ever regretted seeing the sight of the ruins.

Mostly, they came during the summer, for it was too hard a trip to take in the winter on horseback. In the winter, the trip was down the Mancos Cañon and even then there were cliffs twelve to fourteen hundred feet high to climb up in order to reach the ruins. It was impossible to cross the top of the mesa in winter on account of the snow. The trip took three days, whichever way we went.[2]

Between 1889 and 1901 nearly one thousand people visited the ranch to see the cliff dwellings. The first entry in the Alamo Ranch register, which is not a total inventory of visitors, is *June 8, 1889 B. W. Ritter, Durango, Colorado.* And the last is *August 25, 1901 Maj. E. H. Cooper, Chicago.*

It is strange how unobserving some people are, or what little impression the Mesa Verde leaves upon them, perhaps because of its vastness, perhaps because of the fact that their minds can not grasp the grouping as a whole. Whatever makes the first impression is all that can be retained. We can well see the reason: it is all too big to leave room for each and every thing.

Of the people who came to us to see the ruins, my "rememberer" retains many little stories:

On one of the trips to the cliff dwellings, the rough and rugged trail to The Summit almost proved too much for a couple of Germans. At the unusually narrow place one of them called out, "John, John! I thinks I get off here." John said nothing and both horses just kept going as they knew, with their horse sense, that it was no place to stop or even make a change of gait. The man then just shut his eyes and appealed to a higher power to see him safely over. We had to use that Crinkley Edge narrow trail or else go miles around and make lots of climbs in and out of cañons.[3] That narrow trail was not all, for the low hanging limbs of piñon and cedar have a way of reaching out and smacking you, as well as trying to rip all the clothes off you and tear the packs from the backs of the mules (loaded with tin-canned eats and peaceful sleep supplies). That same German made a remark about the biscuits I made in camp. He said, "Dey vass so gude, I t'ot dey vass kek."

Once while going through the low-hanging limbs of the trees, one man caught hold of a branch to keep from being raked off his horse, but [then he] did not let go. He hung on as long as he could and then let the limb fly. The following man was so close behind that it caught him across the face. At which he yelled out, "Sure, Pat! If you had not of helt onto that limb, it would have kilt me entirely and I thank you for it."

Robert Brewster Stanton was a young civil engineer who mapped the country and took invaluable supporting photographs of a boat trip through the Grand Cañon of the Colorado to the Gulf of California. He had all his boats wrecked in Cataract Cañon on the first attempt. On the second attempt he put in either at Dandy Crossing or down Green River. About the middle of Marble Cañon, the photographer got a broken leg and had to be carried out.

The Grand Cañon could never be considered an ideal location for a joy ride but the Denver and R.G.R.R. [Rio Grande Railroad] had in mind running a line through. It would have been an expensive undertaking, but his report gave the first accurate, detailed pictures of the entire length of the cañon (twenty-two hundred negatives in twelve hundred miles). He told me there were only four places where a tunnel would have to be made to avoid some of the rapids on the hazardous trip from Lee's Ferry through the cañon. The tourists and the tourist business would have paid its way, but it would have been impossible to handle traffic going and coming. Dellenbaugh, though, says in time that Stanton's survey will get a road through the cañon.[4]

It is strange how unimpressed some people are but I can never forget one man we brought through all the scenery and over the trails and around the cliff dwellings. When asked what he thought of the ruins and the great stretches of God's country, he just yawned a full-grown yawn and said, "Oh, it's all right. But say, did you ever see the great cornfields of Iowa and Kansas?"

I do not know when I did get so I could ride 'most anything that came along, but I never did ride just to show off. A rider generally loses his nerve to tackle a new bronc, but, if he happens to get on one by mistake, he usually forgets that he is scared of the beast. But one time I really got a medal for riding. We had a young horse that needed to be "uncocked," the expression when a horse had to be tried out before starting in on the day's work. A would-be horsebreaker tried him and came down ker-plunk and everybody laughed. A surveyor who was at the ranch wondered how anyone could stick on a horse when it bucked that way. "Oh, shucks," I said. "I ride that kind for twenty-five cents apiece."

"I'll give you a quarter to ride him," he said.

I rode him, but thought it was just for a joke. A month or so later I received my quarter, but it had been smoothed off on one side and on it was a man riding a jumping horse with my name on it as a top-notch broncobuster.[5]

I never did hobble my stirrups as some did, because I thought it too risky if a horse fell or turned over backward. I have had a horse turn a hand-spring over frontwards, but was never caught but once. I was riding a race horse we had and was coming from town. The horse would never let another horse pass him. This time there was a glare of ice on the road before reaching home. When he struck that, his feet went out from under him and down he went on his side. By the time he got up I was free from the saddle and got up and walked into the house where dinner was ready. I took my place and ate, but it was an hour or so before I came to my senses, thinking I was up to Trinidad where I had been a short time before.

We often had kids from Denver down at the ranch and occasionally one who thought he was a rider. Once, one kid got the best unloading I ever saw. The horse was one of our best cow horses, but always had to be uncocked before he was ready for business. But then, after he had his jumps, he was one of the best horses we ever had. I guess he always wanted to find out if

For a Two-Bit Bronc Breaking:
One of Al's proudest possessions was the quarter he received from a surveyor who came to the Alamo Ranch. The back side of the coin had been ground smooth and reengraved with his name and the figure of a broncobuster.

Alamo Ranch and Point Lookout

Point Lookout "hides an early setting sun," while making a backdrop for the Alamo Ranch. This 1892 picture reveals a problem. For want of a barn, the hay was in danger of loss, so plans were made to build a huge barn on the extreme left of the picture in the space occupied by mounds of hay. Part of the lumber is already piled in the barnyard, but, "the price of nails being out of the question," the Wetherills spent the winter months of 1892–3 whittling pegs for nails to construct the barn in 1893.

the rider was a sure-thing or just a make-believe. Well, that kid got on the horse all right. The horse's name was "Johnny Jump-up" and it fit him proper. About the second or third jump, the kid flew high, wide, and handsome and hit the barn all spread-eagled. He looked just like his hide had been nailed there all spraddled out. When he got up he had to count his pieces to see if they were all there.

When our family had a few girls from the East one time, we went up high in the mountains on a sort of a picnic and to get a supply of raspberries to put up for winter use. About ten miles up the river, but on the mesa through which the river cañon runs, there was a long, sloping cañonside with acres and acres of raspberry bushes just red with ripe, juicy fruit. There was probably a dozen people in the bunch and we all scattered out with someone thought to be congenial.

It fell my lot, or selection, to have a Denver girl wished off on me so that was that (but it was not so bad). We all picked berries and picked berries until most of the cans and buckets were full and then we all scattered, looking for adventure.

The day was beautiful and the air was all that early autumn brings, with its exhilarating effect on people and the other animals that roam the wildwood. The girl and myself looked toward the snowy peaks a few miles further up the river and they looked so good to us that away we went along the riverbed. There our troubles began, what with fallen timber, beaver dams, and slide rock. All that, though, meant nothing to us, for we were both young, foolish things. Distances are so deceiving and the passing of time so quick, that long before we reached anywhere the sun began to get low over the cañon rim to the west.

We hardly looked for berries any more but [enjoyed] the flowers, the birds, the animals, and the immense spruce trees in every nook where they could get a footing.

A frequent splash told us a trout had picked up a fly or bug that happened his way. Almost like shadows, a few mama deer with their children just out of the spotted age slowly drifted from sight. An occasional buck with his newly acquired antlers, just out of the velvet stage, could be glimpsed. He might look back over his shoulder as if undecided whether to disappear or to stand his ground. Grouse, foolish chickens, or sage hens (whatever the distinction between the different classes) were numerous and paid little attention to us. Camp robbers, or whiskey jacks, squawked at us as though we were no good to them unless we had food handy. Magpies made a whole lot of fuss, too, as we passed the bunches of box elder where they were holding reunions of scattered groups of their kind. The ravens were ever present with their caw-caw-caws. And, an occasional golden eagle could be seen high above, circling over miles of sky in the hopes of seeing something to suit his taste—or maybe just doing it for the mere joy of living. No beaver were to be seen, although an occasional heavy splash told us they were at home; but not to visitors. In the rock slides, the squeaking little coney bears (which are not bears at all) would sit up and look at us and then make a dive for their hide-outs. These little fellows are not much larger than a prairie dog and have even less tail.

It is said that water runs uphill in the Mesa Verde country, which is perfectly true. The Little Mancos River has a fall of sixty-nine feet to the mile and the water gets a running start that takes it up the next hill. Keep your fingers crossed when you tell that to your eastern friends, but the water sure gets over the top only when it starts from a higher level.

Traveling down through a Mexican district on a sort of an archaeological expedition once, we stopped at a Mexican store, post office, and saloon all in the same room, which was also the family dwelling. We were three in number (one a lady) and did not know the roads and directions. An occasional signboard was all in Mexican. (A stranger going through the Mexican villages seldom finds anyone who can talk U.S., unless he wants to buy something. Yet these same people away from home in the American towns can get along fine.)

Early in the evening the Mexican population began to assemble for un baile (bailar), or ball. Eventually there were about fifty people assembled. The Mexicans are all musicians. They all dance and sing and those who can possess a guitar are sure to have one. Even the poorest sheepherder who can get a couple of cigar boxes will whittle himself a fiddle that will make enough fuss for a few couples to dance to.

After awhile the lady wanted to try the Mexican dance. I do not know how late she stayed. We had to get going early in the morning and were all ready when the lady showed up. But, she had left her everyday shoes in the ballroom (which was also the family bedroom) and did not know how to get them out. Finally, she made a sneak in and got them.

But now we were up against it for we had all our outfit in the walled yard (or patio) that was all enclosed by adobe walls ten to twelve feet high and the gates barred and locked with iron bars. We looked at the gates for awhile and then got some poles, lifted the gates off their hinges and let them fall. Then we took our outfit out over them and went on our way rejoicing, leaving the whole settlement slumbering peacefully.

Another time, finding it necessary to be in a Mexican logging camp, I was compelled to eat (and almost sleep) with them. I suppose the diet is all right if a person is brought up on it, but it is a hard proposition to one accustomed to a civilized or balanced ration. (There is a saying that a coyote will not eat a dead Mexican on account of the chili seasoning all through his system.)

Early in the morning (daylight) everyone is astir—some to get water and wood; some to make tortillas; some to cook beans and chili; and [some to] make alleged coffee. If you have not eaten tortillas, the experiment would be worthwhile. Take poor flour, a pinch of salt, and a little bkp [baking powder] and mix all to a hard mass by adding water. Then the tortillas are pounded and flipped around in the hands until a sort of a pancake one-fourth of an inch thick and the diameter of a frypan is formed. The stuff is burned and dried until pronounced cooked and a stack of the things, six inches to a foot high, [eventually] stand ready to attack you.

By this time the beans and chili have been mashed and stewed and the smelly coffeepot has done its duty. The tortillas are softened in the bean and chili compound, each party dipping his own tortillas in the semiliquid abomination. All eat out of the frying pan and drink out of tin cans. About a week of this was sufficient [for me] to swear off Mexican diet for life. I could not go the tortillas before this experience but could endure beans if they were not pinto. Now I am off the aforesaid beans for all time to come and have not let a bite of tortilla even get in my neighborhood! Ever since, I have found it convenient to take my own outfit wherever I go. Their dried meat, though, is very sustaining but not much to look at. It is sliced thin and dried in the sun (smoked a little on account of the flies) and you could live on it for an indefinite period.

It always seemed to me that if a person could start a trading store with the Indians—anywhere—the financial part of worry would be settled. To test it out, one of the boys we had helping at the ranch and myself decided to try it a round and to locate down in the Indian country about one hundred fifty miles away in New Mexico. The first store at Pueblo Bonito was established

[October 1895] three years before our father died, by myself and Oscar Buck. We brought down seven burros, loaded with supplies, from Mancos.

Our store and sleeping rooms were two small rooms not more than fifty feet from the cliff. There was an immense rock split off from the cliff, but still leaned almost against the cliff at the top while the bottom had slipped a few feet further out.[6]

First Wetherill Trading Store
In October, 1895, Al Wetherill and Oscar [Orion] Buck opened a trading store in the two rooms attached to the towering walls at Pueblo Bonito, Chaco Cañon, New Mexico.

A large cattle company had tried to run cattle in the sandy and dry desertlike country, but had given it up as a failure and had been gone for a number of years before we drifted in.

The cattlemen had built stone buildings to protect themselves from the Mexican sheepherders as well as the Indians. The Indians were not so bad at the time, but the Mexicans seemed to think that they owned the whole country. Anyway, cattlemen and sheepmen just do not thrive in the same territory.

One sample of the love between cattlemen and sheepmen can be illustrated by the following story of what had happened there. One of the cattle company's cowboys, at a cabin somewhere along the Escavada, was preparing dinner for the round-up boys. Since it was a little early, he was sitting around rolling cigarettes in corn husks or a kind of brown paper, whichever came handiest. He had not been looking around, because they were not having much trouble with the bean-eaters, but the first thing he knew there was a little noise outside so he flopped down to see what it was. Through a crack in the door (I think it was the door), he saw three of a sheepherding gang making a sneak on either him, or the supplies, or to burn the place down. Just at that moment he made a jump for the door on the opposite side of the room as they made a rush to get a crack at him. He beat them at it and was outside before any of them could draw down on him. As soon as he was outside the door, he turned around close to the wall and, as the rush was made for him, took them as they came. The Mexican population was short three hombres. Nothing was ever done about it, for sheepherders were plentiful. But there were three more notches on the handle of his gun.

The thousands of sheep driven in from the mountain ranges of southern Colorado to winter in the Pueblo Bonito area killed off all the range for cattle, because their sharp little feet just cut the grass out by the roots. So the cattlemen finally had to get out of there. They were not a bit sorry, for the water was vile stuff to drink and, if not made up with coffee, was not fit to go down a human's throat.

As the cattle went out, they strung out to the north. Just across the San Juan River at Farmington, and on up the Animas and La Plata Rivers, there was mile after mile of the finest range for cattle, both in winter and summer.

That was about the time of the Farmington War, with Billy the Kid, and others of that cut [being] in the heaven of their existence. They did not last long, because the country was getting too well settled up by law-abiding people to put up with too much of that Deadeye-Dick class.

At the time we went in to the Pueblo Bonito, both cattle and sheep were gone.

We did a swell business as long as our stuff held out. Then the partner took the burros and what pelts we had on hand and headed for Albuquerque to get fresh stock—a trip of over one hundred miles each way—and was gone for nineteen days.

While he was gone and I was there alone, I think I was at a wedding feast. One night I went over to a camp on the opposite side of the cañon where some Indians were having a singing and eating contest, as well as the wedding. Of course I had to join in on the eats, which was a bucket filled with boiled mutton, or goat. The gang would reach into the supply, haul out a big bone with meat on it, take a bite, throw it back in, and try another one. Then the next one would take a turn. I did not make any kick because it was not my game and, anyway, being away from civilization for awhile, I had got to be like the natives.

Up to this time there had been no white man except me across that whole desolate country. Maybe I was homesick by now, or just what? Anyway, a couple of the boys from the home ranch dropped in to see how we were getting along and the result was that I went back with the boys and let the partner run wild with the natives. He was there for only a short time when the Hyde Exploring Expedition came in and went to work and took him in with them.

The only woman tourist who ever had an honest-to-goodness bathtub was Mrs. John Hays Hammond, who took one along with her on their trip to the Mesa Verde.[7] All the seventeen days we were out, Mr. Hammond did not want any mail or telegrams sent to him. We went over trails and saw ruins that the ordinary tourist never saw, since Cliff Palace and Spruce Tree House was their ordinary limit. Mrs. Hammond had a tent and had their handyman carry and heat water, so made the trip in apple-pie order. The whole family was tops, the only bugs in the ointment being the English man's man and their handyman.

Once a delegation of scientific (?) men, women, and children had a great scheme hatched up to visit one of the roughest and least known sections of Colorado—the cliff dwellings—and I was the victim selected to nurse them along the rough and rugged trails and to deliver them back to the alleged civilization of ranches, Indians, and cowboys. To begin with, all were duly assembled and were wild with excitement and mountain exhilaration. Some chose saddle horses; others preferred mountain wagons, thinking there would be less wear and tear to go in that manner. That way, though, we had to go down the main cañon, instead of the regular way. Among the delegation was Professor [Jesse Walter] Fewkes and Frank Hitchcock who was later Postmaster General of the United States.[8]

Camp was made for the night in a beautiful grove of box elder. A roaring campfire was made, [looking] like the pictures you see of such things. Off to one side the cook outfit had a fire about the size of a small washtub. (None of this was to be in the story, though. To get back. . . .) Around the large fire all sorts of war dances, scalp dances, snake dances, and rain dances were going strong until someone suggested toasts to the capable guide of the expedition. The suggestion was received with echoing cheers. I do not know if it is appropriate to tell the rest of the story, but it is true. Each of the members had a turn at toasting and kept it up far into the night. Finally I thought it best to not be so free with the cheers and thanks and suggested that it probably would be necessary to save some of that cheer to get back home on.

The next day told the story: no cheers, no happiness; just heaps of appliances. The wagons had to be dropped after that first day and not more than six out of the more than twenty people made the entire round. The balance of them hung around camp. Most of them never even saw any of the buildings, although there was one just a few hundred feet from where we camped. I guess they came along just for the joyride.

Professor Fewkes and Mrs. Fewkes and two or three others made the climb up to Balcony House and then on up the gulch to the top of the mesa and so across to the noted ruins of Cliff Palace and Spruce Tree House. The climb was rough and every few yards along the way Mrs. Fewkes would have to stop and read in a little book she had along. I wondered about that and found out later that it was a Christian Science book. Professor Fewkes made the rounds in good shape.[9]

[There was] never a more enthusiastic and tireless worker for the preservation of the Ancients' work in the Southwest than Virginia McClurg of Colorado Springs. She became interested in the project soon after our discoveries of the ruins in the Mesa Verde district.[10] From the first her mind was made up to have all things of prehistoric interest set aside to National Parks and Reservations and the Cliff Dwellings was her first project. Her whole mind and time seemed to be devoted to her work. Her persistence overcame all indifference and her efforts with the growing womens' clubs of Denver, Colorado Springs, and Pueblo should have been fully recognized by the state [of Colorado] in particular and the United States in general. She was able, through long and tireless effort, to interest the government, where we had failed in our attempts. It must have required some ingenuity to persuade the Utes to agree to the idea of having the Mesa Verde country overrun with sightseers after their undisputed possession for years of all the high, grassy tableland with its deep cañons and hidden water pools.

After seeing what sort of beings the Cliff Dwellers were, I do not believe any of the folks who came our way ever again tried to date their ancestors back as far as the Stone Age.

Some of the people who came to us became real friends. Most impressive were Alice Eastwood, Gustaf Nordenskiöld, and Dr. Prudden. [More about them follows.]

NOTES

1. Advertising entries in the cashbook were to the *Rocky Mountain World* (Denver), the *Colorado Springs* (Colorado) *Gazette,* and the *Durango* (Colorado) *Herald*. Of these, only the one in the 5 September 1895 issue of the *Gazette* has been found (p. 5, col. 5). The ad carried a reproduction of one of the first pictures made of Cliff Palace.

2. The Alamo Ranch account books show charges of $20 for the three-day trip that included Cliff Palace, Spruce Tree House, and Square Tower House; $5 for the one-day trip to Sandal House in the Mancos Cañon; and $30 to $40 for the trip to Ruin (now called Hovenweep) Cañon, depending upon the number of days required. Other trips, if the Wetherills charged for them, varied according to the time, equipment, and personnel needed.

3. The Wetherills' Crinkley Edge became known as *Knife Edge* to later tourists. The road, constantly slipping downward, required expensive upkeep and has been replaced by a tunnel that bypasses the point. Montezuma Valley viewpoint is now at the southern end of the old Knife Edge. The trail around the point was adopted by the Wetherills as their usual route into the mesa during the tourist years, after the Utes had disclosed the trail in 1889. Subsequent roads continued to follow the route until the tunnel was completed.

4. Al's account is not so accurate as his usual accounting of events. Robert B. Stanton entered the Green River on his first not second trip. The railroad company financing the survey was not entirely the Denver and Rio Grande, but the Denver, Colorado Cañon, and Pacific Railroad Survey Company. Instead of four tunnels, the survey charted seven, possibly eight. The number of photographic negatives is precisely correct, however, for Stanton's notes (p. 176) record that exact number (Robert Brewster Stanton, *Down the Colorado,* ed. Dwight L. Smith [Norman, Oklahoma: University of Oklahoma Press, 1965]). The very fact that the photographic number was correct presents an enigma: Al recorded, at least by 1920, the exact information contained in a book not published until 1965, fifteen years after Al's death.

5. The broncobuster "medal" is one of Martha's prize mementos of her father's cowboy days, in spite of the fact that the name Wetherill was misspelled.

6. A newsclipping (the *Morning Kansas City Star,* 23 January 1941) was inserted between the pages of notes at this point. The article stated that the 30,000 pound slab of sandstone called "Threatening Rock" had fallen, shattering a part of the north wall of Pueblo Bonito, over which it had teetered at least 1,000 years. At the top of the clipping Al had written: "I had my first store in two rooms of the ruin where this rock fell. B.A.W." On the back of a photograph

of the store he had scribbled, perhaps bitterly, "Mamie turned the store into a chicken coop" after she and Richard Wetherill were married and had settled at Pueblo Bonito.

7. On their way from London to California, the John Hays Hammond family stopped at the Alamo Ranch, registering on 29 May 1900. According to Virginia McClurg (*Colorado Magazine*, November 1930), Mrs. Hammond became an enthusiastic member of the Colorado Cliff Dwellers Association and donated the money to blast out the spring at Spruce Tree House, providing an abundant supply of water. Natalie (Mrs. John Hays) Hammond had authored in 1897 *A Woman's Part in a Revolution* (New York and London: Longmans, Green and Co.), her diary of the period of time between 30 December 1895, when it became apparent that her husband would be arrested in Johannesburg, South Africa, during the Boer War, and his release from prison, 12 June 1896. A copy, autographed by her, is still in the Wetherill library.

8. Neither Hitchcock nor Fewkes signed the guest register, but Hitchcock took pictures of the members who visited the ruins and sent some to Al. The pictures are dated 6 September 1901 with "Frank H. Hitchcock, The Clifton, Thomas Circle, Washington, D.C." stamped on them. Virginia Doneghal McClurg claims the honor of escorting the Fewkes on this their first trip to southwestern Colorado's ruin area. If it was Fewkes's first trip, then Gustaf Nordenskiöld's reference to "Mr." Fewkes's explanation of items collected by Nordenskiöld in 1891 (and published in 1893) can not be explained (*Cliff Dwellers of the Mesa Verde*, pp. 56, 100.)

9. Al's use of the word *Professor* establishes the fact that he knew Jesse Walter Fewkes before the title became "Dr." Fewkes. Fewkes's writing provides no indication that he was ever acquainted with the Wetherills, for he refers only to Chapin and Nordenskiöld for source information in making his Bureau of Ethnology reports. Al's account, plus Virginia McClurg's story (*see* note 8 above) makes it certain that Fewkes was acquainted with the Wetherills. In addition, Al's daughter, Martha, remembers him visiting them several times in Gallup when Al was postmaster there.

10. Although the first part has been lost, enough remains to reveal Al's appreciation of Virginia Doneghal McClurg. His outline notes contained a notation to tell about "Mrs. McClurg and the centipede," but the episode is evidently in the missing portion. Mrs. McClurg worked for years to help establish the Mesa Verde as a protected area, yet the United States government never recognized her efforts and her name has practically disappeared from Mesa Verde history. The editor of the *Colorado Magazine* article (*see* f7) noted that France awarded her a Gold Palm of the Academy and an honorary Doctor of Letters degree at the 1900 Paris International Exposition for her indefatigable efforts in behalf of the Mesa Verde ruins (*Colorado Magazine* [November 1930]:217.)

11
Alice Eastwood

J UST before and just after the year 1890 came along, the
Southwestern states were the best hunting grounds for the
scientist. Anywhere in the radius of one hundred to two hundred miles around the point where the four states corner was
rich picking for any who might be on the trail of unknown, or
partly known, varieties of material in Nature's storehouse. The
key to supplying the storehouse to overflowing is a matter of
following up an inclination started far back in childhood days
and of keeping the subject forever uppermost in mind. That
was our friend, the Lady Botanist, from Denver. Our first experience with a botanist was when she came to the Alamo Ranch
in 1889 and camped with us on the mesa. She roamed around
collecting plants and once was lost for a time, but we found
her by the smoke from her campfire.

A botanical research trip became my responsibility in the
summer of 1892 when, with a couple of saddle horses and a
pack horse, I escorted Miss Denver Botanist, Alice Eastwood,
down into southeast Utah.[1] The expedition was also a lost horses'
hunting trip. We lost, or they wandered off, or we had stolen,
a team of roan horses that had been brought in from Utah. Like

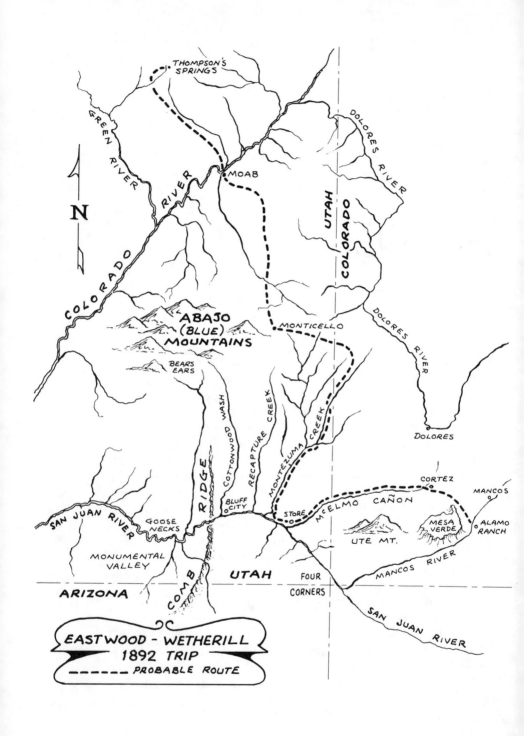

EASTWOOD - WETHERILL
1892 TRIP
- - - - - PROBABLE ROUTE

all Western horses, they try to work back to the grassy meadows of their colthood days. A week or so after they disappeared, we received word that they had got back to their early range district and we had better come, or send, for them. Stock of any kind was often helped along their way, all depending on who did the helping. Monticello, Utah, where they were, was at least seventy-five miles away.

While we were debating the question as to just when to start out on that trip, we received a letter from our friend, Alice. She wanted to botanize the country on a horseback trip from Grand Junction, Colorado, to our ranch in southwest Colorado. We answered that I would be there with the necessary equipment, but that I would meet her at Thompson's Springs, [Utah,] some distance down the river from Grand Junction, and about one hundred fifty miles from the ranch. Although it was a couple more than a couple of days before I got there, it was perfectly satisfactory.

We did not start out that day, since it was too late. We were taken in and made at home by one of the families, the postmaster's, at the Springs. The family displayed the best brand of Western hospitality.[2]

We left early the next morning without any fixed destination. The weather was perfect, the country beautiful with grasses and flowers, and the distant mountains were pictures that memory could never forget or let fade away. The Lady Botanist would always see things that I would overlook, because I was always looking ahead at regular or irregular formations, and she would stop to pick, or examine, some strange or rare specimen of plant that cropped up in protected places or in new territory. When traveling with her we might make only ten to twenty miles in a day, all depending on the variety of the vegetation.

We were traveling along the mail route from the railroad at Thompson's Springs to the farming and mining districts on the Grand and Green Rivers and the mountainous regions in between. We knew we could make it to Moab, Utah, on the Grand [Colorado] River by night, and not hurry. Although we did not expect to use it, we had a regular cowboy's layout—a greasysack outfit. That meant limited camping equipment, a couple of saddle blankets, and a canvas covering for the pack. Grub was bacon, oatmeal, salt, sugar, coffee, and flour and baking powder in the [flour] sack.

We made a dry camp at noon, but did have a canteen of water. We scouted around a bit while the horses were picking their noonday meal of grama grass, or buckwheat, or other sorts of green forage plants.[3]

The first night we made the Mormon settlement at Moab, just about dark, after a long day's work. That is, if the work one does can be listed as work, with all that scenery thrown in for good measure. We stayed overnight with a family I knew and can not say enough for the kindness and hospitality shown us by the folks of that fruit-growing and farming people.[4]

We had been coming down a gradual slope to Moab and from there it was an upward slope most of the way to Monticello, which had the beautiful Blue Mountains behind it for a background. At noon we made another dry camp and repeated the same as the day before. The stop was longer that day, since we were gaining altitude as well as varieties of plants. I think the horses were having the time of their lives, judging from the way they waded into and rolled around in the flat, grassy meadow.

All that country is stock country, but we saw very few head of either horses or cattle on the entire trip and no sheep at all. Of course, cattle and sheep do not thrive together. Sheep are bad medicine on the range anywhere and, too, their little feet cut up the ground, break off the grass roots and, · before long, the country is reduced to just a dust bowl. The valleys of New Mexico, Arizona, Utah, and Colorado were all carpeted with heavy, thick grass at first, which prevented the blowing away of the soil. Along the beds of streams and dry watercourses, you could expect heaps of sand and soil, but in any of the valleys it was possible and [it] was done, to cut hundreds of tons of hay. The stock would keep fat on it. Do not accuse the farmer of causing the barren wastes by plowing the land. Ninety-nine percent of the destruction of the grasslands was made by sheep and the great arroyas cut when stock made their way to water.

We camped the first night after Moab and the following day had mostly level country and wide valleys.[5] During the day we met up with one of the native breed of humans. He was not a Mormon but was something the wind had blown in, I guess. He jogged along a few yards ahead of us for eight or ten miles and then turned off into a side cañon, saying we had better come on up with him. Strange as it may seem, we met up with only that one man and no Indians, all the way to Monticello.

About the middle of the afternoon, the heavens opened up and how the rain did come down! We did not get much wet, for we made a rush for an overhanging ledge of rock. The horses were well pleased with the free bath that Nature supplied, as well as an intermediate lunch hour. How the water did roar down the bed of the gulch! But, in about an hour, it had all run out and then we gathered up our stuff, rounded up the horses (wading in mud up to our shoe tops), and were glad to be on our way again. The horses really got an overdose of free baths and stood humped up and shivering after getting their saddles on.

It was a comparatively short distance to the settlement of Monticello where we were taken in by our Mormon friends. The Mormon people can sure make a person feel at home among them and we always tried to repay our debts in the same kind of coin. They had arranged to have our lost horses ready for us so we could get along early in the morning. But, during the night our lost horses strayed off and it was near noon [of that day] before we got away.[6]

We had inquired for a short cut across the numerous cañons with the idea of getting home the next day. Our directions were to head for the Ute Mountain, which could be seen in the far-away distance of almost seventy miles across ridges and cañons, until we struck the trail into Horse Pasture Cañon. Did we understand the directions? No, but we thought we followed instructions. There was no trail to guide by, except the ability to follow your nose, or by some mountain peak in the dim distance. I do not see to this day why we did not go home via the regular road, except that we thought we could shorten the distance.

It was near dark when we were able to see the cañon, but did not see any trails leading down into it. We just followed along the ridge quite awhile and finally decided to work down the timbered slope of the cañon. We were getting along fine until we were about a hundred feet from the bottom. There, strange to say, was a perpendicular cliff of thirty or forty feet to jump from. Apparently there was no other means of reaching the bottom. We did not hesitate long in agreeing to let Miss Botanist, the camp outfit, and extra saddle down via rope. After that, I was to take the horses back the way we had come and try to get in from the head of the cañon.

I had to tail all the horses together, because it was impossible to drive them, there being too great a risk of losing one or two in the dark. I had five head along in the string and, by good luck, none of them tangled up among the trees, but followed right along in the lead horse's tracks.

In the course of time I found not only the head of the cañon but a perpendicular cliff about seventy-five feet [high] straight down from where I stood to the level below. After that I worked along the edge of the cliff, a sort of shelf, for quite a distance and tried to quit thinking unprintable things. The next move was to get back the way I had come and stop near where I thought the camp below would be.

When I had done that, I just anchored the horses to trees and wolfed it (nothing to eat and no bed). Saddles can not be used for pillows if they are the heavy stock saddles such as are used on the range. They make a fair windbreak but that is all.

I was up at daybreak and started out to look for cattle and horse trails, wondering how the Lady had been making out in the cañon she could not get out of without the wings of something bigger than [those of] a dove. Not fifty feet from where I had passed the night so uncomfortably there were numerous dim trails and, within a short distance, I struck into the one main trail leading right down to a broken place in the cliff. Soon I was beating it down the cañon to where the grub supplies and the Lady must have passed a very uneasy night.

I had not gone very far down the cañon when here came the Lady and I guess she did have a sort of a worried look on her face that immediately changed into a broad grin. She was an Old Timer so far as camping out was concerned and did not fear for herself. Well, we scooted back to camp and exchanged what thoughts had passed in our minds. She was worried some when I did not show up at some late hour of the night and was preparing to backtrack to Monticello and get out a search party if she failed to locate me soon.

What if she had managed to climb out of the head of the cañon just as I was going in lower down! We were both equally pleased to note that the coyotes and other night-prowling varmints had not frightened her to death (which was far from possible) and I was glad for her expressions of thankfulness to see that I was still on the job.

While we were letting the horses make up for the time lost from their meal hours, we had our oatmeal and coffee with a slice of bacon for dessert. As soon as the horses had filled themselves to overflowing and got to rolling around and being

Alice Eastwood:
Wearing her standard attire for botanical excursions, Alice poses at a camp spot "probably in Ruin Cañon in 1894." A skirt she developed is not the one in the photograph. It was one that buttoned demurely down the front for a ladylike appearance, but unbuttoned to become a divided skirt for riding. The original picture was loaned by Mrs. Merle Burch, Alice Eastwood's niece. It was printed on something like blueprint paper, as were a series of pictures in the Alamo Ranch photo file.

pleased with the world at large, we took it as an invitation to saddle up and be on our way.[7]

We thought we would soon be able to cross over to the opposite ridge and on directly to Ute Mountain and McElmo Cañon. Ute Mountain was then about thirty-five miles southeast as the crow flies, maybe fifty by the way of unknown trails. Whenever we came to a break in the side walls of the valley, I would ride up and survey the prospects of a short cut, but there was too much rough country to tackle it. So, we just kept drifting along down the cañon and eventually could see the tops of the big cottonwoods along the San Juan in the distance.

To judge from the bundles of carefully handled and marked bunches, all with unpronounceable names, the botany business was booming. We had gentle little breezes that came strolling along at uncertain intervals. Then the breezes would rest for awhile and, I suppose, go back for more material. Miss Botanist had taken her latest plant specimens out of the papers to dry and had them scattered around hither and yon. I sort of suggested that a small whirley might come along and flop those papers upside down and downside up. Everything seemed so quiet and harmless, though, that it did not look like anything could possibly happen. But in about a minute, here came the most cooling and refreshing breeze you ever saw and what it did to those papers and specimens was a caution. The Lady would have wept had I not been around, I bet, although she was not the weeping kind at all. Anyway, she just sailed into those papers and specimens and got them all safely packed and tied up in their proper places with no loss that I could see. Most of them were pretty green and had not blown far. I did not know how to sympathize, since sympathy could not correct the jumble.

"Let's go," she said. And go we did.[8]

There was an Indian trader's store up the river where McElmo Creek meets the San Juan [River]. (There are really no creeks in all the Western country—just rivers, gulches, or washes.) There our guessing troubles were over, for from there to the end of our journey we knew the country well. We stayed near the store overnight and caught up on the trials and tribulations of an oatmeal diet.[9]

Leaving there early, we made it only about halfway up the McElmo Cañon, for there were many strange and new plants to gather and compare.

We passed the big ruins where the Hovenweep (Yellow Jacket) Cañon comes into the McElmo [Cañon], but did not stop there long. At that time our archaeological education had not been developed and they appeared to be only just big heaps of rocks.

That night we got only as far as the first ranch, Hills. After swapping yarns and news with the rancher, we turned in. There were only two rooms to the house, so the Botanist shared the [bed]room with the lady of the house and the men and myself had the kitchen all to ourselves. Next morning we were out extra early, since the rancher had chores to do and the lady had her usual farm work to keep up.

There are scattered ranches all along McElmo Valley and Cañon. How they manage to get along and raise any vegetation or crops requires even more than a pioneer's background. Talk about alkali water! McElmo has any place beaten by miles. You can drink it if it is made up into strong coffee or tea, but even then it is villainous stuff.

We drifted on up the cañon and made the Alamo Ranch long before nightfall. The folks did not seem to be a bit worried by the long time it took us to get through. I guess we were too much pioneer stock to borrow worries until they showed up. The entire trip was a success, even if we did try for short cuts. But, it proves that the longest way around is the shortest way home—we should have kept to the road.[10]

A long desired trip to Willow Creek, out beyond the Mexican Hat, was made from the Alamo Ranch, which seemed the central point to start from no matter which direction I was for, in July 1895. Willow Creek was fully one hundred fifty miles from the ranch and is hidden from sight as it drops into the San Juan [River] over rough and broken rocks that have dropped off a lookout point in years past, almost blocking any possibility of making a trail between the point and the river far below. Near there, there had been a placer-gold boom for all that San Juan country and [it was the place where] we had a rocker for our claim. While there, I decided that there was something else that the little valley of Willow Creek might produce besides the gold seeker's longings—botanical possibilities.

To have gone by the way of the Four Corners would have been too far out of the way for the place we intended to reach, so we just made a straight line west. Our route from the Mancos [River] was to the top of the divide [between Montezuma and

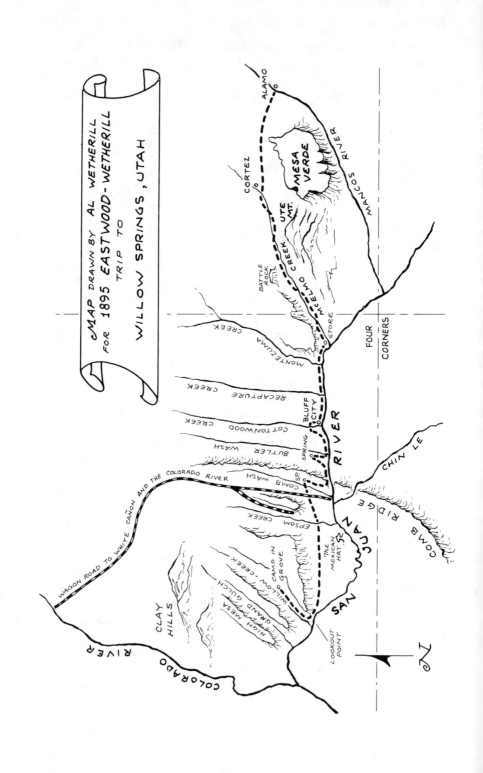

MAP DRAWN BY AL WETHERILL
FOR 1895 EASTWOOD-WETHERILL
TRIP TO
WILLOW SPRINGS, UTAH

Mancos Valleys] that cuts off the Mancos and Dolores waters, the Mancos waters going southwest and on to the San Juan [River], while the Dolores waters run almost directly north to the Grand River. From the top of the divide we look across Montezuma Valley. From this point we go around to the north side of Ute Mountain and strike down McElmo Cañon, down which runs a small stream of the vilest water that humans ever tried to drink. I do not see what the present-day people do about drinking water unless they save rain or snow water. McElmo drains the north side of Ute Mountain and a small part of Montezuma Valley. The water now comes from irrigation ditches carrying Dolores River water, which makes the whole valley almost a garden of Eden, for great quantities and varieties of fruit and vegetables can be produced in that fertile soil.

The seeping drips of water coming through the sandstone cliffs [along the way] shells out places under the rim rock and in such places are to be found varieties of strange plants to delight the heart of any botanist. We were in no hurry to get over the miles because it was the results, entirely, [that] we were after.

We stopped the first night at Harry Hill's ranch, about halfway through the [McElmo] cañon, and the next night at Bluff City, [Utah], following down the San Juan Valley [from the junction of McElmo Creek with the San Juan River].[11]

Bluff City, located at the mouth of Cottonwood Wash, looked like it had had a good wash recently. The channel, or arroya, always looked wide [enough] and deep enough to carry off all the water that ever might come down through the cañon and not bother the settlement by overflows. The folks there did not seem to take in the chance of a cloudburst, which were so common all through the mountain districts. But that very thing happened and the little town was nearly buried from sight by the great rolls of sand and drift trash that poured over the fences, through the houses and gardens, and banked up light sands almost four-feet deep on what fruit trees were still showing. The folks there did not seem to be worried and, so far as I could see, no effort was being made to regulate such a thing in case of another hurry-up-quick water supply. Of course, the main channel was washed wider and deeper, so further washes could not take the toll that the first one made.[12]

We stopped at Allen's place while there, and then kept on

down the riverside to Butler's Wash, which was not a wash, but a jumping-off place to get down to the [San Juan] river level. Here the river makes a little turn and strikes more directly to the west. Ordinarily, it is just a meek and lowly stream, but when the spring rains and melting snows come along, it is a riproaring torrent. Across the river was a stone cabin, vacant for years, where the Indians had killed a trader by the name of Smith. I suppose the Indians were more or less superstitious about going around there. The younger generation has about cut out all the superstitious stuff, unless, like the whites, they have some pet notions that they never let go of.

The road down was largely corduroy, made from poles and logs where the ledge was not wide enough for wagons. I suppose the Mormons made the road when they came into the San Juan basin years ago.

When we had worked our way down to the river level, we turned directly to the right and went on up the slope caused by the uplift from the Comb Ridge formation to Butler Spring, which has fairly good water. We had dinner in the shade of some brushy little trees, much like the buffalo berry, but which the Lady Botanist said was Cascara.

After dinner we followed on down the river valley until we reached the Comb Wash, one side of which is an immense volcanic dike that stretches across the country and was brought into existence by the same shake-up that caused so many blowouts in the Monumental Valley region.[13] The sharp edges of the Comb Ridge are landmarks for many miles, because it extends from the Elk Mountains on the north on down a hundred miles south of the [San Juan] river into Monumental Valley.

We went up the bed of the Comb Wash a couple of miles to where there was a little spring coming out of the rock, close to the cliff side. On the opposite side of the wash, a mile away to the west, there is a trail going up a ridge to another level stretch of desertlike country that eventually leads into White Cañon via Bears Ears in the Elk Mountains.

Turning west again, we went over a number of low ridges. This area is about ten miles wide by fifteen miles long and is bordered on one side by the San Juan River and on the north by a high tableland, raised a thousand feet or more above the little sand flat we were to journey over.

As we left the Comb's rocky backbone four or five miles behind us, we came to a small wash cutting down through the level plateau we were on. In the bottom of it, a beautiful, clear, cold spring was gushing up. We got down to sample it and it was a mere sample! As the saying goes, we were spitting cotton for hours. It was fortunate that we did not empty our canteens beforehand. The spring was rank and vile with magnesia, or "gyp" water. Near where this water, Epsom Creek, gets into the San Juan River, is the Mexican Hat, a tall pinnacle with a flat top to it, and that was the reason for giving it such a name.

As we got beyond this draw, we could see the Mexican Hat on the San Juan River. During the boom for placer gold, there was a store there, but at the time there was no work being done and not another soul within fifty miles. Our line of travel was still west, heading for the far point of the upper mesa that looked like the Point Lookout of the Mesa Verde between the Mancos and Montezuma Valleys, leaving the Hat to our left by several miles.

When we reached the point where the river bumps into the cliffs close to where the high point is on guard duty, there is a narrow, deep cañon leading down to the river, leaving barely enough room to get a horse through. On down, the cañon closes in on the river on its way to the Colorado [River]. As we go along the trail between the point and the head of the cañon, the horses have to lean a little toward the uphill side before they feel safe.

We worked our way around the fallen cliffs, with the San Juan [River] roaring along below us, and came into the little valley of Willow Creek. Up the Willow Creek Valley a couple of miles we camped for the night in a string of ancient cottonwood trees growing along the watercourse. The water here is splendid and [there is] lots of it. As usual, I sat in the shade of the trees while the Lady Botanist snooped around looking for some new world to conquer in the botanical language.

In the morning we started out while it was yet a little cool. A few miles down, along the edge of Willow Creek Cañon, was the trail our outfit had made a few years before down to a lower level, but not all the way to the river bottom. On the trail down is a four-foot flat vein of molluscs (red shells) under a five-hundred-foot-thick cap of sandstone. This time we rode our horses to the top of the trail, hoppled them, and took the cliff down on foot. We had to block the trail behind us to keep the horses from drifting back to the top and beating it for home, as some horses do if they are new to the job of staying with the riders.

At the bottom of the ledge we had to fasten a rope to a chunk of slide rock and go down the last section like circus performers. Getting down off that last level and to the riverbed would be worth dollars to any photographer. The last fifty feet was over broken ledges and you had to edge along the rocks and grab for hand holds and places for your feet. If you kept it up long enough, you would finally reach level ground, or rocks, or "otherwise." This place is where we let our bunch down when we were working placer ground.

There seemed to be very little evidence of either animal or insect life along that narrow strip, where in times of high water the cliffs were washed clean along both sides of the narrow cañon. When we were there during the placer boom, there was a sheep down there. A year or so later when we went there again, there was still a sheep down there. His wool was six or eight inches long and unusually clean. And was he fat? I shall say he was. There are no coyotes down in that little section of the cañon. Not very far up, or down, the river bumps into the cliffs on either side, so he had no worries to put wrinkles in his brow. Since his wool had already reached a white color, he just led a very peaceful life there until we spotted him, eating all the vegetation that might spring up among the rocks.

The altitude there could not have been much more than two thousand feet and, because we did not have a thermometer, we could not tell how much we were suffering from the direct rays of the sun, [rays] that struck us center at that portion of the cañon. There was some cool water in scattered seeps, [ones] that were free from the mud of the river and the rank alkali-saturated water of higher up. Near where we stopped at the river level was the long ledge of onyx, which should be valuable if near civilization.

While the Lady went elsewhere to see what she could pick up to in some way repay her for the tough going she had in getting there, I just looked for shade under some overhanging rock. It was just as hot, though, as if I had picked out a place in the sunshine, because not a breath of air was stirring.

While I was sitting, or lying, down and finding the most uncomfortable conditions, I heard a rattling of stones just behind me and twisted around to see what it was. Coming toward me was the strangest looking lizardlike creature, about two feet long, but heavy. It was a rusty, dull yellow color with darker spots all over. I had never seen a Gila monster, but thought that was what he was, and wondered how one could be that far north. I got up to let him pass, for he seemed to have important business to attend to. But, it was not other business he was after. It was *me!* When that dawned on me, I just shied a fair-sized river cobblestone at him and he was no more. I got to wondering what sort of a diet he had in that out-of-the-way place to make him so fat and clumsy, so [I] cut him open to find out. He had no teeth and had just swallowed whole and let nature do the rest. All I could find in his stomach was a bunch of saltweed leaves. He must have lived mighty hard, for even those plants are very scarce. Later on, I learned it was a chuckawalla. Science says that they are not poisonous, but their looks are surely all against them. They are such a repulsive specimen of animal life.

The Lady Botanist did not harvest much at that end of the trip.[14] We got back to the cottonwood grove early in the afternoon. While she was snooping around the edges of the cliffs and wet spots in the valley, I just sat and watched undeveloped dragon flies coming up out of the water. They would climb up the stems of plants, or anything else that they could get hold of, so that they could dry out and sun themselves. When dried, the shell that protected them in the water could be kicked off and [that would] leave them at liberty to develop and put on the finishing touches of the dragon fly.

While watching them and letting my mind drift along, I remembered something about Butler Wash. In the potholes so common in those rocks, there are hundreds of freshwater shrimp. I found them while looking for water. Some of the holes are nearly eight feet across and a couple of feet deep. How the shrimp managed to live in those holes when the holes were dry is a question. Often, the holes are perfectly dry for months at a time, even the mud drying up like a brick pavement.

The camp at Willow Creek had no flies or gnats to make life a burden, perhaps because there was no stock to attract them. All that holds these oasislike spots is the tangle of roots of the immense cottonwood trees.

Next day we backtracked to Bluff. Whenever we went through Bluff, we always stopped at the Allens's, and it always seemed like getting back from a long journey to a distant country. I made a big mistake in not taking off the dirty yellow and brown hide of the spotted lizard and delivering it to him. He was an expert taxidermist and was quite peeved at me for not bringing it along.

We kept on going [up the San Juan River] to the mouth of McElmo [Cañon] and then on up the cañon toward Ute Mountain and stopped at Hill's ranch for the night. The next day we drifted into the Mancos Valley and arrived at the Alamo Ranch. Home again![15]

NOTES

1. Alice Eastwood signed the Alamo Ranch register 14 July 1889, 25 June 1890, and 6 June and 4 September 1892. Long before that date she was considered as part of the family and so did not sign the guest register on later trips. Although proficient in several fields, she dedicated her life to botany. While teaching school in Denver, Colorado, she explored and collected, alone, specimens from that area and moved her interest to the Four Corners area in 1889. Her Colorado collections at first housed in Denver were later moved to Boulder. In 1892 she became joint Curator of Botany at the California Academy of Sciences in San Francisco, but returned several times to Colorado to finish collections started there. By 1895, she was Curator and Head of the Department of Botany in the Academy, a position she held until her retirement in 1949. With the help of a friend, Robert Porter, she salvaged what she could from the botany department's wreckage after the 1906 earthquake, but lost nearly all her own possessions except the clothes she was wearing. In 1950 she served as Honorary President of the Seventh International Botanical Congress in Sweden and, at Uppsala, was honored by being seated in Linnaeus's chair. Before her death, 30 October 1953, Californians had honored her many times in many ways, even placing her name on the Honor Roll of the Native Daughters of the Golden West, despite the fact that she had been born in Canada (19 January 1859) and, through an error, did not legally become a U.S. citizen until May 1918 (Carol Green Wilson, *Alice Eastwood's Wonderland* [San Francisco: California Academy of Sciences, 1955]).

2. Alice Eastwood was not at all charmed by the management. Her memoirs record that she was subjected to questioning by the woman who was in charge of the place, a kind of hotel. The woman wanted to know if they were married and, if not, if they planned to be. Alice added that it was quite embarrassing to both Al and herself, for Al did not even have any intentions of asking!

3. Alice Eastwood's memoirs identify the location as Court House Wash in southeastern Utah. On the road to Moab, they collected on 25 May a new species of Oreocarya, which she named *Oreocarya Wetherillii* for Al, the first of several plants named in his honor (A. Eastwood, "List of Plants Collected in Southeastern Utah," *Zoe* 4 (July) [San Francisco, California: Zoe Publishing Co. 1893]).

4. Alice added additional detail in her memoirs. The man was a Mormon whose first wife had died and his second had killed herself and her two children, leaving only the widower and a pathetic six-year-old son. Alice prepared a good meal for all of them and, using ripe strawberries, introduced them to a new dish: strawberry shortcake. Carol Wilson (*Alice Eastwood's Wonderland* [San Francisco, California: California Academy of Sciences, 1955] p. 41) provides another detail.

Upon learning that Alice was not going to the Alamo Ranch as a Wetherill bride, the Mormon instantly proposed marriage to Alice and she refused him.

5. While Al digressed to expound on soil conditions, he omitted the reason for them camping that night. Alice's notes tersely state that they had to camp at Hatch's Wash because Al could not find the way to the ranch where he had made arrangements for them to stay, and that the saddle blankets were not sufficient to keep them from being miserably cold.

6. Al, long accustomed to short rations on trips, seldom makes note of hunger. Alice elaborates much more in her memoirs. They were so hungry before arriving in Monticello that she had conjured up a feast in her imagination and had said, "Wouldn't a good beefsteak be fine?" never dreaming that they would find both beefsteak and hot biscuits at the Mormon settlement. Their Mormon host had several wives and, as was the practice, each had her own little house. The children called their father's other wives "Auntie." Alice wrote that it appeared to her that each wife was a financial asset for a male, for they did the farm work and helped just like a man.

7. Excerpts from her memoirs add Alice's version of this experience:

"The next day we started for Mancos with a lunch for the day as we expected to reach another ranch that evening. We had picked up the two other horses. . . . Al tied the pack horse and my horse together, the tail of one to the rope around the neck of the other. He led these two and I led the other. . . . Al decided to take a short cut across country. It was Wednesday. We rode through the piñons and junipers. . . . The horse I led . . . would switch his tail around so that the rope would get under his tail. The first time he reared, I thought that he would throw me. Later, Al changed horses with me and it threw him. . . . [When] Al realized that he had missed the way . . . I was lowered to the shelf and began to fix the camp. . . . I went down to the river . . . [and] dropped some pieces of paper along . . . not only to find my way back but also to guide Al to my camp. . . . I went back to wait one more night before trying to get back to Monticello. . . . In the afternoon Al came along. . . . We had some of the lunch . . . but after that we had nothing but oatmeal with muddy water."

8. Alice recorded that she really didn't mind being lost because she was in new and unexplored territory, although Montezuma Cañon proved to be a prison from which they could not escape until they reached the San Juan River, for only at the bottom of the canyon was there water.

"Finally, about noon the second day we reached the San Juan River and had the last of our oatmeal gruel. I had not been able to spread out my plants to dry, but now . . . I put them in little piles with rocks on top. While my plants were drying a whirlwind lit into them. . . . This is the only time that I felt downhearted."

9. "The men there [at the trading store] took it for granted that we had come from Bluff and we didn't enlighten them. We purchased some provisions— tea, canned tomatoes, and crackers—and went along down the river to camp. I saw a pan of biscuits that looked very alluring but we never let them know how nearly starved we were" (Alice Eastwood memoirs).

10. An interesting comment from Alice's memoirs provides detail:

"We reached Mancos about noon on a Saturday. The poor horses looked emaciated and their tails had lost much hair, while my clothes hung loosely around. We had both lost about as much as the horses, except for the hair on our heads. . . . I have always felt that I can never repay Al for taking me on that trip."

11. Alice's notes almost moan with her version:

"I rode a mule and a new army saddle. Before I had gone 10 miles I was sore for the first time in my riding experience. . . . We stopped at a ranch over night . . . and a most uncomfortable night it was, for it was very hot and I slept on the floor with several others and wished that I could have been out of doors on the ground instead. However, we were then too near civilization to disregard convention. My reputation meant nothing to these people but Al's did."

12. Excerpts from Alice's Field Report ("Report on a Collection of Plants from San Juan County, Southeastern Utah," *California Academy of Sciences Proceedings,* 6, no. 2 [August 1896]:270–379) add much to the story:

"Bluff City, at an altitude of about 5,000 feet, was reached late in the afternoon. . . . [It] is a little Mormon settlement with a post office and two stores and not even one saloon. . . . As we approached, . . . the bluffs . . . arose to a more lofty height. About midway on these cliffs the character of the rocks changes and . . . is marked . . . by a line of green. The water from the mesa above sinks to the underlying strata, and, there on a narrow bench, not more than a yard wide, constantly oozes out. Here is . . . a boreal oasis in the midst of a [S]onoran [D]esert. It was in this place that *Aquilegia micrantha* was first discovered by Mr. Alfred Wetherill. . . . How did these waifs reach that isolated bench, with nothing in the surrounding country in the slightest degree allied? Below . . . was the riparian vegetation . . . of the Upper Sonoran. . . . [There was] not another species . . . nearer than the La Plata Mountains, distant more than a hundred miles. Here these plants have been growing . . . for ages, an instructive remnant of a past flora before the river wore down the cliffs to the present level."

13. Just when Monumental Valley became corrupted into Monument Valley has been difficult to pinpoint. The *Tenth Annual Report of the U.S. Geological and Geographical Survey of the Territories,* 1876 uses the words *Monumental Valley* (p. 191) as a known term. The Wetherill photography account, Al's notes, and the captions for pictures taken of the area all use the term *Monumental* Valley, although Al used the term *Monument Valley* in later years. The Geologic Map of the Navajo Country prepared by Herbert E. Gregory, K. O. Heald, J. E. Pogue, and W. B. Emery from their 1908–13 survey of the Navajo Country (Water Supply Paper 380 [House Document, 64th Congress, 1st Session]) emerged with the name *Monument Valley* instead of *Monumental* Valley, for the area north of Kayenta.

14. Alice recalled in her memoirs that she found several new species of plants, which she named. She was miserable from the discomfort caused by the new saddle and found it torture to dismount, for her underwear would stick to the sore places and it was like being skinned. She did not remember what they ate, except that bread was made in the flour sack, and knew that they did not take any canned goods. Al, she said, was used to slim rations, and she was too interested in collecting specimens to care about food.

15. Alice's Field Report, "Report on a Collection of Plants from San Juan County, Southeastern Utah," (*Proceedings* 6, no. 2 [August 1896] [San Francisco, California: California Academy of Sciences, 1896]:270–379) concluded with a total

of 475 specimens collected, representing 162 varieties (19 that were new and almost all rare) on the 300-mile trip through desert country. New plants discovered on the several trips with Al and named in his honor are: *Dicoria Wetherillii, Oreocarya Wetherillii,* and *Eriogonum Wetherillii.* Another, *Corydalis Wetherillii,* was discovered by Al himself near Bright Angel Creek on the north rim of the Grand Cañon in 1897. Recognizing it as perhaps new, he transported the specimen, via pack horse, several hundred miles, and sent it to Alice in San Francisco. After determining that it was an entirely new plant, she named it for him in 1902 (Ella Dales and Herbert Clair Cantelow, "Biographical Notes on Persons in Whose Honor Alice Eastwood Named Native Plants," *Leaflets of Western Botany* 8, no. 5 (January 1957).

12

Gustaf Nordenskiöld

O UTSIDE of scientific circles there is very little known in this country of the work or life of the Nordenskiölds. The name does not sound like a Finland name, but from Finland the present family came to Sweden.

The grandfather of Gustaf Nordenskiöld was high in the mineralogical world during his life (1791–1866). A sort of coincidence, if it may be called such, is that it was exactly one hundred years from the day of his birth to the time when Gustaf Nordenskiöld started on his trip around the world and became interested in Cliff Dwellers while in Denver, Colorado, where he discontinued his voyage.[1]

G. Nordenskiöld's father, Baron A. E. Nordenskiöld (1832–[1902]) was in line, as a young man, for great honors for geological and mineralogical work in his homeland. But, at some of his college doings, he made a talk that did not agree with the higher powers of the country and he was compelled to leave.[2] Sweden, in 1857, was fortunate in securing him. He was soon after appointed a professor at the Academy of Science at Stockholm. Apparently his work consisted mostly of research and he intended,

so far as we know of his plans, to make a northeast passage
around Asia. The results of the plans are given in *The Voyage
of the Vega,* published in English by MacMillan and Co. in 1883.
I understand that his work on the trip fully justified the title of
Baron.

G. Nordenskiöld, having accompanied his father on a number of expeditions, undoubtedly acquired a desire to see and
know more of distant lands, people, and customs. Possibly as
well, he had a desire to succeed to a title by some worthwhile
scientific work, for a title has to be earned in Sweden and is not
hereditary.[3]

While in Denver snooping around in the archives of history
for something worthwhile, he ran across some of the work of the
Ancient Cliff Dwellers at the Historical Society's rooms.[4] Being
by birth of a scientific mind, he immediately decided that was
the work that was calling to him, so he took the first train out of
Denver and headed for Durango.

Our register shows he arrived at Mancos on 2 July 1891. He
probably left all his baggage at Denver or Durango, because he
drove out to the Alamo Ranch in a light buggy. His first plan
was just to go and take a look-see and maybe write them up in a
scientific manner. There was nothing but Indian trails anywhere
in the Mesa Verde region, so it was necessary to equip himself
with saddle horses, pack animals, and Wetherills to guide him.
Several days were spent in scouting around through the cañons
and mesa tops until he had the entire country pretty well fixed
in his mind. When he returned to the ranch, his enthusiasm had
increased almost beyond his control.

His idea then was to get an outfit in shape and go to work to
find some clue as to the who, the what, and the where of the lost
people. But that question is not fully answered to this day; perhaps drouth [drought], perhaps disease, or perhaps Montezuma's altar fodder.

Finding that we lacked outside support in what we were doing, he expressed a wish to make a collection that would be on
permanent public exhibit in Sweden. He was so taken up with
the subject that he had us get an outfit together for further exploration and excavation and decided that Long House in Navajo Cañon was the most favorable for quick results.[5]

It might not be out of place here to say that we had already
named all the houses and cañons in the Mesa Verde country, except Moccasin Cañon. Nordenskiöld named a section of the Mesa

Verde between Cliff and Navajo Cañon Chapin Mesa and the section west, Wetherill Mesa.

We had plenty of horses and pack animals and a bunch of Mexicans on the Alamo Ranch. A couple of Mexicans were added as workers, but they were a liability, because they were almost as superstitious as the Indians.

Practically all the collection was made from digging in the refuse heaps, which covered the much desired information. Taking turns, Richard, John, and I swallowed more quantities of mummy dust. At first, John was in charge, since Richard and I had tourists on hand for a cross-country trip to the Moqui villages. Only it happened that Brother Clayton and I handled that undesirable-at-times, but profitable job, which lasted a couple of weeks. Then, we were ready to do our part in the development of the unknown C.Ds. [Cliff Dwellers].

We continued at this work until early in November, having cleaned out numbers of old workings and many other new and smaller buildings.[6] By then, we were just duplicating so much of what we already had that we thought it time to call it a day. The collection of photographs and materials, as complete as any of the ancient races could possibly show, was safely taken out and boxed. The transportation in and out of the cañons was just the same as when we turned over the first shovel of the C.D. [Cliff Dweller] kitchen sweepings.

While working in the ruins, Nordenskiöld would mumble to himself that he had to "pay more for help around here in a month" than he would have to pay in his country in a year and that he was paying John as much per day as a professor earned in Sweden.[7] All that, though, fell on deaf and silent ears, so far as we were concerned.

In the course of the summer, G. N. [Gustaf Nordenskiöld] had the spruce tree cut down at Spruce Tree House to try to ascertain the probable age of its growth from the tree rings. The tree was nearly eighty feet high and three feet in diameter a couple of feet above the ground. The count was one hundred sixty-seven and the tree's growth stopped there. The building may have been deserted many years before the growth of the tree began.[8]

The work on the Mesa Verde completed, G. N. [Gustaf Nordenskiöld] wanted to see how the Hopi (they do not like to be called *Moqui*, for they say it means the dead race) village Indians fitted into the picture of the Cliff Dwellers. It was also on the schedule to take in the Grand Cañon for comparison with what Sweden had to show in the way of awe-inspiring sights that Nature produced. We were well equipped at the ranch for just such propositions that he had in mind. A study of the archaeological and ethnological possibilities of the Southwest was a fitting finale to his summer's work.

Our outfit consisted of two pack animals and three saddle horses, for G. N., Roy Ethridge, and myself, B. A. W. [Benjamin Alfred Wetherill]. (I insisted on having a boy along to help in packing and to rustle up the horses, since G. N. was n.g. [no good]; he was helpless as a babe when it was camp work or horse hunting.) [9] We each had a sleeping bag, for we did not know just when the weather would catch up with us and make life miserable when crossing the Arizona desert sands. To use the expression of the time, we had a greasysack outfit and wolfed it frequently.

Was that a trip! It was noon and a beautiful autumn day [Wednesday, 4 November 1891] when we pulled out from the Alamo Ranch. Our most direct route to the San Juan River was by going west and crossing a low divide northeast of the Mesa Verde and on directly west through Montezuma Valley toward McElmo Creek. (McElmo drains the country north of Ute Mountain to the Dolores Divide, as far as Ruin Cañon. From Ruin Cañon to the San Juan, Montezuma Creek is the drainage line.)

About two miles from the ranch, one of the saddle horses (a half-broke[n] bronc) got it into his head that he did not choose to see the Grand Cañon, so [he] proceeded to separate himself from his rider. There was not time for foolishness, so we had to change him to act as a donkey-pack animal. We stuck a heavy pack on him, cinched it 'til he grunted, and away we went, regardless of his objections. All this had used up a good part of the afternoon, so by nighttime we had only made it across Montezuma Valley, not much over fifteen miles from the ranch. But, anyway, we had made a start.

We were at the foot of Ute Mountain. This lonesome peak is really a volcanic blow-out of a part of the dike that is common all through that part of the country. Preparing for a night's camp was an old story after the summer's work. Camping out had contributed greatly to the Baron's limited knowledge of such things, regardless of his experiences on an overseas trip to Spitzbergen. On that trip, he said they had five hundred-dozen bottles of beer

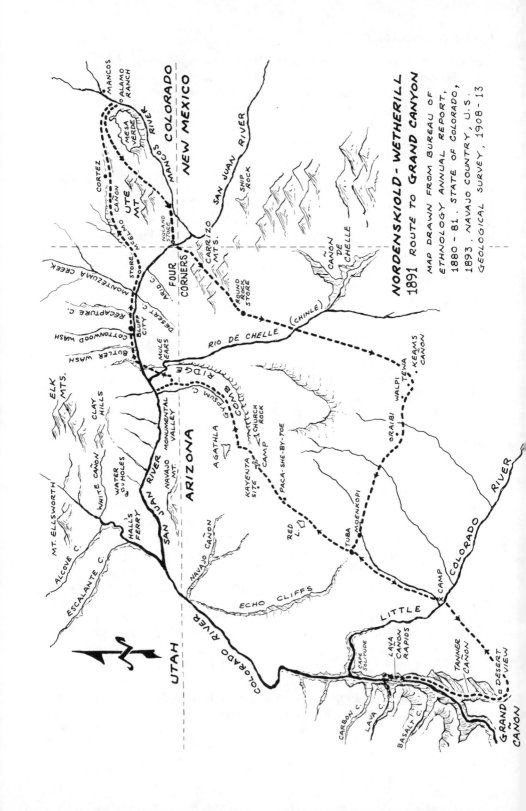

NORDENSKIOLD - WETHERILL
1891 ROUTE TO GRAND CANYON

MAP DRAWN FROM BUREAU OF
ETHNOLOGY ANNUAL REPORT,
1880 - 81. STATE OF COLORADO,
1893. NAVAJO COUNTRY, U.S.
GEOLOGICAL SURVEY, 1908-13

along. We had none and there would be none along the route we expected to take.

It was a question whether to take a longer route around the west side of Ute Mountain. We decided to go along down the [eastern] side and come to the San Juan near the Four Corners. The drinking water at Navajo Springs, where we camped, is fairly good, but McElmo water is vile.

Our camps were made wherever night overtook us, with no thoughts of romance, no songs or poems about beautiful sunsets, purple clouds, towering peaks, gray and scented sage, piñon ridges, prairie-dog towns, or rock-piled ruins. The towering mountain peaks, always visible at some point, meant water and game for the thirsty and hungry. (If you take note, you will find that thirst is more unbearable than hunger and the torture greater.)

From the base of Ute Mountain, we could view the Mancos River and could see Jackson's Butte (a chimney rock) to the east [of us], standing like a guardian angel to all the Mesa Verde country with its wonderful cliff-dweller ruins. To the south is Shiprock, standing out in the sands of the desert and [to the south and west], standing alone as a finished work, are the Carrizo Mountains in Arizona.

From the [southern] base of Ute Mountain we could just see the tops of the cottonwood trees along the San Juan River's fertile valley as it wanders through a tangled up mess of country past the Four Corners. Two and one-half days from the ranch we arrived at the trader's [Oen E. Noland's] store on the San Juan, just a few miles from where the four states meet, but on the opposite side of the San Juan River. From here we were introduced to the Indian in the rough, for it was thought advisable to have one of the Navajos cross over the range with us; there being no roads and very few trails. (We always got along just as well, though, without a guide. We would map out our course and take rivers, cañons, and mountains as we came to them.)

It was a rough and winding route over high and cold scenery, getting over the Carrizos. Our experience with a guide is not worth relating; it was just jog along, hour after hour. We camped one night near the top of the range with about a dozen Indians around and among us, but they seemed all right, for we had tobacco and they had none. We divided with them and everything was peace and harmony. In after years, we never tried to follow that route again, but went around north of the range or through one of the passes that go gown to the Chinle [Valley], for we never got warm, day or night.

Getting down into the Chinle Valley was quite a change from the cold wave we had had. The valley is just a wide, sandy place, with alkali water, and an occasional Moqui mixed in with the Navajos. In the center of the valley is a large pillar of rock known as *Round Rock*. An Indian trading store is.located there and we stocked up with eats, tobacco, chewing gum, and candy, since we were getting out near the Hopi country.

Goods for the store had to be brought in by team from the railroad nearly one hundred fifty miles to the south and prices were in comparison; as well as the prices not paid for wool and hides. In the summer, the goods can be brought in at any time, but in the fall it is necessary to stock up for the entire winter on account of so much high country in the direction of the railroad. Six horses with two wagons coupled together compose the equipment, and twenty to thirty days required for the trip. To the uninitiated, it would look like a great advantage was being taken by the trader over the Indian. But just let the aforesaid sympathizer try running a store out in that country and he will find that the Indian is a natural born trader and expects to be beaten or to be the beater.

As we went on toward the Keams Cañon stores and the [Hopi] Villages, the country was fairly level, but somewhat broken up by the natural drainage system.

Books have been written and libraries have volumes about the Villages from the earliest Spanish histories of the country. Overlooked in the writing about them is the odors that fill the air for miles around, what with the accumulation of trash and rubbish of hundreds of years. Refuse matter is dumped over the cliff from above and then goats and sheep bed down in it at the foot of the cliff. If the wind is in your direction, you can smell one of the Villages for ten miles or more.

These small mesas were, in prehistoric times, level country, but the land has washed away, leaving only the small fragments on which perch the villages. The small mesas were high enough, and generally inaccessible enough, to keep their enemies from cleaning up on them.

The first Indian village is Tewa and it was the only village we visited on that mesa. [Also living there was] the fragment of a tribe of similar Indians adopted by the Tewa people in early Spanish days, they having fled from their own dwellings to avoid extermination (*See* Bandelier's *Delight Makers* for the cause and results of the long trek from the Santa Fe country out to Arizona.) The homes are clean, inside and out; people ditto, but no sanitary conveniences. No water is found on the high mesas where the dwellings are, but is carried from large shallow wells from the valley below. They have beautiful embroidery work, pottery and baskets, blankets, sashes, and lots of turquois workers. We did not see any silversmiths among them, like among the Navajos. The people are easy to get along with and we spend a couple of days with them so that G. N. can get as much information as possible.

The Baron does not have much to say, but he is absorbing great amounts of first-hand knowledge.

The Antelope Clan had one big dance during our stay. It was not so much and lasted only about twenty minutes. In other years when we went through the Villages at the time of the Snake Dance, an Indian coming in with a snake would not stop or speak, since it was all religion with him. Now, the same Indian will stop and make a business proposition of having himself and the snake photographed—religion all gone and business now foremost.[10]

These people are not as bad as the Navajos about stealing everything they can lay their hands on, but anything we left loose around camp mysteriously disappeared. Some of us had to stay around our outfit all the time, even after we rented a room from a decent-looking citizen. (I had a new pair of shoes to get back home on, but the first time I looked for them they were gone. I do not see how they ever sneaked them out of our packs, either at Tewa or Oraibi, without some of us knowing it. When I got ready to put them on, there was none to put on, and I had to take the hind cinch of my saddle, which was made of heavy sole leather, for a half-sole, and whittle wooden pegs from any dry piece of wood at hand. All that proved a very sorry job and I was near barefoot when I reached the Alamo at Christmas time.)

The youngsters were the most affectionate and jealous little beings you would ever meet. There is no need to describe our experiences in that line, though.

Oraibi can be seen from Tewa across the broad valley, perhaps twenty miles distant. We stopped a couple of days there for G. N. to see what he could see and to get our stock rested up. We did not waste any time, because we were not anxious to get

too much winter weather mixed up in our efforts in the ethnological field.[11]

I think all these Village Indians are about the same in most
of their ways. For instance, one of them would go to a store with
a pelt or some wool and hang around the store all day long, just
to get a chance to talk the trader out of another nickel.

One thing about the farming and fruit growing of this valley
is that the sand blows off the land all the time and other sand
keeps blowing in. The Arizona winds are renowned for going
one way until everything is displaced and then blowing the other way until it is all back again to the starting place. When the
crops of beans or young corn starts to grow, the Indian gathers
dead weeds and puts a little barrier up to keep them from getting buried in the ever-moving sand waves. The soil is so fertile,
though, that everything grows. The entire valley subirrigates naturally.[12]

It is different with the peach trees. Acres of peach trees just
stand on their tiptoes, as it were. Or rather, it looks like each
peach tree is a big hand that is balanced on the tips of the fingers. The sand blows under and around the roots, but does not
seem to interfere with the production of fruit, which is most
abundant. The people dry the fruit in some manner so that it
remains soft and is very edible at any time.

Since the Baron is not a very talkative person, all this writing
will be a sort of a general outlook by all three of us. After leaving
Oraibi, we went on to a little water seepage under a bluff somewhere between Oraibi and Tuba. We managed to catch all the
water as it oozed out from the rocks, before any of the Indians
with sheep could mess it all up. If they had, we would have had
a long, dry spell before us for the following day.

Tuba is situated at the end of a long draw, or swampy valley,
which was really a bog as far as we could see up it. It is just off
the Moencopi in a level stretch of valley where water is so plentiful that the land has to be ditched and drained. Tuba is quite a
Mormon settlement and we were treated the best ever.

We stopped at the lower end of the swampy valley with a
Mr. Tanner. Around in different places in his rooms were samples of copper, some native, and in nearly all of its different combinations. He told us of a copper prospect on the opposite side
of the Colorado River in the Grand Cañon and said he would be
going over there in a few days.

When we left the next morning, he gave us all the necessary

directions to reach the crossing of the Little Colorado that is about ten miles, or a little more, before the Little Colorado jumps off into the Grand Cañon. He told us if we wished to go ahead by ourselves to go past a lava butte just visible from his place and to follow down the slope from it into the Little Colorado on the trail that bears his name. On up the other side we would find an old trail leading to the Grand Cañon.

We made it to the Little Colorado all right (which was dry— all sand), but there was such a mixture of trails on the opposite side we decided to wait until Mr. Tanner got along in a day or so, as he said he would.

There was fairly good water and grass for our stock and no Indians to bother or steal, or at least that was what we thought. At the camp were some Navajos to entertain us.

In a couple of days Tanner came along on his old reliable mule. It was about noontime, so, after the chow had been stowed away, we were on our way to one of the greatest wonders of the world: the mile or more deep cut through the formations to the river rushing along the bottom and letting thousands of acre-feet of good water go to waste.

Tanner thought we could make it to the bottom by nighttime. He said he would show us a trail he had made down to the bottom and up the other side to a copper claim he had, about a quarter of the way to the top of the other side. Getting down into the cañon was a tough trip on the stock, as well as ourselves. We took it afoot, but Tanner just rode his mule along down the thing he called a trail, just as though it was level ground. We were afraid to ride. It would have been a tough thing to expect our horses to take it as easy as the Tanner mule and our own pack mule.

It was a fool thing to start down so late, because we had not got half-way when the darkest night caught us. We decided to make camp on any spot big enough to hold our bedding. That was all right, but we had no water. Tanner said there were some potholes somewhere a little lower down and on the next bench. I made my way down to that ledge and I do not know how many more ledges, and still no water. Back to camp I then had to get. I went along one ledge for awhile and then tried another and so on, but still no campfire light or any camp noises. The only way I was sure I was on the trail was the feel of the worn-out rock and soft dirt.[13] When I struck the ledge we were camped on, I was pretty sure I was up above the camp. As soon as I heard the tinkling of the bells on the horses, did I draw a long breath? You can bet that I did!

When we got to the bottom of the cañon, we crossed the river on a log raft made of tree trunks lying there. Because the river was at a very low stage, we made the crossing easily, using our shovels and sticks to keep things moving. Then, we climbed up through a gap in the formations at least a couple of thousand feet. The outstanding stratum showed about four inches of blue-stone, or sulphate of copper, on top of another copper-carrying substance that carried about 12% copper. Tanner had some samples of native copper, but he did not tell us where it came from. (There are copper workings some miles north of Tuba that have been there for years.)

We had no trouble climbing out of the Grand Cañon, since we had scarcely anything in the packs; no grain, no provisions, just the bedding. Of course, we walked the way out to save the horses as much as possible.

Our camp was at the same crossing of the Little Colorado where we camped before. Mr. Tanner went on home to Tuba. In the morning we had everything all ready to throw on the packs and to saddle our horses, but they were all scattered. Whether they scattered with the assistance of a night-prowling Indian or not, it was difficult to determine, since all tracks look old when the wind blows an hour or two.

Ethridge scouted around until noon and came back without any stock at all. It must have been my lucky day, for in an hour I located all the horses, but the old white pack mule was missing. By accident, I spied his shod track where it struck on a rock. The way I got speed out of my saddle horse was a caution. Out on top four or five miles distant, I came up out of a sag in the level and spied an Indian taking a cross trail with our old mule in the lead. His squaw happened to look around and saw me and yelled to him. I did not say a word, but just run around the bunch and cut out our mule. I did not say a word then, either, but just looked mad. The Indians said nothing, either, so that was that. If I had been a few minutes later, I could not have tracked the mule on that grassy soil, and it would have been just too bad for us.

Back to camp, we were ready to pull out and made it to Tuba and Tanner's house, where we camped over the night. As usual, we got the best they had while there and it was funny to hear Mr. T. call out, "More biscuits, Liz."

Before we left, the folks made up quite a bit of milk boiled down and sugared, to do us on our way. They also had a quantity of beans for us. We blessed those folks with all our mights.

Mr. T. gave us directions by saying, "From here, go straight on to the Red Lake, then to Paca-she-by-toe, and then on to the Chinle country in the distance."

When he told us that, I supposed it was some place where the cattle watered over, for I did not know much Navajo then. I could have saved us about twenty-five miles if I had only known it means, "Cow Springs," which is just a short distance from Red Lake.[14]

One of the most conspicuous rocks in that country are the Elephant Legs, standing right along the way and looking like some huge elephant had left his two legs standing there in the desert sands while he went on about his business.

We went on and on, and on short rations. We camped one night at the base of one of the volcanic buttes that are scattered around as if for landmarks. But, since they all look so much alike, there would have to be a great deal of guessing as to which one is which. Anyway, we stopped at the base of one as night was coming along, one where there was a lone cedar tree and no other sagebrush. We pulled off some of the cedar bark, because there were no dead limbs on the tree, and used our canteens of water to make coffee. We did not even take time to pick over the frosted beans to get some solids in our systems. There was not much picking for the horses, but we hoppled them pretty close so they would not quit us during the night. Then we crawled into our sleeping bags and made a sort of a sleep of it, although it snowed most of the night.[15]

I did not recognize the Comb Ridge but headed somewhere near what we thought was it. We could have saved a hundred miles of travel, maybe, if we could have kept going for just a few miles further [east] and crossed into the Chinle Valley.[16] I knew that all the water from that country drained into the San Juan, so we took the first watercourse running north.

We kept north and did not stop until we met up with a Navajo woman with a bunch of sheep and goats. We made a swap with her for a yearling kid, giving her some coffee and frosted beans in exchange.[17] Soon after we were in a sort of a sagebrush flat where we stopped, fired up a bunch of brush, and had goat ribs right hot from the fire. The Baron said the results were the best he had ever eaten (they were covered with ashes and burned in places) and when he said how good they were, I told him he would not feed such looking stuff to a dog. He was a good sort, though, and everything was just the right thing for him.

We were getting near where I thought the San Juan River should be. As we neared the river, there was a little branch cañon off to one side of the main one and, as an experiment, I thought we might gain a little by going down it and get to the river quicker. We could have done just that, but it would have been by jumping off cliffs and over boulders. A couple of miles down the branch cañon I felt in my bones that I was not right, so, when it seemed to be closing up on us, we went back. We then climbed over a ridge and tried to work back toward the Chinle Country.[18]

Away off to the west we could see the monuments and peaks of Monumental Valley and knew we were getting somewhere. Soon after, we were able to see the two points known as the Mule Ears and felt quite at home, for I had been that far before [from the other direction].

Monumental Valley in the Distance
Carrying its own title, the outlines of monolithic-appearing buttes silhouetted against the sky were a signal of hope to the weary, lost party. Al wrote that now he knew he was getting someplace. In his notes, G. Nordenskiöld predicted that the original virgin wilderness of the wonderland would some day draw thousands of visitors from all corners of the earth to see and to treasure in their memories the sight of the monumental natural structures. (From G. O. Williams's translation).

It was a clean sweep, then, up the Comb Ridge. We felt sorry for the horses, whose feed did not compare well with what we had been eating. They had only the tops of sage and greasewood to browse on and were getting weak. When we reached the [San Juan] river we camped without crossing.[19] If we had crossed, the horses would have pulled out to greener pastures instead of eating the dead cleome (or beeweed) stalks, which was the only visible feed around.

In the early morning light we were on our way to Bluff City, where we knew everyone and everyone knew us. We were quite at home for the time we were there, but did not stop overnight, for it was high noon when we arrived and there was still time for us to get miles up the river. We wanted to sample real human grub and would have been welcome to stop over, but Christmas was just a few days off and we wanted to get home for that occasion.

The Baron was suffering from some awful itching ailment (he was all broken out on his stomach, ankles, and wrists) and wanted to see a doctor and get his skin disease straightened out before leaving the country, but did not want to stop at Bluff. Of course, everyone who goes through the Indian country needs to change clothes and bathe frequently, to keep free of the B-flats and B-sharps.[20] We had taken no extra clothes with us on the trip and G. N. was wondering early in the game what he had contracted by being among the Indians. (He had caught a full crop of lice.) It is the general custom to put your clothes out on an anthill every night and then the ailment will not be so troublesome. When it was cold enough at night, we did lay our clothes out in order to freeze out the tenants as much as possible.

In coming up McElmo Cañon, we arrived at a ranch long after dark and we certainly looked tough. Western hospitality insisted on our going to the house and making ourselves at home. We just as strongly refused, without giving a reason. (We were too dirty and lousy to go in the house.) The friendly rancher finally gave it up and went back to the house.

Out from the house a distance was an overhanging rock with some straw and leaves, so we took over for the night. We spread out our bedding and hustled some grub down where it belonged in our systems and fell into our nests. During the night, a bunch of hogs came along and tried to root us out. We rocked them away, big and little, and went to bed, scratching away at the B-sharps and B-flats. Maybe we slept a little; but it was very little. The next morning proved our bedground had been a hog roost for years, I think. Perhaps all kinds of creeping and crawling things off the hogs were everywhere present. But, so far as that was concerned, the hogs had nothing on us. Poor hogs!

As soon as day showed up, we were again on our way and there was no stopping until we were 'way up Montezuma Valley where school was just out. My horse had a lame back and I wanted the kid [Roy or Roe Ethridge] to stay with some people we knew and come along in the morning. But do you think he would do it? He just started crying like a small child and said if he stayed he might never get home. So, I stayed and let the Baron and him go on. I got to the ranch the next afternoon.

The fatted calf was killed and there was much rejoicing in our stomachs while we put on pounds and pounds of adipose. And, too, there was a gladness to be back under the paternal roof. We had made around eight hundred miles since early November.

Nordenskiöld's collection was held up for shipment. A complaint had been made some time previous about the destruction of the buildings and the carrying off of the articles found in the ruins, but that had quieted down. Now, the groups of people who had refused to cooperate in any work or to show the slightest interest sprung to the front ranks as conscientious objectors and demanded that the authorities stop the shipment.[21] The articles were examined, pronounced as being merely of nominal value, and stamped for export. How about that! His book, *The Cliff Dwellers of the Mesa Verde,* the results of the work done during his stay, is the only reliable work on the subject, for it so fully describes the country, the people, and the work of the Cliff Dwellers.

NOTES

1. Gustaf Nils Adolf Nordenskiöld, born 29 June 1868, was the second child of four children born to Baron Nils Adolf Erik Nordenskiöld and Maria Mannerheim Nordenskiöld. Gustaf grew up in the atmosphere of the Academy of Science in Stockholm, where his father was chief of the Institute of Mineralogy. In 1890, G. Nordenskiöld developed tuberculosis as a result of an expedition to Spitzbergen. Going to Berlin to conceal his illness, he stayed there in a clinic until February 1891, when he embarked upon a trip around the world. In Denver, Colorado, he broke off his intended journey, going to the Mesa Verde instead. Returning to Sweden the first of the year, 1892, he married in December 1893, and his daughter

was born in September 1894. Again he developed tuberculosis and died on 5 June 1895. His gravestone bears an Indian swastica, proof of his attachment to the cultures of the American Southwest (Dr. Olaf Arrhenius, unpublished Nordenskiöld biography).

2. It was the Russian authorities of Finland who considered him very radical and who ordered him to leave the country after a speech he made at the conferment of the master of arts degrees in 1855 (Arrhenius, Nordenskiöld biography).

3. The Wetherills were responsible for creating a legend about Gustaf Nordenskiöld. They understood that the title of *Baron* could not be inherited and must be earned by extraordinary endeavor, and were so sure that Gustaf would earn the title for his work in the cliff dwellings that they almost immediately dubbed him "The Baron." From their use of the title, it has become entrenched in Mesa Verde history. Nordenskiöld's daughter (Mrs. Olaf Arrhenius) has asked that he not be called by the title, since he was not, and had never pretended to be, a Baron (Letter of 7 September 1964).

4. G. Nordenskiöld's own notes record: "Cliff Dwellers. Pueblo Alto near Chaco Canyon. Met Miss Alice Eastwood in the library at Denver. She gave me letters to Durango and Mancos" (Arrhenius, Nordenskiöld biography).

5. It is doubtful that Nordenskiöld's intentions were entirely altruistic, for he wrote his father that the cost of the excavations, about $400, could be recovered several times over, but, even if his expenses could undoubtedly be financed by the sale of the collection, "it would be better if a definite grant of about $600 could be obtained." He also confided that he "must keep on good terms with the Wetherills for they are the only people who know the labyrinths in the region." In the same letter, he commented that the Wetherills were "cowboys, but with a surprising degree of education" and, since the Wetherills were already acquainted with Baron Nordenskiöld's arctic exploration, asked that a copy of the Vega voyage and other voyages be sent to them (Arrhenius, Nordenskiöld biography).

6. One of the new buildings they "discovered" brought great disappointment to Nordenskiöld. After much difficulty in reaching the ruin, they entered it two days after observing it from the opposite mesa. The building was cleaned out of whatever it might have contained and they found only "a poor stone axe lying below the ruin. People from Cortez had visited the ruin earlier" (G. Nordenskiöld notes, 6 August 1891 entry, Nordenskiöld biography).

7. In an article G. Nordenskiöld wrote for a Swedish newspaper, he commented that he was privileged to stay in bed a little longer than the rest of the party each day, while "John Wetherill, the foreman (who has three dollars a day, almost as much as a professor in the Old World), makes breakfast" (Arrhenius, Nordenskiöld biography).

8. G. Nordenskiöld counted 167 tree rings the first count and 169 the second, neither count satisfying him (*The Cliff Dwellers of the Mesa Verde*, p. 56). He was attempting the tree-ring method of dating nearly forty years before it was credited with being a newly formulated process in the late 1920s. Even earlier, F. H. Chapin in 1889, reluctant to destroy the namesake tree, had proposed cutting down one of equivalent size near Spruce Tree House, to try to determine the age of the ruin (*The Land of the Cliff Dwellers*, p. 151). Later The Denver *Republican* ("The Cliff Dweller," 22 January 1893, p. 7) revealed that A. F. Willmarth "has in his collection a section of a spruce tree found growing upon the ruins of one of the houses . . . ,

[which] contains nearly 300 rings, . . . each ring appearing in the heart of a tree stands for a year in the tree's existence." Mr. George O. Williams (unpublished American English translation of G. Nordenskiöld's *The Cliff Dwellers of the Mesa Verde*) included some annotations regarding attempts to date tree age by growth rings as far back as Leonardo da Vinci, who had recognized the character of tree rings and had concluded that the width of the rings indicated the moisture or lack of moisture for each year.

9. Nordenskiöld admitted his inadequacy in cooking matters. Once, when Al had gone to Mancos for foodstuffs, he was faced with the problem of preparing his own meal or going hungry. After much debate, he decided that it would have to consist of porridge without salt, tea without sugar, and bread without yeast. He succeeded, eventually, in getting a lump of dough into the frying pan, where it promptly turned a blackish brown, in contrast to the white flour he had on his nose, arms and surroundings. The porridge never became more than boiled oats and water. Even then he went hungry, for two Indians appeared just in time to devour what he had prepared (Arrhenius, Nordenskiöld biography).

10. An unpublished "American" English translation by George O. Williams ["Across Northern Arizona," carried in the *Stockholm Dagblad* in 1892] provides details of Nordenskiöld's record of photography charges made by the Hopi people in 1891. Small boys would pose for 5¢ to 10¢, but a young girl was insulted when offered only 25¢ for posing and complained to one of the leaders, who informed them that the least amount offered should be $1. Nordenskiöld appeared to drop plans for pictures, but obtained his photographs by tucking the "instantaneous-film" camera under his arm and "snapped" his pictures while apparently strolling about.

11. A marginal note added later reveals Al's hesitancy to make statements concerning the ethnological habits of the Hopis: "Tried to get N.'s trip to Moquis and Grand Cañon from his book *The C. D. of the Mesa Verde*, but his is free from any opinion, as I have been, but he does not speak well of their morality. They still have a regard for women the same as when the negro Estaban was killed for attempts, and so on. He uses pages and pages of quotations, so I have a free hand to say what I will about the trip."

12. A narrow band of saturated sand occurs in the valley between four feet and six feet underground. Above and below that level, surveys show that the sand is dry (Gregory, *Navajo Country Water Supply Paper*, p. 128).

13. If the rocks were worn, the trail could not have been a new one. Edwin Corle supplied the answer (*Listen, Bright Angel* [New York, New York: Duell, Sloan and Pearce, 1946], p. 224) when he found that three prospectors, Tanner, Bedlias, and Bunker, had improved the old Horsethief Trail in 1889. The Horse-thief Trail, down to and across the Colorado River at the bottom of the Grand Cañon, was originally a deer trail, later a Navajo trail, and became the Horsethief Trail in the 1870s. Horses stolen at either Flagstaff, Arizona, or Kanab, Utah, were driven across the Grand Cañon by the trail and sold at the town opposite the theft locale.

14. The names given are all in a northeasterly line from Tuba, Arizona, to Bluff, Utah. Although they must have had a compass, neither Nordenskiöld nor Al mentions use of one, but Nordenskiöld's log notes barometric pressure both morning and evening until about the first of December (Arrhenius, Nordenskiöld biography).

· 15. The picture taken by Al does not reveal where they were, but a letter he wrote from Kayenta many years later commented that from his window he could see the "volcanic pinnacle where we camped with Nordenskiöld in the snow so long ago." The only volcanic extrusion visible from that point is the one just west of Church Rock, near the southern entrance to Monument Valley. Although Al almost discounts their situation, Nordenskiöld revealed the fright the three-day snow-fog had created. His horse had sunk to its belly in quicksand but succeeded in getting out. The white mule sank with its pack and only the united efforts of the three extricated it (Arrhenius, Nordenskiöld biography). Had there been visibility, they would have discovered the ruins in Marsh Pass that year, for Richard and Al sent to Nordenskiöld, in July of 1895, an exceptional piece of red pottery with black-and-white design from "the long valley where you and Al were lost in the snowstorm."

16. From their camp in the snow, Nordenskiöld's log states that they headed due north toward what is now known as Agathla. Al took a photograph of that peak from a point close to the southern side, but then, according to Nordenskiöld, they decided they were going in the wrong direction and turned east. By going north from their camp, they went around the southwestern tip of the Comb Ridge so that when they turned back east they were then on the western face of the Ridge but several miles north of the tip.

17. The frozen beans became a source of amusement for them later. Upon his return to Sweden, Nordenskiöld jokingly wrote to request that Al send him some of the Mormon's pride (the beans) to see how they would do in Sweden's climate, then added, "They would probably come up all frozen" (Letter of 21 February 1892).

18. Perhaps in chagrin Al almost omits the fact that they were again lost due to his "experiment." Nordenskiöld's log plainly reveals the fright at being lost. Actually, the only creek or drainage they could have gone down (by combining their notes) was Gypsum Creek that originates to the east of Agathla Peak in Monumental Valley and drains almost due north into the San Juan River.

19. Although there was no trail there at the time, later maps show a trail running just to the west of the Comb Ridge through the Monumental Valley area and crossing the San Juan River where the Chinle Creek breaks through the Ridge. One branch of the trail then went north several miles before turning east while the most direct route followed the river closely into Bluff, Utah.

20. In another chapter, B-flats are explained as being the result of bedbug bites. Al states that Nordenskiöld had caught a full crop of lice, which, from the description of the irritation, must have been body lice. Evidently the expression "B-flats" or "B-sharps" were the polite words to use when referring to bedbug bites or lice infestation.

21. Contrary to tales that trainloads of material were shipped out of the United States for years, the controversial shipment amounted to seven boxes and two barrels, none of which carried, according to G. Nordenskiöld's list of relics, the storied "princess wrapped in a robe of bluebird feathers." Nordenskiöld had obtained permission for himself and his helpers to visit the Ute and Navajo Reservations from Fort Lewis officials. The Indian Agent, a Mr. Bartholomew, had told Nordenskiöld, through an attorney, that he would not be disturbed so long as the buildings in the ruins were not damaged. When the shipment of artifacts from the ruins arrived at Durango, the press raised such objections that the railway

officials refused to accept the goods. On 16 September 1891, Nordenskiöld was arrested on a warrant issued at the request of Agent Bartholomew and trial date was set. During the interim between his arrest and trial, the press raised such a hue and cry about Nordenskiöld and the collection that echoes were heard in the Swedish newspapers. Bartholomew, although he was in town, did not appear in court during the trial and excused his actions in the matter by saying that some Indians had lied to him about Nordenskiöld's activities. The court held that no breach of the law had occurred, dropped the charges, and released the collection for shipment. G. Nordenskiöld was offended at the slanderous allegations made against him and noted that no apology was ever made to him for the incident (Arrhenius, Nordenskiöld biography).

13
Dr. T. Mitchell Prudden

A SSOCIATION is one of the greatest of teachers and whatever is acquired in this manner leaves a permanent effect
on whoever might be fortunate enough to experience or accept
the teaching. A boy could not go far wrong to have a man of
Dr. Prudden's character to associate with.[1] All of us considered
it a privilege to be able to accompany him on any of his trips
through the Southwest.

He usually came to the Alamo Ranch in the summer and
set up a tent under the trees along the irrigation ditch. It was
a heavenly place, cool and breezy on the hottest day, with no
flies, no bugs, and no 'skeeters. A hammock strung across the
ditch between two cottonwood trees was his favorite place.

Always, he made long trips on his summer vacations, but
this long, drawnout journey, trek, or trip was to be the longest
he had ever requested, for it meant at least thirty days duration.
We had made other trips with him and knew his habits. There
were many days through desert sands or mountain forests when
we were often short on food; many a dry camp with trail-tired
horses; days of blistering sunshine or frosty nights in the high

233

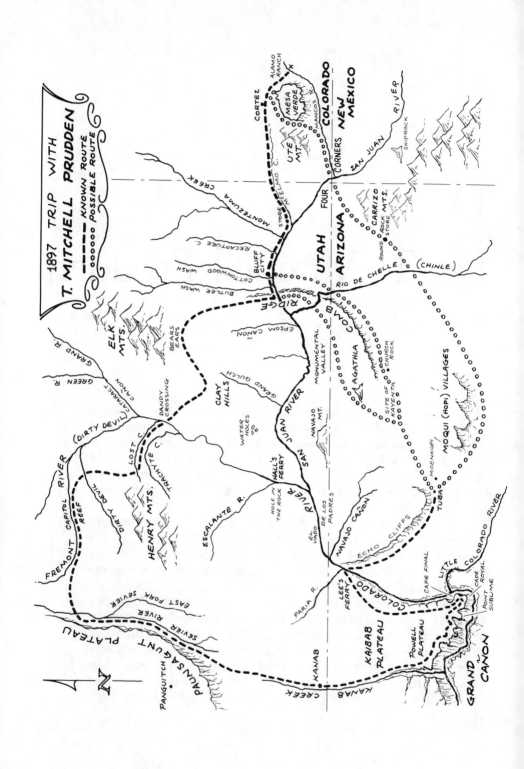

1897 TRIP WITH
T. MITCHELL PRUDDEN

————— KNOWN ROUTE
ooooo POSSIBLE ROUTE

country—but never a complaint from the Doctor. We knew his stomach often troubled him something beyond words to express. No one can take, three times a day, the hurried cookery of camp and trail, drinking all grades of water from purest mountain streams to the saturated solution of gypsum in the lower country, and not have, finally, stomachs needing attention and dispositions to correspond.

This trip was to be as far as Kanab, Utah, on or near the Arizona line, and to return by way of Lee's Ferry.[2] The route was the same as a previous one as far as the crossing of the Col-

At Ease in the Front Yard of the Alamo

Usually strung with hammocks tied to the cottonwood trees on each side of the irrigation ditch, the spot was a favorite retreat. Marion Wetherill stands on the left with Julia Cowing seated in front of her, while Debby Mason drapes herself in the hammock. Al Wetherill and a tourist to the ruins sit on the grass at the right of the picture. The two people in the background are not identified, but Dr. Prudden's tent is pitched in its accustomed spot that Al described as a "heavenly place, cool and breezy on even the hottest of days, with no flies, no bugs, and no 'skeeters to annoy." Sumner W. Matteson made the photograph in the summer of 1899 and presented it, along with other pictures, to the family.

orado at the place known as Hite. But, no matter which route you decide on, you will be going over a more ancient world [that has been] buried for a million years. Far across the country toward the Colorado River, and on about the same level as the Mesa Verde, are miles of water-washed cobblestones. How many ages they have lain there, glazed with heat and weather, no one can tell. They were there evidently long before the Colorado River made such a gash in the earth.

We headed toward the Henry Mountain country via Elk Mountain and White Cañon.[3] At one place on the way out, we passed a place where there were many short cañons, or really gulches, and in such places there were often overhanging cliffs. In these places there was no outside evidence of the existence of an earlier race of people who were not akin to the Cliff Dwellers. By digging away the dirt and dust of many hundred years, there was evidence enough to put lots of enthusiasm into our digging. One day we were all taking a rest and a blow at the same time, never saying a word or even opening our mouths, unless it was to spit out the dust of an unknown people. While we were deliberating a bit and trying to think, an old Ute or Pah Ute poked his head through the bushes in front of the place where we were working. We did not move nor say a word and his eyes kept getting bigger and bigger. The next thing we knew, he was tearing down the brush in getting away. Soon after we met up with Mancos Jim (a renegade Ute or Pah Ute) and he asked us about it. When we told him he laughed and seemed to think it was a great joke on the old codger.

When we got to the [Colorado] river at Hite Ferry, it was a ripping, roaring torrent, as usual, I suppose, and we could not get across the alleged ford. There was a cabin on the opposite side and a woman there. So far as we could find out, there was no man around anywhere. There was a small boat on that side and we made all kinds of noises to have someone come across with it. But the woman let on [as if] she did not know how to manage it in the current.

The Colorado River is known as the Grand River until after the Green River enters it in Utah and is one of the greatest points of interest in the West; well worth a journey by water or otherwise. What a short time [it has been] since the first sign of civilization put its foot down on the land, or a boat in the waters, of this country! Imagination can not picture, nor words express, what the mind registers in traveling over the high and

rough tableland surrounding the deep gorges of the Colorado
River, or what is to be seen in a rush trip down just a small
section of the river, a mile or more below the world above, for
anyone having the nerve (or courage) to take the trip. From
the Green River [junction with the Colorado River] to the
mouth of the Virgin River [at the western end of the Grand
Cañon], the difference in altitude is five thousand feet. Words
will not disclose the sights seen along the roaring, tumbling
water of the deep gorge.[4]

The thirty or forty miles above Hite Ferry and Dandy Crossing (as us natives call it), is undoubtedly the worst part of the
entire two-to-three hundred miles of cañon, for great sections
of the walls and perpendicular cliffs topple over into the bed of
the stream from time to time. This part is known as Cataract
Cañon and is the part avoided by all the hardy pioneers and
explorers seeking renown. Major Powell lost part of his outfit
here, and Stanton had all his boats wrecked in the first attempt.

Below Hite Ferry are added the wonders of the San Juan
River Cañon, which has cut its way down to meet the grand
old father-of-many-waters at the point where Glen Cañon begins, squirming around through a cañon as deep and wild as
the cañon of the Colorado. At seasons, the San Juan has no water during dry spells, because farmers hundreds of miles up
toward its source have to irrigate their crops with it to raise
anything.[5] Navajo Mountain is right at the junction of the two
rivers.

Glen Cañon is nearly as opposite to the Cataract Cañon as
it is possible to imagine. Instead of rough, roaring, tumbling
waters, we have a still, quiet surface, with little coves and an
occasional island. Cañon walls extend thousands of feet above,
their rough points weathered and softened; places where ordinary speaking will echo and reecho. All this gives one a desire
to be at peace with all the world, to sing songs of long ago—
simple, quiet songs—so as not to disturb the stillness that seems
to be over everything.

In Glen Cañon is what is known as the Crossing of the Fathers, or El Vado de los Padres, the latter name [from] some
Spanish missionaries [who had] crossed on the rocks there hundreds of years ago. The Spanish Fathers found the rip in the
formation when they were journeying to or from the California
settlements and the Spanish soldiers were looking for gold, or
silver, or more worlds to conquer. Here, too, is where the Mor-

mons crossed [at Hole-in-the-Rock Crossing] when coming in to colonize eastern Utah, as well as northern Arizona, and it has been the route of traders and trappers to the Hopi villages.

Here at the Ferry, though, it was up to us to see that the Doctor got across. I took two of the horses and started to make my way across on their backs. I was somewhat suspicious of one of the horses and, as a precaution, fastened two empty gallon canteens on my shoulders as life preservers. I could swim well enough, but was sort of afraid to tackle it if the horses got tangled up in the rope or passing drift. One of the horses thought that water was just made for drinking and that he could wade across, but when he got to walking on his hind legs, I thought it time to call a halt. If he could not swim, another step would have put both of us out of sight, since the water was then 'way up on his back. He was just going under when I turned the saddle horse around and managed to get to the bank a little further down. It was a mud bank, with heaps of bushes growing down into the water. We struggled and pawed mud and finally got a foothold and were back to the starting place.

Up the river just a little way, near the mouth of the Dirty Devil, or Fremont River, is Dandy Crossing, but the Colorado River forbade getting to it. We tried to make a trail around a narrow ledge and get on up to the crossing. We worked on the ledge and then got to a place where it was impossible to go any further without the use of powder [dynamite] and of that we had none.

The Doctor suggested that we were to get him across and that it was our affair to see how it was to be done. So then Big I took myself in hand and worked my way around the aforesaid ledge and up to the so-called ford. There was a shallow spot in the middle of the river, but on the opposite side the heavy current was washing strong. Halfway across looked like fairly good sailing but the balance of the way was a tearing volume of water. A couple of water-logged chunks of logs were stuck in the rocks and mud along the bank, so I worked one loose and started to sail over to the other side. But, the chunk of wood and the current, bouncing along, seemed to laugh at my efforts, so I turned the log loose and it gouged into the opposite bank like it was shot out of a gun. I put in my best licks at swimming and managed to get through the roaring current and crawl out on the bank. I had been a good swimmer when

I was a kid, but for years had seldom had anything bigger than an irrigation ditch to swim in. I made the landing on the other side without losing either my head or my clothes, which were on top of it.

Just after getting my unmade tailor suit on and going a couple of hundred yards, here came the Doctor looking for me or my fragments. It seems the woman finally relented and brought the boat over.

In getting our outfit over, we had to really tow the four horses over, and the one that could not swim did not try to commit suicide or anything. I had to hold his head on the edge of the boat and drag him across—he might have thought we were just giving him a bath.

We stayed the night there. It was the only house anywhere around and was a sort of a lookout point for the Robber's Roost, which was named because it was a hiding out place for uninnocent cattlemen for the Four Corners. It was in a sort of a "stay out" region, but we were treated the best ever by the lady of the house, and gave her our blessings for help and directions.

The directions sent us up the Dirty Devil [Fremont River]. We went up and went up that dry and dusty bed of the river for miles and miles to Capitol Wash. Finally we got out on a beautiful, grassy highland where the horses could get something to eat besides the hard, dry, saltgrass along the borders of the river.

We had a letter of introduction to the various Mormon Bishops, which directed anyone at any time to give us help in any way along our route. We called the letter our passport, but we never used it, for we found the people the best ever whenever we passed through a Mormon town. (There was a regular road to travel on, on up the country, but we did not know of it at the time.)

After getting across this high country in a direct line, we came to the jumping-off place. Looking down into the Panguitch country, the streams and cañons below run 'most any way they want to. There was a broken place in the rocky face of the mesa, which seemed to reach all the way down to the farming country at the bottom. We did not attempt to ride down and the pack mules had to take their chances, since there were rocks, brush, and trees all the way to the bottom. We slipped, slid, and rolled down, and if we had found it necessary to try to get back up to where we came from, we never could have made it.

(The notes I have taken regarding the country and the trip are lost or misplaced, so this is from memory.) [6]

We stopped at the first house we met up with and found the folks most pleasant and agreeable. We stopped over a day and thought we would like a little extra food. There was a boy standing around, so we asked him if he could get us some eggs. He said he could, so off he went.

In a little while he came back with a dozen nice-looking henfruit. I do not remember what the cost was, but it was not much. We got everything ready to eat and had the frypan and the grease hot and dropped in egg number one. Uuuck! Also number two and three and so on. The boy had gone home with his few cents, but the man of the house was still nearby and saw what had taken place. He sent for the boy and asked him how he came across such a soiled bunch of eggs. The boy said he had found a nest under the house that had all of them in it. When he saw the condition of them, he handed back the money and said he was sorry and would get us some more if we wanted them. But we had had enough of eggs for the time being.

Our next object was to get to Kanab [Utah], 'way down on or near the Arizona line. There were villages and towns scattered all along the route and at one place we came across a large dam that had been built for a number of years, but had broken in the middle, letting out not only the water, but also about one hundred-sixty acres of fish. They looked like they were all great big carp and who wants to eat carp? Or, maybe the dam was cut to let all the undesirable fish out to fertilize the soil. Soon after seeing the broken dam and the fish, we noticed the scarcity of water all around and supposed that the broken dam was the reason for so many dried up farms further along the route.

We popped into Kanab all at once, for it was out of sight until we got right to it. We got directions on how to get over toward Mount Trumbull and the Uinkarette Valley, as well as [where to find] some water back in the hills where there was timber and a mill, too.

Our destination was Mount Trumbull and the Uinkarette Valley and down that to the Colorado River near the Black Cañon and to come back through the Buckskin Mountains. Instead of going miles around to get to a certain point, we started down a break in the mesa, or mountainside. We could not lead or drive our horses but they skidded along down anyway. Fortunately, there were no abrupt cliffs or jumping-off places. What water we found was in a sandstone pothole and somewhat ancient, but it answered.

It was a whole day's journey to go down that valley to the top of the cliff where black formations of volcanic rock and lava seem to be the main body of the cañon sides as far as we could see. The Black Cañon is named for the black walls that line the cañon for miles. From the place where we were, the [Colorado] river slips silently along between the towering cliffs that look like rough, terraced, stepping-stones for imaginary giants.[7]

While trying to get away from the hot sun, Clayton laid down under the shade of an overhanging rock and had just got settled when a rattler came out of a crevice to investigate and perhaps get a feed. He certainly was surprised to see what was before him and made a quick coil-up to do business when my brother heard him. Did Clayton scatter! A few well-aimed rocks put the snake out of commission, but the boy was not interested any more in cool, shady places.

The Grand Cañon is worth anyone's journey, but it does not take long to see enough of the great works of Nature and the destruction that is going on wherever a great body of water gets to work changing the appearance of what has taken ages to build up. Layer after layer of the formations are being swept away. With a controlling plan, the destructive waste could be stopped. We decided that we had seen enough of cliffs, gorges, and cañons, and dry, barren land with a drink of water fully a mile away—and that down, with no possible way of making connections with it.

We left that so-called camping place without regrets and made a direct line for the Buckskin Mountains [Kaibab Plateau]. Late in the evening we arrived at the western end of the plateau and it certainly was a rest for weary eyes and tired bodies. All the dry and rocky country was now just a bad dream to us. A person who has not been around and over a sandy desert with its mirages, [or] with tired and thirsty horses, and cranky companions, can not know what it is to get into great forests with water and grass everywhere. We could now make a sort of vacational stop whenever we took a notion.

We stopped one afternoon in a little open park where there was quite a good-sized pond, or little lake. The entire forest, at least the part that we were over, was dotted with sinkholes. They are sort of basinlike depressions, most likely caused by caverns beneath the surface. The caverns were either formed by some upheavel or by water dissolving the rock for thousands of years and carrying away much of the stratum. Then the weight above caused the top to sink down, leaving the places that formed waterholes for animals and bird life in the great pine forests above. These are called Jacob's Pools and are some distance from Kanab.

While we were sitting around doing nothing and scarcely thinking, a couple of deer came out of the timber, just gave us a glance, and kept on going to the water for a drink. Soon after, a grouse came moseying down to the edge of the water, just like a chicken would, not saying a word and ignoring us entirely. It was a hard thing to pry ourselves out of that stopping place, but it had to be done.

Our next move was to get out and across a wide flat where cattle and wild horses ranged. The wild horses were a nuisance and were shot whenever the cowboys had time enough to go after them. The wild horses sneak the saddle horses away, and when once a gentle horse gets in such a gang, he gets to be the wildest of the bunch.

Near the edge of the plain some cowboys were having a roundup, but we did not stop over with them, although we would [have] be[en] perfectly welcome, because such is the custom whenever you strike a bunch.

Here on the plain, there are freshwater shrimp in the potholes in the rocks, rocks that are perfectly dry the greater part of the year.[8] Also in this desert land, little frogs come out after a rain and express their happiness in song.

We spent one night at Lee's Ferry. The crossing is at the mouth of the Paria River, a stream coming in from the west side. Lee's Ferry is named for John D. Lee, the head of the gang of Mountain Meadows Massacre fame (?).[9] He had a ferry there and a small farm up the Paria. A small colony of eight Mormons was located there.

At the ferry, we were entertained by an old English Man-o-War sailor. He took us for a ride in his boat up the almost still waters of the [Colorado] river—it looked like one long, quiet lake. This section of the great cañon should have a more romantic name [than Glen Cañon], for its stillness, without one ripple, makes one feel that he is out of the world entirely and all the universe belongs to him. We all sang songs that we thought might be appropriate, nothing loud or funny, just sane and old-style holdovers.

Glen Cañon ends at Lee's Ferry and Marble Cañon begins,

entirely different in character and scenery. In this part the Little Colorado comes in [to the Colorado River] in a part of the cañon where there are almost perpendicular cliffs nearly a mile high. Here the Colorado roars by or silently slips along.

Sitting along the bank in the sun was a large government lifeboat—probably one of Powell's—no doubt donated as surplus from some former expedition. I guess the boat was too deep and narrow to go over the hidden rocks, too big to take the rapids kindly, or to stand the sideswipes from crosscurrents, so it was discarded.

After crossing the river on a cable boat, we camped a short distance away from the ford. Since there was a small spring and some grass on that side of the river, we made our camp early that afternoon, expecting to make it down to some seeps the next day that were said to be enough water for our stock and ourselves. All the next day we had no water, although we were still along the river, but were getting higher and higher above it.

When we reached the place that was to wet us all up, there was nothing to be seen but a little patch of moist ground. We had made a full day of it and so had to get water. We made camp after a fashion and had dry rations, because the seep was not good enough to fill our canteens. Still, we did not worry. The ground looked pretty wet, so soon brother Clayton and I were digging away where the spring was. Always the water seemed to be just a little bit lower. After awhile we thought the hole might fill up if we left it alone a bit. When it did, we scooped up the water with a frypan and dealt it out to the horses as often as we could get the pan filled. They were standing around trying to get first place at the pan. We kept on handing out sups of the water until after midnight and knew by then that the horses could get along until we got down around the point of cliffs that would put us over Tuba, [Arizona,] way, where water was as common as dirt. There was not much sleep for us, but we had to do it, for a horse will go to pieces quicker from lack of water than from any other cause.

We were well out of there the next day and had no more troubles. We did not do much stopping from then on, for we were getting on the last leg of the trip and began to think of, "Home, Sweet, Sweet Home." From Tuba, it was then Chinle, San Juan, and a direct line the balance of the way, unless Bluff City caught us in the meantime.[10]

Nothing funny, nothing strange from then on to the Alamo

Ranch—just a keep-going proposition. When we arrived at the ranch, not only one fatted calf as usual was killed, but two, or possibly three. All along our trail, it was a case of bacon, bacon, and more bacon, baking-powder bread three times a day, and dried fruit occasionally. I still do not look with pleasure at that sort of combination and our Doctor friend had a beautiful case of indigestion that stayed with him the rest of his days, as near as I could make out.

NOTES

1. Theophil Mitchell Prudden (1849–1924) became a pioneer pathologist in 1878, serving admirably in the field of medicine. A graduate of Yale Medical College, he became an authority, not only in the field of medicine, but also in zoology, botany, geology, ethnology, and archaeology. After 1892 he became intensely interested in archaeology and, in order to publish his many articles of ancient Southwestern cultures, he often assumed the entire expense. Acquiring, eventually, a representative collection of cliff-dweller artifacts, he presented it to the Peabody Museum of Yale University.

2. Dr. Prudden registered 20 July 1895; 10 August 1896, and 17 July 1897, the year of the trip described in this chapter. Succeeding years show no registration in the guest register, but the Prudden account shows tiny matchsticks to indicate meals taken at the Alamo Ranch, meals that averaged 30¢ apiece.

3. Al's account eventually identifies the "we" as Dr. Prudden, Clayton Wetherill, and himself. Dr. Prudden lists the "we" as three white men and one Navajo (*On the Great American Plateau* [New York and London: G. P. Putnam's Sons and The Knickerbocker Press, 1906], p. 36) . The rest of the outfit consisted of "two horses, one pony, one broncho, and two mules."

4. Twice in this paragraph Al makes vague reference to a trip down the Colorado River. When some of the Wetherill unidentified negatives were printed and several were found to have a strip of water in the foreground, it became necessary to identify the landmarks they contained. One picture, that of Hole-in-the-Rock Crossing, established the fact that Al had taken it from the middle of the Colorado River. Several other statements in this chapter (pertaining to Glen Cañon and Marble Cañon) indicate a knowledge of the area *at the river level*. Martha, upon questioning, admitted that Al and Wirt Billings, a friend, had made a trip down the Colorado around 1890, but whether the trip began at Dandy Crossing and ended at Lee's Ferry or the Little Colorado River she did not know. Either Al did not think the trip important enough to write about or the account has been lost.

5. The map included in the *Bulletin of the Geological and Geographical Survey of the Territories, 1876* (Hayden, vol. 2 [Washington, D.C.: Government Printing Office, 1876]) shows the lower San Juan River as a dry watercourse west of the 109° 30' meridian, so even before the water was consumed for irrigation purposes upstream, the lower reaches of the San Juan was dry much of the time.

6. Not only has Al lost or misplaced notes, but time and deterioration have also destroyed still more. Although he usually, as he wrote Alice Eastwood, "would write up our trips soon after the making," it is apparent that great chunks of some detailed accounts have disappeared, leaving only fragments of an incident or a brief notation in a logbook.

7. Dr. Prudden had also been waiting expectantly to see the Grand Cañon from that point and to observe the reaction of their Navajo companion. When they reached the brink of the great chasm, the Navajo uttered a verbal expression that Al and Clayton interpreted for him as being equivalent to, "Well, I'll be darned." The native then dismissed the whole panorama by turning his back on the view, lying down, and taking a nap. Thereafter, during the days they skirted the brink of the cañon, he paid little or no attention to the views. Dr. Prudden, evidently disappointed, excluded the incident from his account of the trip (*On the Great American Plateau*), but his students included it in his biography, *Biographical Sketches and Letters of T. Mitchell Prudden, M.D.* (Yale University [New Haven, Connecticut: Yale University Press, 1927], p. 142).

8. Proof that freshwater fairy shrimp do exist in the potholes was cited by Dr. A. S. Packard in "New North American Phyllopoda," (*American Journal of Science and Arts* 2 [New Haven, Connecticut: Tuttle, Morehouse, and Taylor, 221 State Street, 1871] July–December, p. 109) with the Utah specie named *Apus newberryi* for Dr. J. S. Newberry who first collected and reported the type. Larry Smith, writing for *Sunset Magazine* ("The Mountain States Have Fairy Shrimp" 138, no. 5 [Menlo Park, California: Lane Magazine and Book Co.], May 1967, pp. 62, 89) describes the phenomenon and supplies photographs. The fairy shrimp hatch out in freshwater pools that form briefly after seasonal rains. After laying their eggs in the bottom of the shallow depressions in the rocks, the adults expire when the water dries up. Several years may pass before there is enough rain to refill the pools and hatch the eggs. Adapted to the environment, the shrimp thus continue their tenacious survival cycle.

9. In September 1857, an emigrant train of 150 people from Arkansas and Missouri, led by Charles Fancher, was waylaid at Mountain Meadows on the west fork of the Virgin River in southwestern Utah. Some controversy still exists as to whether the conduct of some of the emigrants provoked trouble, but the fact remains that the Mormons did induce a preliminary attack by the native Paiute Indians. Then, John D. Lee, under a flag of truce, approached the wagons and convinced the party that they would be given Mormon escort to safety if they followed his instructions. When the party was separated, however, the Mormon militia opened fire, killing everyone in the party except seventeen or eighteen young children. Although Lee was known to have settled at the Paria River site and was operating a ferry across the Colorado River there, it was several years before he was arrested for the crime. Following his conviction, he was executed on the same ground where the Fancher party had been slain, nearly twenty years to the day following the massacre (Juanita Brooks, *The Mountain Meadows Massacre*, revised edition [Norman, Oklahoma: University of Oklahoma Press, 1962]).

10. There is a great deal of variance in the Prudden account and Al's narrative. Prudden gives their return route (*On the Great American Plateau*, p. 70f) as being past the Hopi villages, across the Navajo Reservation to the western side of the Carriso Mountains, then across the San Juan River near the Four Corners and along the western and northern side of the Mesa Verde to the Alamo Ranch, a trip of "thirteen hundred toilsome miles." Neither Dr. Prudden nor Al explain the pictures of Monumental Valley that were included in Dr. Prudden's book as part of the journey or the photographs that Al took for his own records. A route through Monumental Valley would be still yet another way from Tuba, Arizona, to the Alamo Ranch.

PART 4

AFTER 1895

A WELCOME FOR A BRIDE

The dust is thick in every room and papers line the floor.
There's pancake dough in every dish, with soot and crumbs galore.
Old duds are in the kitchen and wet ones in the hall.
The closets reek of moth balls, if you know that smell at all.

The weeds out in the garden are higher than the fence.
Old clothes still hanging on the line are filled with awful rents.
Now if there was a kindred soul who'd to our needs arise,
We'd get them here at double quick and would not advertise.

Benjamin Alfred Wetherill

14
Dear Hunting

AFTER several years, the boys and girls got the habit of
marrying themselves off. The first was Anna. Charles, the
son of the Masons we knew in Joplin, married sister Anna
[1885] and they tried farming, but it was not a success, so they
finally went up on the headwaters of the Rio Grande and started
a fish hatchery. In the course of time it was a success and he was
fairly well off.

John and Lulu [Louisa Wade] were married in 1896. They
farmed and worked at the mines at Mancos, but finally quit and
got an Indian trading store at Tiz-na-zin (Ojo Alamo) down in
New Mexico, about fifty to sixty miles south of Farmington.

Winslow went to school, married, and went to Mason City,
Iowa, and worked in a lumber yard for Uncle Winslow Tompkins for awhile, but came back to Mancos, tried farming, and
was a failure. (Later he got a store at Two Gray Hills and did
well while there.)

The Hyde Exploring Expedition took over Brother Richard.
Then he married [Marietta Palmer on 5 or 12 December 1896]
and made an exploring and collecting party in southeast Utah

and northern Arizona. Then he took his outfit to Pueblo Bonito and, under the direction of Professor George H. Pepper, worked over quite a part of that ruin. Also, he had a large store to keep supplied for the Indian workers. He had thousands of sheep in the surrounding country as well as cattle and horses. (Once he sent up four hundred sheep from Pueblo Bonito for me to keep all summer. I had a family of Navajos look after them for me. In the fall of the year there were still four hundred; not an increase of a single one when there should have been at least three hundred lambs. I should have got Mexican herders instead of the Navajos and [would have] made a good thing out of the business.)

Clayton and myself pulled together the finest ever until after Father died, and then Clayt sort of drifted away and went down to Pueblo Bonito with Richard.[1]

The boys, the daughter, and the cousins were all gone into other work. Some were in archaeological work and others took up the Indian trading business. Indian trading was a moneymaker in those early days because the business was not overdone as it is now, and the government had no restrictions to hold the trader down.

Mother wanted to go up to where sister Anna and Charley were living, but she did not want me to live at the Alamo alone and try to carry on.

But, things will happen and be worked out while you sleep. Mary Tarrant, a schoolteacher from Atchison, Kansas, was visiting a cousin in one of the mining towns and was being a tourist in the mining districts of Telluride, Silverton, and the Red Mountain scenery. She heard of the cliff dwellings and decided to see them as part of her educational objective of that vacation. Of course, she heard our names, since we were well known all through the mining districts.

She wondered if we might happen to be the family that lived diagonally across the street from them years and years before in Atchison. In the summer, the boys would play baseball and marbles and such, or would mix up with the girls in sissy games like ring-around-the-rosie, or something equally silly, it seemed to us. Or, when the crawdads were ripe, she would often get a part of the crop, for the boys were always on the lookout for her. In the winter, we would go coasting together when the snow was on the ground and she would snowball us, making life a burden to all young male fry who happened to be around.

Mary Tarrant Wetherill
Mary Tarrant was photographed by Babberger Studios in Atchison,
Kansas, where she taught school before her vacation in the mining
districts of Colorado brought her into contact again with Al Wetherill.
She had written from Telluride to inquire if the family was the one
she had known in Atchison years before and if she could come to
the ranch to see the cliff dwellings. "Well, she came, we were, she saw,
and she conquered," Al wrote and so they were married on 27
December 1899, and she became Mrs. Benjamin Alfred Wetherill.

Well, she came, we were, she saw, and she conquered; not
only the cliff dwellings but also your most obedient. She landed
at the ranch while I was away, but I returned some time during
the night and mother routed her out to meet me again. In a day

or so we had a trip to the ruins. By then, I was hog-tied and led around like a regular range broncho broken to harness. There did not seem to be any balky tendency at all in my makeup, which must have been the result of having fairly good ancestral stock. On the trip over the Mesa Verde and down to Cliff Palace and home again, we took two neighbor girls along to protect me, but——!

A few more days at the Alamo and I was hers for sure and certain. She had to get back home, though, to think over the risk she was taking and to gather up her doll rags and send a letter back that would look like "no, no, no." It still sounded like "yes, yes, yes" to me, and that was that.

In full swing, I went back to Atchison on my dear hunt, took a room at a hotel, and started out on foot to get to number 600 something, south of town. I was not long in getting there, but things and houses did not look just right—no hills or hollows in sight—but I went up to number 600 and asked the girl who opened the door just where I had drifted to.

She grinned and said that I must be from the West (for I had on a Western cowboy hat and duds to suit) and that I was in *North* Atchison and that it was *South* Atchison where I wanted to go.

I said, "But how do you know?"

To which she replied, "Everybody in town knows that Mary Tarrant has a boyfriend out West and he is supposed to be here by now and you sure look like Exhibit A!"

I fled and grabbed the first [street] car going in the opposite direction and landed on territory that now looked familiar to me. But that was not all the grief I was to encounter, for, after the hitching-up process was accomplished, I had to go out with the newly made Better Half and call on diverse and sundry lady friends of hers.[2] Some of them took advantage of my innocence and kissed me. Was I scared? I will tell the world I was!

While I was off on the marry-go-round, the Alamo Ranch had been the halfway stopping place for ranchers and cowboys for miles and miles around—Mother had gone on up to Sister Anna's home—and as soon as they got notice of my return from the Matrimonial Bureau, they all beat it. Was the house cleaned up and everything in order? Not on your life! It looked more like wild hogs had been busy and knew that trouble was brewing. There was sourdough on the floor, dirty dishes on the table, and bedding strewn everywhere. The sight of things should have made the Better Half beat it back to her Ma. She never tooted a toot, but the way I beat it over to a Mormon woman friend, who had always been the helper in the past when we ran full blast, was a caution. And soothing conferences sort of healed up the cloudy atmosphere.

Fortunately, we did not have any tin-can orchestra to announce our homecoming, and we were properly thankful, but in a few days we had the swellest party that had ever happened in that part of the valley.[3]

Before we were in running order, she really did wish she was back with her Ma. When the first effort at cooking went into effect, I wished I was back with *my* Ma. The Lady of the House wanted some information about pancakes, so I told her to stir up a batch of batter. But she wanted to know what a batter was. I thought she was trying to put something over on me, but found out she was *not*. I let my countenance drop as low as the safety notch. But, as past master camp cook I was able to eat anything that had the name of grub attached to it, so took on the job of making her into an enthusiastic farm wife.

We got along merrily while the education was growing, but some of the eats she turned out——! Pancakes, or biscuits, and meat and milk were the main articles of our diet. As long as the stuff bubbled, the biscuits were passable. Later on, we worked on the sourdough proposition.[4]

I do not remember when the lightbread managed to get around among us, but I do remember the first grand effort at cakemaking came along because brother John happened to be with us for dinner one day. In honor of his visit we had cake. Well, we had it, and gnawed at it and kept sliding slugs of it into our pockets to dispose of later. We had to brag on it, of course, and John said he would have to have Lulu get the receipt and then went on his way, snickering to himself. Some time later when Mary could really make something worthwhile along the cake line, brother John came by again and when she asked him how he got by with that first experiment he grinned and said, "Wasn't it awful?"

Soon everything seemed to jingle along all right, just the same as any other Westerner who has to make the best of any condition. She soon began to see and know all the advantages and pleasures of a ranch life in the Rockies.

NOTES

1. A letter from Dr. Charles H. McLean, dated 3 June 1898, advised B. K. Wetherill that only an operation would cure his kidney problems. The operation, performed later that year, was not successful, and he died on 18 November 1898.

2. He neglected to mention the date: 27 December 1899.

3. The "tin-can orchestra" no doubt means a charivari, an old American custom of serenading newlyweds with a concert of discordant noises made with any and all objects that would make a loud noise when struck or blown.

4. Al was not immediately successful in teaching her the art of making light-bread. Martha Wetherill Stewart says that it was Julia Cowing who finally succeeded.

15
Tenderfoot Wife

ALL the winters are about alike, with worlds of sunshine, even with heaps of snow. During the winter, since it was sort of quiet around the ranch, we decided to make a trip over to Pueblo Bonito where brother Richard had charge of the H. E. E. [Hyde Exploring Expedition]. We had nothing to go for but just went so as to be doing something. We got our doll rags together, as well as grub and bedding, and grain for the horses. We had a good team and a light mountain buggy and, with our stuff closely packed in the back, started by going out a side cañon four or five miles and up a branch of that cañon a mile or so.

It was impossible to go around by the regular road because it went 'way up nearly to the foot of the mountains and the snow up there was what is usually found at eight to ten thousand feet altitude in winter. Although it was February it was like the middle of winter.

Up the branch of the side cañon a mile or so, a trail starts up the side of the hill, with a rise of a thousand feet or so to get to the top. Although there was snow on the sides, we thought that when we got to the top it would be like late fall. We had been shaking hands with ourselves to think how easily we were going to get to the top, because the snow along the sides did not worry us. But now our troubles began.

When we got to the foot of the trail and looked up, we knew we were in for it; the snow had drifted over the road and, where the grade was cut, had filled everything to the level. Up the slope, the snow was packed, partly thawed, and frozen afterward. It was not so bad at the start, but when we were about halfway up, the snow was up to the horses' bodies and the axles and bottom of the buggy pushed the snow along ahead of it. The horses plunged and snorted their objections, so I passed the lines over to the side partner and got out ahead of the team and broke trail. We did not know just how to tell which was road and which was hillside. If the snow had not held the buggy and kept it from slipping over the bank, we might have been going down 'til yet, with no one to tell the tale. The Missus looked and felt scared, but she just sat on the seat and let the horses drag her along like a snowplow.

All this sort of outdoor life did not seem good to the Better Half and I shall bet she wished more than once along that road that she could get back to her Ma, but she did not even cheep until we were almost out on top and struck an extra deep patch of snow that hid the view ahead. Then she wanted to get out and go back. I know it was brutal, but I laughed at her and told her to hang on a bit longer and we would be out, since that was the last pull. We got to the top in a few jumps and the horses heaved great breaths of relief. It was almost night, the horses were all in a sweat, and the tenderfoot wife about in tears.

We skipped along and made for a thick bunch of piñons. We quickly unloaded, fed the horses, and started to make ourselves a comfortable place to pass the night. We cut piles of piñon branches and pulled the small sprigs off to put under our bed. Then we took a great quantity of the large branches to make a windbreak. The piñon is a species of dwarf pine and has short needles, which are dandy for putting under the beds or for making a nearly windproof shelter. We built our fire just in front of the windbreak, cooked our supper, drank quarts of coffee, and had a second helping of eats. We also gave a sort of a Christmas dinner to the horses and hoppled them out. Before turning in, we sat and built pictures in the flames of the campfire. And did we have a warm and cozy bed on that brush-spring bed with piñon feathers!

The next morning we had a red-hot breakfast concocted by the cowboy method of cooking. When we had cleaned up the dishes and such like, we stuffed all we could locate into the transportation department and were then ready to move as soon as we made connections with the motive end of the works.

It seemed, however, that something was wrong with the power works. But, because the land was more or less of a rolling disposition, I thought just a few extra steps beyond the hummock of ground we were on would find the beasts. I left the second-in-command in charge of our temporary home and drifted out on the trail of those old plugs who had probably got a sniff of green alfalfa from the lower La Plata and San Juan [Valleys'] fragrant fields.

The horses were hoppled, but that did not seem to make any difference, and it proved to be a long, long trail before they were spotted. They must have left us immediately after their supper and a moment's rest, since it was nearly fifteen miles before I spotted them moving along with their hippity-hop, hopple-gaited means of escape. (Later, up in the mountains, they pulled the same stunt on me. But that is another story.)

It was high noon before the old skates and myself got back to camp. There was a worried look, and maybe tears (which I pretended I did not see) to greet my success. There were not words enough in our combined vocabularies to express all we said, or thought, about dumb brutes that fail to appreciate "the merciful man who is merciful to his beast."

We just had a cold snack of what was left over from breakfast, coupled up the team, and, when we started, let no grass grow under the horses' feet, for we hiked them along at double-quick. Since starting at noon, we had been coming down to a lower altitude, over long, grassy flats, but we did not stop to enthuse at grass or flowers, if there were any, or at the birds. Romance was all gone out of us, so we said nothing.

We stopped at the first ranch we struck when we got down to the La Plata River. The ranch folks greeted us as if we were some long-absent kin, but people always were like that. (If no one was at home, it was all right to go in and help yourself, but you should leave your name or brand on the doorpost, or the table, to let them know you had passed that way.) We were put in an attached room, called the cold storage, that everyone who came along slept in. I slept beautifully, and the side partner did, too, we thought, until we got down to Pueblo Bonito.

Early morning found us on our way, since there were no stray horses to look up or breakfast to get. We had about fifty miles to make and a team could easily make it that day if we did not push them too much, but just let them take their sort-of-fox-trot gait.

We struck the San Juan River at the old ford and noticed it was up some on account of an ice jam breaking loose somewhere up the river. The high waters are responsible for the uncertainty of a ford. One time it is there, and the next time it is no more. Because the ford was running in quite a wide channel, there seemed to be no occasion for worry, even though heavy whirlpools and sandrolls looked like the border of the hereafter, both above and below it. With my usual sangfroid, I just snickered and drove right in. The horses seemed to fret a little, but, with a little urging, made the plunge into the deeper water. Was it a plunge! This time, the jumping-off place was right at the bank and the horses went in nearly over their backs. They tried to turn back, but I held them into the water.

As they started ahead, the buggy swung off downstream and water rushed in nearly up to the seat. I had to get out on the buggy tongue and onto the back of one of the horses to keep up his nerve while Mrs. Tenderfoot held onto the lines. The buggy swung around and whirled with the current. The side partner tucked her feet under her to keep them from getting wet and, strange to say, let out no shrieks and did not turn pale. The horses had to swing about and head upstream. Just a few more jumps and we were free from the deep hole we had dropped into. We made it to the other side with nothing worse than getting ourselves and everything in the buggy soaked. Getting out of the water and cleaning up was like doing a day's work.

The quicksand on the San Juan is just the same as it is the world over. When we strike such a place with a bunch of cattle, the best practice is to push a few head across and back a few times. That hardens the sand and makes it possible to get your wagon, the horses, and the herd through in safety. Just the same, though, keep away from it unless it is absolutely necessary to make a run for it. All kinds of animals are found in it now, and there are probably all kinds of horses, camels, mastodons, dinosaurs, and sloths in it from thousands of years ago when they wandered around the ancient watering places.

As soon as we had our nerves adjusted into the proper channel, we went merrily along over the rolling country. The better half was learning great gobs of pioneer life and there was still more to follow.

About halfway between the river and Pueblo Bonito was where brother John had his trading store at Ojo Alamo. By taking a shortcut on an old Indian trail through the Bad Lands of northern New Mexico, we could shorten the total distance a few miles. John had told us he had crossed that way and it looked all right to me, for we could see some old wagon tracks and I knew that if anyone else had made it, we could do it, too. So, we took down the Indian trail and left the wagon road far to the left.

Of course, that shortcut was one of the "shortest way around is the longest way home" things.

The first step-off was not so bad, but there were no more that easy. After awhile we got along where we could look down into the little valley from the last rough and rugged place and felt pleased. But we were glad too soon, for the trail slanted very badly to one side and was rocky as well. I had been riding on the brakeblock iron every time we came down the hillsides, but the last one was a fright. The Lady Love sat heavily on the upper side of the seat and let the horses pick the road. I was leaning 'way out from the buggy and weighing heavily with all my might. The side partner sort of held the lines and kept her eyes shut and maybe searched her soul to find sounds to tell how scared she was. The buggy was going along on only the two upper wheels, the others touching the ground only when the ground reached up to meet them. I do not know how she felt inside, but she was sure absorbing Westernism in great big chunks and seemed very much like an old timer.

When we reached the bottom, it was just a couple of miles up the cañon to Ojo Alamo and if John and Lulu were surprised to see us coming in from that direction, they never said a word about it. I think the reason was that, as boys, we were always ready to try anything once and this, also, was another once.

The Bad Lands extend from near Pueblo Bonito north toward the Mesa Verde. In the Chelly formation all sorts of bones of prehistoric animals and fossils and petrified wood can be found. Near the mouth of Chaco Cañon we have found ants inside of crystals. Brother John's place had huge blocks of ancient trees, now rocks, around the foundation of his buildings.[1]

The balance of the road from Ojo Alamo to Pueblo Bonito was a boulevard in comparison to the rough places we had been over. Crossing the Escavada [Wash] though, a few miles from our destination, the sand blowing out of the dry watercourse was just about as bad as sticky mud.

That night when we arrived at Pueblo Bonito, Mary was sure she had caught some infectious disease and spoke to Mrs. Richard [Wetherill] about it and Mamie said, "Let me see where you are broken out."

All around Mary's neck and shoulders there were hundreds of bright red spots. Mamie looked carefully at them and said, "You stopped at that first ranch when you struck the La Plata, didn't you? Oh, well, you'll be O.K. in a day or so. Those are bedbug bites. Out here they're called B-flats."

It is not necessary to describe the immense ruins of Pueblo Bonito here. At that time, they were just great big heaps of tumbled stones and crumbling walls.

The return trip from Bonito to the Alamo Ranch was not quite the same route we took down and was uneventful until we reached Thompson's Park, near the head of Cherry Creek, where the valley closes up into a cañon. The park is right at the foot of the La Platas and is just a broad, natural valley in the pines. There is a cattle ranch at the upper end and a number of German families are in a little settlement, farming the level ground. All were making good so far as dollars were concerned.

But please deliver us and forgive us for even stopping at the place where we stopped! The man of the house perhaps was not a high-grade German; maybe just some low-grade stock mixed up and put in human form. When we went into the house, what we saw upset us and we would have kept on going, only our team was taken care of before we went in. One look and we saw such a mess that even a decent hog would turn away: dirty dishes, days old; dirty bedding, and all the house to correspond. How we managed to get by was by cleaning up things and cooking our own grub while the man and his wife were still out looking after stock and chopping wood.

The woman was a mail-correspondent victim and was unable to quit and go back to where she came from. Though we felt as sorry as we could for her, that was all we could do.

We used our own bedding and slept in the bed of the mountain buggy. Luckily, the people were early risers and that suited us beautifully, so we were on our way, after paying a pretty good hotel bill.

All the names of streams or valleys are not of a romantic or inspiring nature. Just below the German's ranch is a side cañon that comes into the main cañon and is called Dead Man's Gulch. A human skeleton was found there, probably that of some poor prospector who had met up with early-day Indians. Just over the ridge dividing this gulch from the main traveled road is Starvation Creek. Some men who were snowbound, it was said, got so desperate that they drew lots to see which one would kill the other and thus save the life of one of them until he could get out. I really do not think trappers or prospectors could be caught in such a predicament, for, just a few miles below there, plenty of deer, elk, bear, and beaver could be had as late as 1890.

The view from the height that divides the La Plata and Mancos waters is always inspiring and our nightmares of the night before were soon forgotten. By noon we had reached our ranch.

In time, the rough-and-tough life of the West initiated friend wife into real ranch life. Life was an out-of-doors playground as the seasons of planting, harvesting, and herding tourists came around. When the tourist season came on at the ranch, we had to hire a girl or two to help out. We also had to have some extra men and a number of extra horses to handle the tourist trade and the farm work.

When people come along from all parts of the U.S. and foreign countries, one is sure to meet up with the congenial as well as the others. It was a busy time for everybody as long as the season lasted. Wifey-dear had lots in common in the line of conversation with all of them, for she could adjust herself to conditions and personalities. She was a star entertainer and so was a great success.

Every once in a while she would make the trip over to the ruins with some of the schoolmates and teacher friends of other days. One of these friends went back home and told that she had thought Mary Tarrant had married a Cliff Dweller, or some sort of a wild Injun, but was *so* disappointed to find that Al Wetherill was just an ordinary man!

On one trip, or rather, the return trip, the better half was riding along toward the rear of the bunch and was leading one of the pack mules. Being still a tenderfoot, she had wound the lead rope around her hand instead of using the saddle horn. By and by there was a log across the trail. The horses went along just the same gait as always, but a mule always has to stop and investigate. As a result, the hand had to take the consequences, which resulted in a thumb being jerked loose from its location, causing much anguish to the would-be Western wife.

Pack mules know an awful lot. We had an extra-large pack on that mule one time when he went under a low-hanging branch of a piñon tree. He had been in the habit of going under and not getting caught. This time he hung up and could not go either forward or backward until we took an axe and cut off the limb. Ever after that when he got to the tree, he would not go through where he had been caught, but would go around on the other side of the tree trunk.

The parties going out to the cliff dwellings would be out one day, or two, or three, whatever time required. All would come in ragged, dirty, and hungry. They had to have baths (in big washtubs), and, looking as they had, it was a delight to their souls. But the Home Department made good, which was a miracle, since no notice of when we would get back was very often possible.

Think of what a gang [it was] to burst in on the house when we got back to the Alamo Ranch! The better half made a reputation as a real hostess in feeding the hungry people. The rations for the ruins trip was the simplest we could handle—meat, bkp [baking powder] bread, and coffee—so everyone came in starved. For a meal at the ranch on our return as many as fourteen young rabbits were fixed in a hurry, along with all sorts of vegetables and fruit, buckets of milk, and ice cream, maybe.

When there were quite a few at the ranch, the women took up all the rooms and beds in the house, so the men took blankets and quilts and slept in the big hay barn, with its sweet-smelling alfalfa.

Everyone went away happy and the better half had cause to feel like that old timer who said, "I came, I saw, I conquered."

To be real citizens, we began to see that we should try to discover what was going on in the world and to adjust ourselves to citizenship. In the course of time we quit talking in terms of cows, horses, hay, and grain and adopted civilized ways. We went joy riding behind fast trotting horses, went sleigh riding and coasting in winter, and picnicked in the high mountains in summer. We acquired considerable ability along the lines of neighborly society without much effort, but at the expense of success in acquiring a bank account.[2]

Generally on Sundays or holidays, we would bundle up a bunch of grub, a wagon sheet or two, and yell to any of our near neighbors to hitch up and come along. Or sometimes we would go alone, taking all of the ranch help for company. More often, we had four or five families to go with us, or us with them.

About ten or twelve miles up the [Mancos] river, the valley closes into a narrow channel with open spots covered with grass and berry bushes. We would make one big campfire and cook meat and bread, cowboy style. We would have either fresh or canned fruit and a cake from home. To see us stow away the food, a person would think that we had spent years in prison. After the eats, we would sit around and compare notes, and tell yarns, and finally start games of some sort.

Those picnics did not always turn out in such a joyful manner. Cloudbursts in the mountain regions are common. On one picnic, there was a little rumble in the sky, a cloud not much larger than a man's hand came rolling over the mountain top, and the next thing we knew, we heard the sound of water. We got up all our wagon sheets and doubled up under the wagons just about the time someone yelled, "Look out! She's a-comin'."

We had already hitched our horses to the wagons, but did not think the water could get high enough to reach us. But, because the river bed was narrow and not deep, maybe only twenty feet wide and two feet deep, the water spread from edge to edge of the banks at once.

We landed in our wagons arunning and managed to get to higher ground before the water got more than knee-high to the horses. We dragged ourselves home, singing all the songs we knew, and really did not get too wet at all, since the wagon sheets were ample protection. When we got out of the cañon and into the pines, it was raining and snowing all at the same time. I do not remember any thundering, but the lightning was shooting through the trees in a very weird manner. Friend wife did not enthuse much, but we did not catch cold.

The other half was supposed to be a good rider, but cow-country horses were not in her line at all. Once we decided to go for a horseback ride out through the cool-looking timbered slope reaching down from the high points just back of the ranch. We went skipping along at a pretty good gait and when the horses struck the timber they did not slacken their speed, but just tore along as though there were some cattle to get out [of the trees]. I did not look back, since I knew the horse was a timber-splitter and would keep shy of any low-hanging limbs, but the other half did not see it that way, for she was hugging the horse's neck and yelling to me to wait and let her get off. She was a good rider in the city, on city-trained horses, but the timber-splitters of the cow camps were not in that line at all and it was many a day before she had a wish to go horseback riding again.

While the wife part of the family was still green to the public in general and to myself in particular, my mining partner and I found it necessary to go well up toward the nearby range of mountains to work out our assessment on a mining claim we had been carrying along for some time without results.[3] Of course, friend wife went along. There were plenty of prospect holes all over the face of the one important peak, named the Hesperus. That name should have been enough to warn us that it was all a failure.

We had a small prospector's cabin to live in and [to] keep our supplies away from the coney bears and the nervy camp jays, or whiskey jacks, which were so numerous all through the slide rock. We also had a tent, which was more in keeping with the ordinary prospector's equipment, since it could be moved over the range to new fields. Actually, the tent was better, for us old timers felt we needed the outside fresh air in our lungs and lots of it.

Coming from a lower altitude to one touching the ten thousand foot mark makes your heart go pitty-pat and, if troubled with a weak heart, it would be best to stop somewhere at six thousand or less. People not familiar with the high altitude think there is nothing to the idea of shortness of breath and take risks by being too speedy in action.

At that cabin one time, one of my brothers noticed a broken board in the floor, just over where a skunk traveled. He had heard that if you catch a skunk by the tail, he can not get his smeller discharger to work. So, my brother just waited for a spell until along came Mr. Skunk. As he came within a few inches of the broken place, brother nabbed him and dragged him out of there. But that tail hold did not seem to be a preventive to action by the skunk. He dropped the skunk and flew for home. We could smell skunk for weeks after that. Skunks are plentiful in the mountains and they never bother you if you leave them alone. At night they will play around where you are sleeping on the ground and act just like a lot of kittens. At first I was a little nervous, but soon saw they were not up to any mischief, so we got along. There is also in that country a little spotted cat called either a civit cat or hydrophobia cat, but I think the skunk is neither one. The real civit cat is an African production and is two to three feet long and more than a foot in height.

Friend wife was doing the cooking by then, but 'most anything you cook will deal you misery at that altitude unless you know how to handle the eats. Boiling, or trying to boil, is n.g. [no good], but it is O.K. to use a frying pan or Dutch oven. The boiling point of water is such that there seems to be something wrong in Nature's makeup. Beans should be ground up like coffee and spuds cooked in the frying pan, if you expect to eat them like a human should. Otherwise, you would have to digest food like a cow and you simply can not get it back up into your mouth so as to rework it into a digestive condition.

During our time there, it happened that the mining partner was off at a prospect hole when I had to go to town for supplies, so the tenderfoot wife was left alone at the camp. Just a short distance away, there was a camp of burro punchers; a sort of a relay camp for a big outfit. We did not see much of them or they of us. We just knew they were there and tending to their business as we were with ours. When they discovered that no one was at camp but the lady of the house, one of the toughest of their gang (who also was alone at his place), came over to entertain the bride. She was scared stiff when he demonstrated his remarkable knife throwing and asked him why he was always practicing.

"It makes no noise," he said. "That's why I like it." But, since he was a real decent fellow, he soon worked himself into her graces and she got over being frightened. The first thing she knew, she was laughing and talking with him and in a bit he had a burro saddled up and she was riding around just like nobody's business.

After that the whole camp of men would come over at night and we would play cards and tell yarns, often until the wee, small hours.

Late in the winter, when the burro camp was gone and the Mrs. at home, the mine cabin needed supplies. So, with pack horses loaded, two of us at the ranch wallowed up to the mine when the snow was three feet or more deep on the level. We did not make camp until quite late, because one of the pack horses had slipped off the trail and rolled over a couple of times. If dynamite is as terrible as it is supposed to be, this yarn would never have been written, since the horse was loaded with the aforesaid stuff. We camped alongside a spruce log, anchored the horses to it, fed them a few bites of grain, then dug a hole in the snow down to the ground, made a little coffee, rolled up in the saddle blankets, and passed the night in feeling sorry for ourselves.

In the early morning, we looked across the way and saw a cabin we had never seen before. There were a couple of prospectors there. Did we enjoy their company and hot grub! But, to get along our way, we had to make the long-legged horse plunge ahead in the snow and make the others follow in the trail.

It did not take long to get the supplies housed up and then beat it back to the lowlands and home again.

[Mary Tarrant Wetherill's memoirs include a few incidents that Al omitted or have been lost. The incidents are so germane to the life of the times that they are included here.]

I shall never forget my first experience with the Utes. I heard a noise one night. It was winter and I asked Al what it was. He said it was just some of our friends. In the morning we went out to the summer kitchen, a big room 14' x 28' in size, with a huge hotel range in it. The room was full of Indians! They had a roaring fire there and were making themselves comfortable. Al introduced me by telling them I was his "squaw." I had on a red dress. Those men never took their eyes off me and I was frightened all the time.

Later, I learned that if they could reach the ranch, they would travel until they got there, even if it was two o'clock in the morning. They felt safe there. These Utes are short, fat, with broad faces, and wear their hair in two braids, brought over each shoulder. Their moccasins are always beaded and they often wore beautiful, beaded leggings. They would come carrying a tent—they called it a wickiup—made of canvas. They used that when they could not get into our kitchen. They would tie all their worldly goods on two poles bound close together and then fasten the poles to the saddle of the horse.

There was one old Ute we were very fond of, Mancos Jim. He was a little fatter than anyone has any right to be, but very friendly. He would come and stay and we fed him. One day I thought I would fill him up, if I could. I told Sadie [Halls] to give him all he could eat. Afterward he hunted me up and rubbed his stomach and told me, "Heap eat. Plenty good."

That was about a month before our boy was born. [Jim]

came a few weeks after [the baby] was born and asked about [him]. I told Jim the baby was dead. He put his arm around my shoulders and said, "Poor baby. Poor mother."[4]

One afternoon when Al was gone, Colorow [a Ute Chief] came. I happened to be all alone, with the exception of a man who was working around. Colorow came up with his family, which was large, and asked for "Ale." I told him Al was gone. Then he asked for Mrs. Wetherill.

"Gone," I said. "John?" "Gone, too."

Then I knew what he thought. They [the Wetherills] had all gone and I was living there. Then I thought it would be a chance to quit keeping so many Indians. So, when he asked for bread, I told him I did not have enough, which was true.

"Lache?" (Milk?) That I gave him. "Syrup?" None. Then he said, "What matter? Pretty poor?"

"Yes," I told him.

When Al came, we kept him hidden out, never dreaming Colorow meant to stay. The next day he saw Al. He rushed at him and cried, "Oh, Ale, mine friend, Ale."

Honestly, I felt ashamed of myself. Later, when he came back, I was walking with Al and he was holding my hand. Colorow said, "Your squaw, Ale?"

"Yes, my squaw."

"Oh, no, no, no, Ale."

"Oh, yes."

"Good."

When they pitched their tents in the big open space in front of the yard and spread their blankets, furs, and sheepskins down, it looked clean and cozy enough to rest in, although I never went inside. In their way, they were very honest. They would sometimes borrow a rope or something they needed without saying anything. It might be two or three months before it was returned, but they always brought it back. Al lends them small amounts of money, and they pay it back. They get an allowance from the government, so, for a little while, they are rich.

In looking back upon my life at the ranch, the tourists, the Indians, and the cowboys march before my eyes; the tourists eager to see the West, the cowboys attending to their duties, the Indians always picturesque. Of the Indians, some were friendly, but often seemed morose. There were a few whom we felt were really friendly, but, after all, we knew (or rather, I felt) that it was just what they got from us.

NOTES

1. A letter to Alice Eastwood (6 January 1929) contained a newspaper clipping and a comment from Al:

> The clipping of the wonderful scientific discoveries that have been found in northwestern New Mexico makes me laff and laff. Prehistoric animals and fishes and saurians! Thirty years ago John had his store walled up with the fossil remains of these same animals and reptiles that are now being 'found.' There is a stretch of country through there, nearly one hundred miles of it, that have long been known as the Bad Lands. There is another such formation over beyond Ute Mountain in what is called Nancy Patterson Cañon.

2. The habit of taking Sunday dinner at the Alamo Ranch for the whole community was always costly to the Wetherills, but none of the uninvited "guests" ever contributed toward the costs. One of Dr. Prudden's letters to Al inquired about the practice, so it was very commonplace. When Mary Wetherill realized what financial circumstances existed at the Alamo Ranch, she unexpectedly charged Sunday uninvited diners 25¢ apiece for the meal. This reduced considerably the Sunday congestion and those who continued to come expected to pay for their meals, like at any hotel or eating establishment.

3. Colorado mining laws for unpatented mines required $100 worth of acceptable work each year on each claim, in order for the holder to retain mineral rights to the mine.

4. Al could never bring himself to write about the birth, at 6:30 P.M., 12 July 1901, of Benjamin Alfred Wetherill, Jr., who lived until 3:30 A.M., 13 July 1901. Al and Mary could not bear the stark severity of the bleak cemetery at Mancos, so they buried him in the yard of the Alamo Ranch, where the yellow roses on the white picket fence created a bower of beauty.

16

Last Trip
to the Summit

TRYING to enlarge our cattle industry and buying up additional land and horses at the Alamo Ranch was the millstone about our necks, since we mortgaged everything we had to reach that end. I was not so smart, but I knew enough to balk at that sort of thing. It was done anyway, and when the place was left to me, the mortgage still hung over it. If we could have all hung together, we would not have hung singly. When the boys and girls married off, the union, broken up, never got on its feet again. The tourist business did not ever pay enough to pay off what was due. Although we seemed to harvest plenty of money, it was something like pouring into a bucket that had no bottom to it.

Actually, we were about twenty years too late in starting the cattle business, because, just as soon as we had worked up to a paying bunch, the prices were all shot to pieces and we were glad to get ten dollars for a three-year-old steer that would

$40⁰⁰

4 Months after date, without grace, for value received,

DURANGO, Colorado, Jan 18 1895

promise to Pay to the Order of HARRY JACKSON, at the office of Harry Jackson, (the Novelty Carriage Works,) Durango, Colorado, Forty — Dollars,

with interest at the rate of 1 per cent. per month, from date until paid.

If this Note is not paid when due, or is collected by Attorney or by legal proceedings, we promise to pay an additional sum of ten per cent. of the amount of this note as Attorney's fees.

P. O. Bluff Utah

P. O.

P. O.

B K Wetherill

Jn R W.

Richard Wetherill

Aug 28 Cash 25⁰⁰
Dec 16 " 15 —
14⁰⁰

Int Due 4⁴⁰

Hard-Times Financing
The money borrowed was to finance the Wetherills in a "bit of the supposed gold gathering" along the San Juan River. Repayment of the $40 took until 8 May 1896. These facts are inconsistent with tales of Wetherill wealth gained from the sale of artifacts.

have brought seventy-five a short time before. And, even at that price, no one wanted beef unless it was a loin steak, cooked and on a plate. Also, we always seemed to have had too much help in the branding process, for larger outfits than ours, who had more men than we, acquired the habit of putting their brands on our calves because they did not seem to remember just what our brand was. What cattle we had left we traded for more horses.

Then the horse project got the upper hand of our whole outfit, and, as one of our friends told us early in the game, when we got to going in the horse business it would be all over with us in the cattle business. But, we had to prove it to be that way, which we all did with a vengeance.

Sheep, too, were destroying the ranges and our whole world seemed to drift back (or go ahead [as the case might be]) into the agricultural projects. Sometimes a cowman would take over a bunch of sheep to make a living and, if you wanted to stir up real trouble, all you had to do was ask him how he and his woolies were getting along. The sheep business was a long way beneath the dignity of a cowman and he sure had to be on his uppers to step over the line into that sort of a business.

We continued on, paying interest [on the mortgage] and not reducing the principal until the death blow mopped us up clean.

We lost everything. Fred Hyde wrote me out a check to cover the amount of the mortgage, but I did not use it and later gave it back to him because, if we had stayed on, we would have been just a sort of a hired-help pair and that did not set well with us, since we were young and energetic.

When we left the ranch [January 1902] we had only our clothes and a few personal articles. The bulk of the Alamo Ranch museum collection we gave to the Colorado Historical Society.[1]

But I wanted a last view from the edge of our small world. It was talked over and decided upon while sitting in front of the large fireplace that was glowing with the coals of huge piñon chunks.

Before the sun even started to peep over the rough and jagged peaks of the La Platas [mountains], we were already on the move. Before mounting to ride, we could never resist the every-morning look toward the east where the sun was just beginning to color the snowy peaks of the La Platas with the most beautiful pink. It was such a contrast to the darkened cañons below, where the spruce and aspen cover all the lower slopes with an everlasting shadow, protecting the winter snows from melting and [becoming] lost by midday suns. By conserving the moisture and gradually drawing it away, it provides the source of the irrigation projects of the early pioneers, as well as [maintaining] the life of the beautiful flowers that grow around the borders of the forests.

We closed our eyes to the thoughts inspired by all that grandeur and beauty and returned to the earth where our horses were impatiently stamping and pawing to be on their way.

Our way to the top of the Mesa Verde is to cross the valley of the Mancos, heading west toward Point Lookout, which stands at the most northern point of the Mesa Verde. The ride across the valley is through sagebrush, rabbitbrush, and greasewood. In places, where we cross the arroyas, or gulleys, great balls of white adobe abound. They cave off the banks somewhere above, will not dissolve by ordinary treatment, and get stickier and stickier after every shower. I have seen wagons held up with that mud clogging the wheels until the freighters had to dig themselves loose or camp until it dried up. Nothing much grows in these spots, for the water is of the vilest kind and undrinkable by man or beast.

We stuck to the main trail of the level valley for between five and seven miles until it reached the old Indian trail that winds its zigzagging way up to the top of the gap, passing behind Point Lookout. The whole hillside is covered with piñon and cedar trees and bushes of buckbrush, chaparral, mountain mahogany, and squaw apple. No matter how careful you try to be, they seem to reach out and tear at your clothes or packs.

Before going over the top, we had to have another squint back toward the La Platas and the few scattered farms that lay like crazy-quilt patches up and down the Mancos Valley. Down below the farms, the high mesa closes in from both sides and the river goes down for fifty miles or more to where it pops out into the San Juan Valley and is lost among the beds of quicksand where it joins the San Juan River, almost where the four states corner.

After that last look at the La Platas, the trail passes through the gap, or saddle, as it is generally called, and drops over into a little valley only about a mile wide and maybe five miles long. It is pinched out into a deep cañon by the cliffs closing in on it from both sides. The valley itself can never be pictured on canvas in a way to do it justice, for it is different for each of the seasons. A couple of miles down the little valley is a grove of heavy pines right in the center; not more than twenty trees in all, but all grand old fellows of many years growth. All this valley is a sea of blossoms or color, depending upon the season, and the trees appear like a small island of green in the midst of it all.

What a contrast this valley is to the rank smelling and mouse-colored black sage of the plain we cross before the beginning of the climb up the Mesa Verde trail. This, Nature's flower garden, has immense primrose blossoms, mariposa lillies, lupine, shasta daisies, and so forth, and grasses such as bluestem, grama, buckwheat, and long musquite, along with saltweed and white sage; all for the support of free-running life over these natural parks and winter retreats for ancient man and animals.

The most conspicuous flower is the primrose, with many of its blossoms being fully four inches in diameter and the fragrance noticeable long before seeing them. Next is the lupine, with their lovely blue clusters; then the larkspur, so pretty yet so deadly to stock early in the season. Locoweed, a member of the pea family, grows about a foot high, mostly where there is an abundance of alkali, and is covered with bright flowers. Everyone knows its effect on horses. Some of the prettiest and brightest colored are the gilia and penstemons, both of which grow from the lowest land to the highest land. The gilia, often called shooting stars or wild cypress, is the most noticeable. The penstemons are actually wild honeysuckle. Indian paintbrushes, or castilleja, invite attention and everyone who goes into the hills will gather great handfuls in spite of themselves. The sego lilly, mariposa, or tulip lilly (the Utah state flower) covers miles and miles of mesa and plain with color in the spring and early summer. It would seem impossible for them to stand the dry, alkali soil and the freezing temperatures, and then come out after spring showers with all their delicate structure to gladden the hearts of children and grown-ups alike.

Thousands of others, known and unknown, are seen hidden away in nooks and ledges wherever there is a little moisture to encourage them. It has been said by a noted botanist that the mountain flowers are of a greater variety and have more beautiful colors than can be found in the tropics. One could go on ad infinitum about flowers, trees, and plants. It is really a duty we owe ourselves and our children: to take more interest in the beautiful that Nature has placed before us to enjoy. If we want to cultivate the finer instincts, there is a satisfaction in being able to forget the opposite things we see too much of all the time and go back to Nature through the medium of the ever-beautiful flowers. They can well be classed as **Nature's** smiles.

After crossing this valley we climb back up to the same level as Point Lookout and then have a case of ups and downs in the crossing of the various heads of Moccasin and Cliff Cañons until we reach what we call The Summit. A good part of the distance is along the crinkley edge of the cliffs where we can look [west] down into the wide open spaces and across the magnificent distances of Montezuma Valley and on and on. The trail there is a rough and rugged one, but we use it, because it is miles and miles around, with lots of climbs in and out of cañons, just to miss that few feet of scarey pathway. The narrow trail is not all, for the low-hanging limbs of piñon and cedar have a way of reaching out and smacking you, as well as trying to rip the clothes off you.

Looking back along the trail, there is a perfect resemblance of the sphinx [in the distance] as well as an immense pyramid. All the while, eighteen hundred feet below, the plains stretch for miles and miles northward to the high mountains in the dim distance.

The Summit is really just a hump above the surrounding level and may have been a station or lookout point for the aborigines for hundreds of years, because fragments of pottery and an occasional arrow point may be picked up after a summer rain. It is not a barren spot, for a few pines and a heavy growth of scrub oak cover the greater part of the space, but leave a bare section at the very top for the observers to get a clear view of what may be coming their way. There is a dim trail leading down from this part of the rim to the valley below. A man or deer might make his way up; but going down you must lead, skid, or roll your horse.

While the horses are standing asleep or picking off the heads of the grass around them, we sit and begin to open our eyes to what is before us, both near and far. The snowy La Platas, with the jagged peak of the Hesperus, stand as sentinels to the east. Their extension [goes to the north] around Silverton and Ouray [to] Lone Cone near Rico, and on west to the La Sal Mountains, one hundred twenty miles north of us. All raise snowy peaks to the sky. Seventy miles to the northwest are the Blue Mountains, while just to the west is Ute Mountain. Going toward the south, Shiprock and the Carriso and Chuck-a-Luck ranges stretch away off into Arizona and New Mexico. Directly south, over an open plain of more than one hundred miles, are the Zuni Mountains and, east of them, Mount Taylor. It seems they were all intended as guardian peaks and ranges for the protection of that lonesome little piece of country so cut up with dikes, blow-outs, and deep, narrow cañons: The Mesa Verde.

The Indians call the view from The Summit the "rim of the little world" with Mount Hesperus, Navajo Mountain, Mount

Taylor, and one of the peaks of the San Francisco Mountains being the four corners of their world.[2]

As we sit quietly upon a hummock of grass, a small cloud goes drifting by just below us in the valley, and sprinkles a few raindrops on the ground. And then it is gone. It seems queer to be above a rain cloud, but it seemed to have business of its own on hand, coming from Ute Mountain and keeping on its way to the higher country of the La Platas. With it all clear now, we can see everything that makes the heart of the Nature lover respond to what has often been claimed as sights that can not be duplicated, not even in the Swiss Alps.

When we look across the spaces between the mountains, the timbered peaks have a rather cloudy appearance, while the untimbered ones look clear. All the mountain ranges above eight thousand feet are covered with fir or spruce, while below that comes the pine, with aspen and bunches of scrub oak slipping in where they can. Sometimes fires raged around the mountain sides, started by lightning or otherwise, and burned for weeks until a change of wind or a summer rainstorm would stop them. Until silver went dead, all the mountains to the east and northeast were covered with mining boom towns.

Directly in front of where we sit, the Dolores River, which begins in the northern part of the La Plata range, turns directly north and makes its way through rough and jagged formations for nearly a hundred miles before it flows into one of the forks of the Grand [Colorado] River. All the valleys to the north and west were considered good only for stock range to begin with. Later, dry farming was attempted. Finally, water was ditched into reservoirs from the Dolores. Then, the country showed the world what the earth, with plenty of water, could produce.

To call this view enchanting, for even the most unimpressive being, would be too mild an expression. It is grand, superb, sublime, and, although in the land of magnificent distances, it is unsurpassed by any other. Yet there are people who have eyes and see not. What is the enchantment this land holds: climate? magnificent distances? sunshine and clear, blue skies? blessedness of solitude? These are not the expressions to use. It would be more appropriate to say that it is the exhilarating sense of feeling; the joy, mainly, of living; and the lack of fatigue in doing.

To us sitting quietly on that high point, gazing across the miles of sublime grandeur, we know that it is the land that the

Lord, thy God gavest to us, where we could work and grow in peace and happiness. Never will I forget—nor cease to long for—just one more soul-inspiring view of this vast panorama of Nature's handiwork.

Facetiously, we always said we would erect a monument to ourselves at The Summit, which to us was the grandest view in all the beautiful Rocky Mountain region. Now I am alone: the last of the six. I hope the powers-that-be will think of us kindly.

As the sun starts down toward the west, we mount and ride away ranchward, with no loud exclamations, no laughing, no talking. The view and the silence speak volumes that can not be expressed by words. The snow on the La Platas beckons to me, but I can not answer the signal.

Buenas noches, con Dios,

Benjamin Alfred Wetherill

NOTES

1. Keeping only a few pieces, for the most part the miniature sizes of pottery and others that had sentimental value, the rest of the collection, Al thought, went to Denver to join the pieces from the first one and the one they called the "State Collection." A search for the pieces has resulted in failure to find any evidence that it arrived in Denver, or the Colorado State Museum. What happened to it remains a mystery.

2. Mount Hesperus, a 13,150-foot peak of the La Plata Mountains, is just northwest of Durango, Colorado; Navajo Mountain (elevation, 10,388 feet) lies just south of the junction of the San Juan River with the Colorado River in Utah; Mount Taylor, 11,389 feet, is a peak of the San Mateo Mountains near Grants, New Mexico; the San Francisco Mountains are north and slightly east of Flagstaff, Arizona, ranging in height from 9,000 to 12,611 feet.

PART 5

EPILOGUE

CRITICISM

There's a bunch of would-be critics for everything you do.
Not a word for good attempted, not a smile to help you through.

Success results from failures and not from wrongful praise
And judgment, whether good or bad, goes but a little ways.

An effort made will please a friend, no matter what the line,
And scoff and scorn that's shown me now can't dull what will be mine.

We can work along unaided, but it comes almighty hard,
When just a little honest praise would help and not retard.

Benjamin Alfred Wetherill

Epilogue

CONSCIOUSLY and subconsciously the snow on the La Platas beckoned to Al for the rest of his life, yet he never faced the fact in the open, leading to a constant, inexorable battle with himself. Many references to the yearning he carried for the mountain views and the arid country of the Four Corners occur throughout his account of his life. It is understandable, when viewing the occurrences in retrospect, that he wanted to close his mind in order to escape the trauma of remembering. First and foremost, his first child and only son had died. Second, the ranch could not be redeemed without accepting money from friends, a thought abhorrent to him, even if accepting meant saving the Wetherill monument of boot-strap endeavor and achievement: the Alamo Ranch on the Mancos. Also, borrowed money would have to be repaid and there appeared to be no way, ever, to amass sufficient funds to do so.

With his world crumbled to rubble, even as the cities of the ancient peoples had crumbled, he vowed to part with the past; to bury his Alamo Ranch life; to sever all memory of the Mesa Verde; to be born anew someplace else. That determination led to years of moving from place to place, always pursued by a relentless restiveness, but resisted by that stern resolution to never look back.

Running like a bright thread through all the succeeding years and binding them together are Al's references to the pro-

279

vocative light of the snow on the La Platas. Had he stayed near enough to receive the inspiration from the sight of the snow on the peaks, the succeeding years may have taken a different course, not only for him but also for Mesa Verde history as well.

When Al and Mary left the Alamo Ranch that January of 1902, they had little more than the clothes they wore. They had shipped C.O.D. to Mary's parents two trunks containing books, the Alamo Ranch records, the first photographs and negatives of the Mesa Verde ruins and some of the Four Corners country, and the very few, mostly miniature pottery pieces, of the Mesa Verde artifacts that Al could not part with when he started the bulk of the collection on its way to Denver. Heading toward Thoreau, New Mexico, where he had a job in a trading store, Al probably could not resist looking once more at the La Platas as they drove across the irrigation ditch at the corner of the ranch. That was the last time he was to view the snow from the Alamo.

From that time forward, there were no Wetherills at the foot of the Mesa Verde. It was four long years before interested citizens succeeded in making the Mesa Verde a National Park in the summer of 1906 and many more years before a permanent camp was established on the mesa itself.

Arriving in Thoreau in February 1902, Al and Mary began all over again with quiet Quaker fortitude. Fortunately, trading was good, they managed to save a little money, and with part of it purchased a half-interest in the store by the time Martha Cecilia was born in Atchison, Kansas, in December. When Martha was three months old, Mary returned to Thoreau with her.

After a time Al sold back his interest in the trading store to his partner, Horabin, and moved to Denver to manage the Wetherill Navajo Indian Blanket Store. Their sojourn was brief, for Al made a mistake that plagued him for years: loaning his savings to Richard and Winslow, even though they gave him notes for the amount. Early in 1904, Richard and Winslow removed all the stock from the store to Saint Louis for the World's Fair. That action left Al with no job and no prospect of one. He was acutely conscious of the conspicuous item he had left: a pocketful of paper notes.

Returning to familiar territory in Farmington, New Mexico, they arrived with fifty cents, an ill child, and few hopes. Taking on the job of managing a boarding house, they lasted until the owner's "dead beat kith and kin started drifting in casually, singly, and then in bunches."

Managing to trade one of the notes he held from Richard and Winslow for a team and wagon, they began a weary trek southward, hoping to find employment with the American Lumber Company in the Zuni Mountains southwest of Chaves, New Mexico. Dejectedly pulling into Pueblo Bonito, Al traded back to Richard one of the fifty-dollar notes for the "worst piece of walking horsehide that ever drew the breath of life into a thing called horse."

And that, though he later went so far as to engage an attorney to collect the rest of the money, was the sum total he ever recovered from his savings, but admitted his "own weakness for not pressing matters" to a conclusion.

Dragging through deep sands and an early snow, with weak horses and a still-ailing child, they eventually made their way through Seven Lakes (stopping there temporarily with a kind Mexican family who would not take any money for their hospitality) to Chaves where John had a trading store near the railroad tracks. Leaving Mary and Martha with John and Lulu, Al went on to work at a lumber company in the Zuni Mountains. That job was soon terminated when all the horses died as the result of deep snows and no fodder. Al lost not only the horses but their harness as well, for the carelessness of one of the men set fire to a log on which the sets of harness had been laid.

Al returned to Chaves just a few days after John's small son Benjamin (Al's namesake) had been thrown from a horse, then dragged and kicked in the face. Flagging a train, Ben had been sent to the hospital at Albuquerque where he was recovering except for the loss of sight in one eye.

In desperation, Al took his family to Atchison, Kansas, where he was soon working for the railroad as a freight hustler. Life was quite difficult, because the climate was too humid after all their arid country life but "even that could have been endured if the pay had been anywhere near living costs." Mary would have returned to school teaching but Al was adamant on that subject.

So, using his Santa Fe recommendation that had been given him when he terminated his employment in 1881 to move to the Alamo Ranch, Al obtained a job in the railroad office at Gallup, New Mexico. There they were immediately a part of the community, the Mayor and his wife calling on them as soon as Mary and Martha arrived to make a home. To Al it "seemed [as if] we had been wanderers from the fold and had at last wandered back to where we belonged."

Within two years the old restlessness aggravated him until he decided to pull up stakes and settle in the fertile "Banana Belt" of Montana where one would be rich in a year or two.

His plans were changed when President Theodore Roosevelt appointed him postmaster at Gallup. From 1908 to 1916 he attempted to cope with the burdens of being the postmaster while the post office grew from Fourth to Second Class rating and Parcel Post and Postal Savings accounts were added to his responsibilities. Although he was allowed to hire an assistant, the monetary allowance was only half the going rate so he had to pay half the assistant's salary out of his own pocket. In addition, Mary eventually had to work nearly full time, at no salary at all, to keep them from becoming inundated with postal matters.

When word came in 1910 that Richard had been ambushed and slain *by an Indian,* Al was stunned with the incredulity of the story. Quakers are invariably on the fringe of violence but, since 1872, the Wetherills themselves had been closely associated with the Indian peoples around them, often serving the Indians over their white associates. Forced to accept the fact that Richard had indeed been killed by an Indian, Al was never satisfied (nor were any of their friends, for that matter) that the death was fully and efficiently investigated. Included in Al's grieving notes is an unfinished poem:

The graveyard we have chosen in the 'dobie and the sage
Don't seem a fit surrounding_____
This choice of a last resting place is the neighbor to perdition
_____while the coyote howls around
And the sun's most glaring brightness is forever on the ground.

To be laid away in an alkali spot on the borderland of hell
Where the lingering glare of the sun so hot_____
_____
But in a pine tree's shade on the mountaintop
Is a rest we know full well.

During those years at Gallup many old friends visited Al and Mary. Alice Eastwood, for whom Mary had harbored a secret jealousy, stopped often and became as dear to Mary as to Al. Jesse Walter Fewkes dropped in occasionally. Although Mary privately referred to Fewkes as that "snide old goat," Al welcomed the visits and would listen closely to everything he had to say.

Fred Hyde came as often as his wanderlust brought him

through town. He usually arrived disheveled, dirty, and hungry, from his habit of riding the rails or just pointing himself in the direction he wanted to go and putting one foot in front of the other until he reached his destination. Mary and Al would take him in, clean him up, repair his clothes, and feed him for as long as he would stay. One of those trips nearly frightened Martha to death, though, for she was awakened by rapid footsteps and vehement argument. Creeping toward the living room she tremblingly picked aside a portion of the portiere and peeked through the slit. Relieved to see her father and mother alive, she was puzzled to see Fred Hyde and her Grandmother Wetherill pacing the floor. Marion Wetherill was stamping an emphasis each time she repeated, "Mary, *make* him do it. *Make him do it.*" To squelch the disturbance Al said,

"Fred, even if I did agree to go back to the Alamo, it would be a financial impossibility, for your family would never let you have enough money to buy it back." Whereupon Fred reached down and removed his shoe. Turning it upside down, he slid the heel forward to reveal a hollow shell. Extracting several tightly rolled pieces of paper, he triumphantly counted out before their astounded eyes *seven one thousand-dollar bills.* More than enough to take them all back to the Alamo Ranch! But Al would not accept the money; Mary refused to force him; Marion Wetherill's pleas had no effect and, with the rejection, Fred drifted out of their lives permanently.

Overwork forced Al to resign from the post office in 1916 and he soon engaged himself in a frenetic race. Dashing first to Manuelito, New Mexico, he quickly returned to Gallup only to rush on to Durango and Silverton in Colorado. Thinking he had at last conquered himself he settled down to being Indian trader again at Salane, Arizona, situated on a colorful shelf of cream-white-to-pale-pink cliffs sculptured into beautiful figures overlooking the Chinle Valley in northeastern Arizona. But only for a short time.

Returning again to Gallup, he went to work for the railroad, a job that lasted until January 1922 when he was dismissed at the insistence of a railroad workers' union on the grounds that he had performed manual labor that was outside the realm of management personnel. Extenuating circumstances had forced Al to repair a hot box on a railroad car at a time when there was no one around to perform the labor and the car had to be used.

Sixty years old and jobless, he was unable to obtain adequate employment for the rest of his life, due to the stigma that plagues the elderly.

Leaving the West for all time, Al moved his family to a rural area of Arkansas where they lived until he and Mary moved to Sand Springs, Oklahoma, to be with Martha and her family. Then, in 1943, the whole family moved to Tulsa, Oklahoma.

In reviewing his life to that point, Al observed that poverty was an endemic factor in the Wetherills, for "going broke was always a habit, but without fail we would pop up somewhere else to do it all over again." It seemed that all his life he had

just skipped around without any real aim or prospect. Many is the time I have said, "Just give me ten years and I can put myself on Easy Street." That was easy to think or say, but may have been the truth because I never stayed ten years on any project or proposition after the Alamo. Nine years was the most time I ever hung onto anything.

Occasional visits to John and Lulu at Kayenta, Arizona, relieved the tedium of the years, although he was rejuvenated each time he returned to the land where he still preferred the term *Monumental Valley,* for the majestic monoliths and mesas. One letter he wrote from Kayenta exposed his yearning. He sketched a picture of teardrops and wrote

My mind has been dead and my thoughts paralyzed ever since leaving this country.

These are the teardrops for leaving

This is the stream flowing away.

Then, by the 1930s, neighbors, friends, and relatives returning from trips to the Four Corners area hesitatingly repeated stories they had heard about the Wetherills to Martha and Al. Conspicuous in the tales was the assertion that the Wetherills, identified as the "early explorers," demolished many of the ruins of the Mesa Verde, using dynamite to open up the ruins; had ruthlessly collected from the dwellings and had sold the material collected for tremendous sums of money, the amount specified ranging from an ever-persistent $3,000 to as much as $100,000.

In a letter written to his best friend Alice Eastwood, Al exclaimed in consternation, "What's happening to us? What is somebody trying to do?" Ever after that time he shadowboxed with a tangible, yet unidentifiable darkness surrounding the Wetherill name. He was never able to discover who was responsible for Wetherill traducement.

Incongruous in the tales was the application of the word *vandal* to the "early explorers." That term has never been used to imply anything but willful destruction of valuable or beautiful things. Even the commercially minded pothunter never destroyed deliberately, for every object found meant money, while indiscriminate handling of the buildings brought forth only unmarketable fragments. Also inconsistent was the tale of the use of dynamite. No fragile "mummy" or delicate piece of artistic pottery could have withstood the concussion. Therefore, *if* any of the ruins suffered from blasting, it could only have been attributed to those who still believed the ruins hid the proverbial "great pots of gold moons" allegedly hidden by the Spanish, for only hard metal could have endured.

The whole situation carries a striking paradox: by making plenty of money selling artifacts, the Wetherills lost everything they had acquired in ten years of back-breaking endeavor. For writers and historians to have lacked the sagacity to question the inconsistency is astounding. Had the Wetherills accepted the smallest amount allegedly paid them, that fictitious $3,000 would have gone far in paying off the $3,404.30 mortgage against the ranch and spared their tumble into obscurity and denigration.

Some of the ache was transmitted to Al's grandsons who were serving in the armed forces, bringing a resolute determination for one of them to stay alive until he could return home and take his Pops back to meet the government personnel at the Mesa Verde face to face. That fierce fixation on the future sustained him through Peleliu and many more horrendous campaigns.

Eventually came the day in 1946 when he, Al, along with the grandsons, returned to the Mesa Verde and listened to the remarks that not only confirmed the fact that the tales were told by park personnel but also that those tales had persisted for many years. Al climbed up the crevice exit to Cliff Palace and tried to view again the La Platas. But they could not beckon. It was summer and there was no snow to glint and glisten with that old inspirational light.

Returning to Tulsa, Al began an intensive research to find a reason for the guide's statements. He and Martha studied government publications about the Mesa Verde National Park, much as the Wetherills had done while perusing the Hayden Survey Reports in the 1880s.

Part of the answer was found in the text of the Mesa Verde National Park brochures. Until 1934 the discovery of Cliff Palace was credited to Richard and Alfred Wetherill with the 1934 edition also including Charles Mason's name. Then the 1935 edition omitted Al's name from the credit, using only the names of Richard Wetherill and Charles Mason. Subsequent editions carried the 1935 version. More specifically they found an almost exact duplication of the guide's spiel in the Smithsonian *Bureau of American Ethnology Bulletin 51,* written by J. Walter Fewkes and published by the federal government in 1911, which was still being used in the park material, although the author's name was not identified as Fewkes. Included in many of the subsequent brochures was an almost synonymous use of "early explorers" and "pothunters" to denote depredations committed in the cliff dwellings between 1889 and 1906. Since no explanation to the contrary was carried, it was apparent the terms intended to cast aspersion on the name Wetherill.

Belatedly reporting the indignation produced by the 1946 trip, protesting the Wetherill traducement inferred by the publications, and claiming credit as the discoverer of Cliff Palace, Al and Martha wrote to the Secretary of the Department of the Interior in April 1948.

Representing the Secretary, Assistant Secretary C. Girard Davidson replied. He assured them that the National Park Service went to great lengths to assure both accuracy and justice in the information provided the public. Chiding them somewhat, the letter stated that it was "easy to exaggerate the importance of the discovery, since the existence of the major cliff-dweller villages on the Mesa . . . had been known . . . and photographed by Wm. H. Jackson in 1874" revealing his abysmal ignorance of the facts as recorded by Jackson himself. He then continued with, "I believe it would be of great value if you might prepare a detailed account . . . as fully and factually as possible. . . ." *As fully and factually as possible!* The absurdity was ludicrous. The correspondence had been brought about partially in an effort to induce the Department to return to its own factual account of the credit as carried before 1935. Yet the office of the Secretary appeared to cling to its own discrepancy as fact, but requested veracity from Al to support its own facts as carried before that date.

Nonetheless, Al obediently began the chore of condensing and compiling a summary. Once again he wrote Alice Eastwood, requesting her help in restoring some semblance of truth and fact to Mesa Verde history. He wrote that he and Martha were

> digging up the past events as much as possible; of course. we have considerable [amounts] of the early-day notes and letters to refer to. I do not know what outfit it is, but we are being cut out entirely [in Mesa Verde history]. Hayden, Holmes, and Jackson never saw those ruins and all their photos were taken years after we had found them. None could even find the main ruins without some of our outfit along. Our grief is in proving now to the Department of the Interior that us boys were the first to discover Cliff Palace and numbers of the ancient buildings of the Mesa Verde. Do you think you could send me your idea of the discovery of the [Cliff Palace] ruin, since you were one of the first to work over Mesa Verde and the surroundings. You have seen the ruin from both sides and the middle in your search for new material; the one that had the wild potatoes in that flat across from the ruin. . . .

On 16 June 1948, Al and Martha mailed to the Department of the Interior their summary of the Wetherill activities, activities that were supported by extracts drawn from various early publications and their notarized affidavits. While waiting for an answer, Al turned to his journal to record:

> The actual discoverer of anything of importance is generally soon forgotten and it is he who goes ahead and develops that article whose shoulders receive the honors. It is not our intention to say how good we are, or how bad the other fellow may be, but too many people just make a mental note of points that suit their purpose and fail to read the other side, or put any credence on what the other side may say. We created an interest in the work and people of an ancient race all through that S.W. country and later worked under scientific observation. We did not in any case destroy buildings and now our work is classed as vandalism. We met opposition, but that was to be expected and no one, at the time, cared to join in the atmosphere of the stirred up dust of untold ages. The actual value of anything found would not be worth all the dust and dirt you swallow in bringing to light those things that have been buried for hundreds of years. The point I

want to bring out is that we made the trails, named the cañons, located the water holes and springs. We uncovered the field and showed the possibilities, doing all the pioneer preliminaries for the latecomers to finish, and now all our work is called *vandalism*.

It was not until August 1948 that the June letter was answered. C. Girard Davidson, speaking as the Secretary, informed Al that "careful study has thus far failed to yield sufficient new evidence to authenticate in the minds of critical historians the claim that Cliff Palace was discovered before Richard Wetherill saw it. . . . In the meantime, the National Park Service has withheld from the 1948 edition of the Mesa Verde booklet any reference to the discovery of Cliff Palace. . . ." (It not only was omitted for that issue, but it was also deleted for ten years. When credit was again used in 1958, the booklet carried the erroneous 1935 concoction, as have publications since.)

Regarding criticism of the text of an article written by Don Watson, then Mesa Verde Park Archaeologist, he added that "it would be contrary to the policy of the National Park Service to hamper the free expression of its scientific and professional staff regarding matters of fact and interpretation on which they had conducted careful research." Just where those "facts" were located he did not volunteer. To his credit he did not close with a jocund "best wishes for the future" as one of his predecessors had done, but he might as well have, for the callousness was just as telling.

Al was completely bewildered. He could not understand the situation: The Department of the Interior, through the National Park Service, had originally carried the factual record of the discovery of the major ruins and carried those credits without discredit to the "early cowboy explorers," yet it now resolutely refused to admit either error or to recognize as factual their own earlier material. Just who the "critical historians" were who furnished the brochure information or to what lengths their "careful study" took them was never disclosed.

Time became an endless succession of days running downhill for Al. His life was terminated with that brusque and curt rejection, but it took his body a year to die. Attempting to wind up his thoughts while he had energy to write, he recorded a short paragraph in his journal, a paragraph he entitled *Finis*:

There is not need to draw a long breath when a person tries to make a comparison of all that has taken place over the Southwest in the past generation or two, or even three. Where deserts were, there are many miles of farming country; all wheat and cattle. Villages, towns, and mills are where we once could go for days and see no one. The only stopping places were where there happened to be a water hole or a good patch of grazing grass for saddle and pack horses. And yet, when memory drifts back to those early days, there is a deep-down longing to live over again, and go over again all the wide open spaces that once were and are now no more. I would like ever so much to go again over all that dry and dusty country, where time and high water have cut through the soft sandstone levels and sown miles of river-washed cobblestones through the valley during many changes of river channel. I often have a fine time all by myself when thinking of the bygone days. I guess I started to go over the things of the past a number of years too late, for no longer do I remember the things I used to know so well. Only the snow on the La Platas do I remember clearly.

It was not until the 5th of January 1950, in his eighty-ninth year, that Al found his way back to the range of his colthood days, only a few days after rounding out a full fifty years of marriage to Mary Tarrant, the little schoolteacher from Kansas. Mary, then blind and bedfast, did not need to be told that he had gone. In a soft voice she called Martha to her and, with calm serenity, told her, "Richard came for Al. They rode off together toward the La Platas and when they went over the ridge, Al turned and waved his hat to me."

There was no need for the snow to beckon any longer. Al had answered the signals, at long last, and the mountains had welcomed him home forevermore.

Appendixes

APPENDIX A. REGISTER OF TOURISTS TO CLIFF HOUSES 1892

July 9	J B Harris	San Francisco 300-18 st / 1633 Garden St / Sonoma ... Cala
	Mrs J B Harris	" " Cala
	A F Willingarth	Denver Colo.
	Elizabeth Willmarth	Denver Colo
25	Geo W Sumner	Omaha Nebr
	Chas. M. Sumner	Durango Colo.
	Jac. M. Rich	N. Y. City 50 West 38 Street
	W. D. Dowd	Denver Colo
Aug 10	M L Scudder Jr	Chicago 240 La Salle St.
	Marvyn Scudder	"
	Harold Scudder	"
12	F. C. Hyde	New York, N.Y.
	Talbot B. Hyde	" " "
	F. C. Hyde Jr.	" " "
	J. C. Seyl	Chicago
	E. J. Elzner	"
	W C. Taylor	Bensonhurst
	Miss Grace Taylor	"
	Geo E. Thompson	Wilmington Del.
15	F. G. Uhlich. Druggist	St Louis Mo
	Mrs. F. G. Uhlich	St Louis Mo.
	J W Foreman M.D.	Jonesburg Mo
	D. D. Dykeman	Logansport Ind
	Mary ... Dykeman	" " "

Tourists to Cliff Houses

May 5   Alexis J. Fournier (artist) 3500 Chicago Ave Minneapolis Minn

      Henry Smith   Minneapolis Minn.
      Art Director Minneapolis Industrial Exposition

May 19   J W Ayres. Chief assistant Historical
      Department Colorado Worlds Fair
      Board — Durango.

May 21st 1892

C. F. Boyle   Durango
Anna Boyle
Helen Peyton   Parsons Kansas
Gratia Edwards   Parsons Kansas
Lizzie L. Jackson   Durango Colo
Henry Carson Jr
W. S. Wingfield   Durango

June 6   Alice Eastwood   Denver, Colo.
" 23   Mrs J. W. Ayres   Durango Colo
" 25   Julia R. Cowing   Brooklyn N. Y.
"   Mrs T. Sumner   Durango Colo.
"   " Bennett Bishop   Durango Colo
"   " Lida Harkness   Brooklyn, New York.
"   " Jennie M. Scovell   Durango
"   " Hellen Sumner   "
"   " Charles Sumner   "
"   " Dora M. Sumner   "
"   " Anna Boyle   "
"   " Mrs Robert Coleman   Buena Vista Colo
"   " Henry Carson Jr   Durango Colo
"   " Nat Coleman   Buena Vista Colo
"   " J. W. Ayres   Durango

Tourists to Cliff House 1894

May 6	Frank A. Putnam	Boston Massachusetts
	Elizabeth Putnam	" "
	Laura E. Hayes	Foxcroft - N. Hampshire
	Emeline F. Rucker	Chicago, Illinois
Apr 24	R. R. Diehl	Montrose Colo
May	H. S. Ferguson	Denver
	W. A. Bowman (1621 Wazee)	808-16th St Room 9
	A. M. Buchanan	Cleveland Ohio
Jun 28	Edith A. Eames	Iowa Falls, Iowa
	Terrell W. Croft	Denver Colo
July 3	G. Law & wife	Greeley Colo
Aug 4	Fred. E. Stimpson	Lawrence Kansas
	Wm C. Stimpson	Brooklyn N.Y.
	B. Talbot B. Hyde	New York City
	Frederick E. Hyde Jr.	
	D. C. Baldwin	Elyria O.
	E. C. Baldwin	Cleveland O.
8	Wm Cross U.S.A.	Washington D.C.
	" " Asst "	" "
17	J. W. Hullinger	Junction City, Kan.
	Mr & Mrs. Frederick O. Vaille	Denver Col
	Miss Harriet W. Vaille	
	Agnes W. Vaille	
	Edith A. Vaille	

APPENDIX B. LETTERS

[The file of correspondence between the Department of the Interior, the Mesa Verde National Park, and the Wetherill family, as well as M. S. Fletcher, has, of necessity, been abbreviated and those letters that have been used are condensed, but what is quoted is quoted verbatim. The letters written by Martha Wetherill Stewart sometimes ran to ten pages, giving detailed history of the events at the Mesa Verde during the years the Wetherills lived at the Alamo Ranch.]

Sand Springs, Oklahoma
May 24, 1933

Superintendent, Park Service
Department of the Interior
Washington, D.C.

Dear Sir:

Sometime around 1880, Benjamin Wetherill and his family homesteaded a few miles from Mancos, Colorado, and homesteaded more, calling it the Alamo Ranch. They gradually built up a good herd of cattle and were fairly well fixed. The boys had some knowledge of botany and mineralogy and did a little exploring while rounding up stock. In this way my father, Alfred Wetherill, and his brother Richard found the Mesa Verde Cliff Dwellings. They took tourists to the ruins, but guarded against the destructive tendencies of souvenir hunters by protecting the ruins themselves.

My father was the last of the brothers at the ranch and started Professor Fewkes on his Mesa Verde career. I think Professor Fewkes would tell you that.

Since the ruins were his very own to take care of for so long and since you do have men at the park, maybe there's some place for him there now. He has studied archaeology extensively and knows the primitive peoples of North America intimately.

He's a Western man and my mother is a Western woman; they want the mountains and everything that the West hold for those who love her. He and mother dream and wish and I do so hope that, some way, their dreams can come true.

Yours truly,
(Signed)   Martha Wetherill Stewart

United States Department of the Interior
National Park Service
Washington, D.C.
June 1, 1933

Dear Mrs. Stewart:

I have your letter of May 24, which you have written in the interest of your father, Mr. Alfred Wetherill, who with his brother Richard discovered Cliff Palace and other ruins in the Mesa Verde National Park. I am very sorry that we can not consider Mr. Wetherill for an appointment to the park. It is impossible for us to deviate from Government rules, much as we would like to do so.

With very best wishes for the future, I am

                    Sincerely yours,
(Signed)   Horace M. Albright,
                    Director, National Park Service

                    Tulsa, Oklahoma
                    August 3, 1946

Park Superintendent
Mesa Verde National Park

Dear Sir:

My father is Al Wetherill, the last of the Wetherill boys. He should arrive at the Park in the next few days. He's eighty-five now and I know that the return is going to be emotionally difficult. Will you please help him over the crisis? It will mean only being a bit friendly, acting as though you thought the fifteen years of working in the ruins were a contribution to American archaeology and not the devastation of "pot hunters" as recent newspaper articles infer. Because, after all, pleas to the Government at that time were coldly received and so it was a project carried on by individuals who were convinced that they had discovered something worth while and wanted it recognized.

Will you please meet him as a friend who shares a common and important interest with you?

                    Sincerely,
(Signed)   Martha Wetherill Stewart

[No answer was ever received.]

Tulsa, Oklahoma
April 11, 1948

Honorable Julius C. Krug
Secretary of the Interior
Washington, D.C.

Dear Sir:

It's spring in Oklahoma and it will soon be spring in Colorado. It is almost tourist time again at the Mesa Verde and there is still an error in the information that is given at the Park by the guide and in the bulletin. I am enclosing a copy of a letter that I wrote two years ago, which remains unanswered.

When my son Donald returned home from the war in the Pacific, it was because he had a dream to see him through the physical exhaustion, the agony and the death and the stench and the horror: he would take his Pops back over the old trails and to the Mesa Verde once again.

They didn't expect fan-fare when they reached the Mesa Verde but they didn't expect to be hurt, embarrassed, and bitterly indignant. Ensuing remarks about the Wetherills gave the tourists the impression that they were pot-hunting vandals and ignorant cowhands. Nothing at all was said to show that fifty years ago the Government had no interest in the preservation of the ruins of ancient peoples; that the Wetherills did endeavor, without success, to interest the Government; that the brothers were pioneers in early American archaeology. And now guides tell strange stories about that early work, and the trip that was to have been the fulfillment of a dream just became another heartbreak.

Will you please not pass this over lightly for life is a day to day proposition with my father.

                    Yours very respectfully,
(Signed)   Martha Wetherill Stewart

The Secretary of the Interior
Washington, D.C.
April 28, 1948

Dear Mrs. Stewart:

Your story of the visit of your father and your sons astonishes me. The courtesy of the National Park Service rangers and naturalists is of so high an order that I feel sure no discourtesy was intended.

Few agencies go to such lengths to assure both accuracy and justice in the information given the public as does the National Park Service. In order to avoid the possibility of a misstatement, the statements regarding the discovery of Cliff Palace are being omitted from this edition. I think it is easy to exaggerate the importance of the discovery, since the existence of major cliff-dweller villages on the Mesa Verde had been known for some years and some of them were photographed by William H. Jackson in 1874. To me, the more important matter is the part played by your father and his brothers subsequent to the discovery of Cliff Palace; I believe it would be of great value if you might prepare in writing a detailed account of what they did, as fully and factually as possible. You may be certain that your father's connection with Mesa Verde will be treated with fairness when we have all the facts.

> Sincerely yours,
> (Signed)   C. Girard Davidson
> Assistant Secretary of the Interior

Tulsa, Oklahoma
June 16, 1948

Mr. C. Girard Davidson
Washington, D.C.

Dear Mr. Davidson:

I am sending herewith a number of enclosures, respectfully submitted for your approval: (1) Direct Quotations, Exhibits A through G, from Printed Material; (2) notarized affidavits from Mary and Alfred Wetherill; (3) a copy of "Desert Magazine," and (4) my father's report [a twenty page summary from the original journals], picked out from countless miscellaneous pages. It is strictly original and truthful. I was merely the typist.

> Yours very truly,
> (Signed)   Martha Wetherill Stewart

United States Department of the Interior
National Park Service
Washington, D.C.
July 1, 1948

Dear Mrs. Stewart:

We have received from the Assistant Secretary of the Interior Davidson the enclosure regarding the claim that Alfred Wetherill was the first discoverer of the Cliff Palace at Mesa Verde. An historical study is now being made of the first discovery of Cliff Palace. In the course of the study, we shall give careful consideration to the evidence you have assembled as well as to other pertinent historical source materials. We shall advise you of the results of our historical investigation. It has been very kind of you to assemble the data.

(Signed)

Sincerely yours,
Hillory A. Tolson
Acting Director National Park Service

United States Department of the Interior
Office of the Secretary
Washington, D.C.
August 30, 1948

Dear Mrs. Stewart:

Upon receipt of your letter of April 11, in which you raised the question of historical fact, the National Park Service began the reexamination of all available evidence concerning the respective claim of Alfred and Richard Wetherill to the discovery of Cliff Palace. Careful study has thus far failed to yield sufficient new evidence to authenticate in the minds of critical historians the claim that Cliff Palace was discovered before Richard Wetherill saw it.

When the final report is ready, it will be available for examination. In the meantime, the National Park Service has withheld from the 1948 edition of the Mesa Verde booklet any reference to the discovery of Cliff Palace, as I stated in my letter of April 28.

The excellent article by Don Watson in *The National Geographic* was prepared many months before the above-mentioned reexamination. In any event, it would be contrary to the policy of the National Park Service to hamper the free expression of its scientific and professional staff regarding matters of fact and interpretation on which they have conducted careful research.

Your interest in this matter is understood and I appreciate your getting in touch with me about it.

(Signed)

Sincerely yours,
C. Girard Davidson
Assistant Secretary,
Department of the Interior

Tulsa, Oklahoma
November 26, 1951

Mr. Don Watson
Mesa Verde National Park

Dear Mr. Watson:

Some time ago, while my father was still living, we read your article in the *National Geographic*. I wished then, and still do, that at some time you had "hunted him up." Each summer someone we know here in Oklahoma makes the trip to the Ruins. Each time when they come back, there is the same question: Why don't you tell the Park custodian the Wetherill angle?

I don't know how old you are, I think quite young, but I think perhaps you lack the weight of years that bring with them understanding. It is difficult in a day of government appropriations, good roads, and modern methods to get the perspective of a group of men over sixty years ago.

This probably doesn't make much sense to you. It's just that I'm trying to let you know the heartache and desperate homesickness that my father lived with all those years still breaks out in hurt feelings on the boys and my part when we think someone is speaking disparagingly of what they did at the Mesa Verde.

I think, Mr. Watson, that if at any time someone connected with the Park had been big enough to say, "Al Wetherill, you boys did a good job for the time in which you lived. You pioneered for present-day archaeologists to follow," it would have been some of the bread you hear about that gets cast upon the waters.

Sincerely,
(Signed)   Martha Wetherill Stewart

Mesa Verde National Park
April 3, 1952

Dear Mrs. Stewart:

Your statement that you sent your Father's notes to the Department of the Interior comes as a surprise to us. They were never sent here. At the present time one member of the staff is writing the history of the Mesa Verde. It will take many months, since there is so much historic material to be sifted, for there are many conflicting stories.

Your statement that your Father saw Cliff Palace from the bottom of the cañon is a fact we have always accepted.

Visitors often say, "Isn't it a shame all of that material was taken out of the ruins? Isn't it too bad the early explorers took all those things away?" Frankly, we don't feel that we need blame those men for what they did. When those men took the things out of the ruins they thought they were doing the right thing.

I think we have a fairly decent outlook on those early days—certainly our effort is to weed the facts out of all the stories that have come down to us. As I mentioned before, your Father's notes would have great value to us and we will make every effort to get them. If they can not be obtained from Washington, do you have a copy we could borrow?

                        Sincerely,
     (Signed)   Don Watson

Tulsa, Oklahoma
September 24, 1952

Dear Mr. Watson:

Here 'tis! The manuscript is not my writing. I was only the typist. If you find you are able to utilize any of this in your account of the history of the Mesa Verde, will you give Papa script credit, please?

                        Sincerely yours,
     (Signed)   Martha Wetherill Stewart

United States Department of the Interior
National Park Service
Mesa Verde National Park Colorado
October 12, 1952

Dear Mrs. Stewart:

The pictures and text which you sent on September 24, have been received and we want you to know how much we appreciate your generosity. I am sure you realize the value of this material; the text because it is a record of events and the pictures because they record the condition of the ruins at the time of discovery.

Sincerely,
(Signed)   Don Watson, Park Archeologist

United States Department of the Interior
Mesa Verde National Park, Colorado
November 9, 1954

Dear Mrs. Dunkelberger:

We are, at present, trying to write the history of the Mesa Verde. There is so little information available about the early period of discovery that we feel we can not do justice to that period or the men who made the history. Do you have information, photographs, notes, or other papers your father might have kept, that you would be willing to loan us?

We are always interested in meeting park friends and we would [be] even more interested and pleased to meet the daughter of one of the discoverers.

Sincerely yours,
(Signed)   Jean M. Pinkley
                Archeologist National Park Service

Tulsa, Oklahoma
July 2, 1960

Superintendent
Mesa Verde National Park
Mancos, Colorado

Dear Sir:
   Friends just returned from the Mesa Verde tell the same old story: tourists are told that the Wetherills were vandals who stole everything out of the ruins. I demand that these lies be stopped. If I had unlimited financial resources, I'd bring suit against the Park Department, the Department of the Interior, the Superintendent, and all the "90-day wonders" who act as guides.
   Yes, I'm more than angry. I'm furious.

                    Al Wetherill's daughter

cc   Department of the Interior
     Senator Robert S. Kerr, Oklahoma
     Congressman Page Belcher, Oklahoma

                    United States Department of the Interior
                    Office of the Secretary
                    Washington, D.C.
                    July 22, 1960

Congressmen Page Belcher
Senator Robert S. Kerr:
   We have your letter to Director Wirth of the National Park Service. We have no information about the incident referred to in Mrs. Stewart's letters. Mrs. Stewart's letters are returned herewith.

                    Sincerely yours,
     (Signed)   Roger Ernst
                    Assistant Secretary of the Interior

United States Department of the Interior
National Park Service
Mesa Verde National Park Colorado
July 26, 1960

Dear Mrs. Stewart:

I wanted to personally and thoroughly investigate to see if there could be any basis in fact for your statement. I can find none whatsoever. If you can furnish instances, we can deal with individual cases. I note that you have been critical of the National Park Service since you first started correspondence in 1933. The Wetherills were controversial people almost from the time they settled in the Mancos Valley. The National Park Service is perhaps the one organization that can do more than any other to set the record straight. This we are doing. We do not need to be clubbed over the head. I wish there were some means by which we could convince you that we have not in any way given out information that could be construed as "lies."

                    Sincerely,
         (Signed)   Chester A. Thomas
                    Superintendent

[Note: The full contents of the following letter carried the names of those who reported their experiences to Martha, as well as listing the particulars.]

                    Tulsa, Oklahoma
                    August 1, 1960

Dear Mr. Thomas:

Your first paragraph indicates exactly what I have been trying to accomplish for many years. I did not realize it had been since 1933 that there have been yearly uncomplimentary reports. I have no axe to grind; only a drum to beat. If it has a blatant, discordant sound it was because it was—and IS—necessary to my piece of mind that the distinction be made. I'm nobody, but even so, I am one of those formidable creatures; a woman with a cause.

                    Yours most sincerely,
                    Martha Wetherill Stewart

Tulsa, Oklahoma
September 15, 1964

Mr. Stewart Udall, Secretary
Department of the Interior
Washington, D.C.

Dear Mr. Udall:

I am putting together, for publication, the notes that Mr. Benjamin Alfred Wetherill left of the period of time in his life that carries through the Mesa Verde years. Among the files is one folder that contains the correspondence with the National Park Service and/or the Department of the Interior for the past thirty years. The text of that material concerns the reports related to the Wetherills by visitors to the park as to the role the Wetherills played in the early years at the Mesa Verde, and subsequent denials by the Department.

Through it all, two statements from the Office of the Secretary are consistent: one, the department has full facts to substantiate every statement made and, two, the Wetherills are being treated fairly. This implication, along with one letter that states that "the Wetherills were controversial people almost from the time they settled in the Mancos Valley" prompts me to ask where such information is available and if I could have access to such records.

Sincerely,
(Signed)   Maurine S. Fletcher

Washington, D.C.
October 6, 1964

Dear Miss Fletcher:

Any such documents as you mention are probably in the National Archives and you should send your request there. Similarly documents originally at Mesa Verde National Park, if not still there, would be in a nearby Government depository. The Superintendent of Mesa Verde could assist you in this matter. These documents are, of course, public ones and you are certainly welcome to study them.

Sincerely yours,
(Signed)   N. O. Wood, Jr.
Director of Management Operations

Tulsa, Oklahoma
October 29, 1964

Dear Mr. Wood:

Policies Professed *east* of the Potomac can not compete with the Practices Persistent *west* of the river. I was not able to view the material I asked for in Mesa Verde National Park. I had a letter from Dr. Arrhenius giving me permission to use any of the material he had deposited there, yet I was told that Dr. Arrhenius had not made the photograph deposit in the amount he claimed, that there were no letters from Al Wetherill in the material, and there were no Nordenskiöld notes such as I claimed. Finally, after arguing, I was permitted to view briefly a small portion of notes. I spent over $400 in making the trip to do the research I felt necessary, but was denied access by employees there.

                                        Sincerely,
(Signed)   Maurine S. Fletcher

Department of the Interior
Office of the Secretary
November 16, 1964

Dear Mrs. Fletcher:

Your letter indicates you feel there are some documents relating to Dr. Arrhenius and Al Wetherill that have not been made available to you at Mesa Verde. Everything that the National Park Service has received from Dr. Arrhenius has been deposited without exception at Mesa Verde National Park. Mrs. Pinkley took you out to the Wetherill Mesa Archeological laboratory on your visit on September 27, and this material she made available to you there.

We very much regret that for some reason known only to yourself you chose to spend only a few moments with this material. So far as Mrs. Pinkley and the staff knew, you were completely satisfied with your rather cursory examination of the documents deposited. The material is still there and available to you, just as it was on September 27. It is not possible to ship this material to you since it is Government property entrusted to the custody of the Park. All of [the] early notes, letters, or other documents have been made available to you and are still available to you in the Park.

                                        Sincerely,
(Signed)   N. O. Wood, Jr.
                                 Director of Management Operations

Tulsa, Oklahoma
November 20, 1964

N. O. Wood, Jr.

Dear Mr. Wood:
"Out to the Wetherill Mesa Archeological laboratory." What and where is it? With the exception of about five minutes when he went to the infirmary for some medication for Mrs. Pinkley's condition, my husband and I spent the entire time in Mrs. Pinkley's office. We waited for two hours to see anyone who could and would talk to me about the material. I talked by phone to Mr. Thomas, who did not offer assistance, but who did not necessarily need to do so.

"Rather cursory examination of documents." It is impossible to give any examination, cursory or intensive, to material never seen.

"Documents have been made available to you." It may tend to inflate your ego to call me a liar, but what service do you perform for the U.S. government when you call a citizen a liar upon no more evidence than you have?

Obstinately yours,
(Signed)   Maurine S. Fletcher

Tulsa, Oklahoma
November 20, 1964

Mr. Stewart Udall, Secretary
Department of the Interior

Dear Mr. Udall:
I am enclosing a carbon of my latest letter to your office. It is probably quite confusing to you, but no more so than the puzzle it and previous letters concerning the Department have made for me.

The serious matter is that all the Wetherill material will be placed in a depository when I am finished with it. For it to be deposited without letting the present Secretary know what has occurred over the past thirty years is not right, to my way of thinking. Therefore, I am still attempting to contact you so that you will have the opportunity for the file to contain at least one letter that will leave a commendable impression of the Department of the Interior and the role of the Secretary himself in Mesa Verde history.

Sincerely yours,
(Signed)   Maurine S. Fletcher

Washington, D.C.
December 4, 1964

Dear Mrs. Fletcher:

We are sorry you did not agree with the information on the Wetherill Mesa that we gave you in our letter of November 16. We are checking further and as soon as information is available you will be advised.

Sincerely yours,
(Signed)   N. O. Wood, Jr.
Director of Management Operations

Washington, D.C.
December 17, 1964

Dear Mrs. Fletcher:

The Secretary has asked us to reply to your letter to him of November 20, concerning certain documents you allege are at Mesa Verde and which presumably pertain to Al Wetherill. To our best knowledge no such documents are on file with this Department. All material relating to Al Wetherill on hand at Mesa Verde has already been made available to you. It is regretted that you insist on believing that this Department has in its files certain material that we will not allow you to review. The material you desire is not in the possession of the National Park Service nor in any other organizational unit of this Department.

Sincerely yours,
(Signed)   N. O. Wood, Jr.
Director of Management Operations

Tulsa, Oklahoma
December 22, 1964

Dear Mr. Udall:

May I have some communication from you—a postal card will be sufficient—telling me that Mr. N. O. Wood, Jr., has been requested by you to handle my communications with your office? If you have authorized him to speak for you and if he does write under your permission to represent the Department of the Interior and if you will only give me your assurance that the foregoing situation exists under your authority, then that is all I need to know.

Most Sincerely,
Maurine S. Fletcher

Washington, D.C.
January 23, 1965

Dear Mrs. Fletcher:

Your representative has brought to my attention your letter of December 22, 1964, which you had addressed to me and submitted to him for transmittal.

I have had the matter looked into by my staff, and I believe our Interior employees have extended their fullest cooperation in your search for information. I regret the material you seek is not available, but if it were, we would be happy to offer it for your inspection.

I am sure you understand that I personally, can not possibly handle the hundreds of communications addressed to the Secretary of the Interior that come to this office every day. Of necessity these are referred for handling to our most knowledgeable employees for their action. Your letter was handled just exactly that way, and again, I believe that we have done all we can to assist you.

Sincerely yours,
(Signed)   Stwt Udall
Secretary of the Interior

January 19, 1970
Hon. Walter J. Hickel, Secretary
Department of the Interior of the U.S.
Washington, D.C. 20240

My Dear Secretary Hickel:

What is the policy of the Department of the Interior (including the National Park Service) concerning use of letters sent by the Department? I have been under the impression that letters from any branch of our government are considered public property and can be used for publication. If not true, I would appreciate your advice. . . .

Sincerely yours,
Maurine S. Fletcher

January 29, 1970

Mrs. Roger C. Fletcher

Dear Mrs. Fletcher:

As a general rule official letters from this Department may be used in connection with a publication by a private citizen. If the letters were addressed to you or you otherwise properly received copies . . . it appears . . . there would be no objection to your use of them. If a letter in full is not used, I suggest that the reproduced material indicate that the material is a partial quotation.

Sincerely yours,
Bruce Wright, General Legal Services,
Dept. of Interior

Bibliography

Bennet, Ralph. "Scion of Wetherill Clan Returns to See Mesa Verde." Durango (Colorado) *Herald*, 31 August 1952.

Bernheimer, Charles L. *Rainbow Bridge*. Garden City, New York: Doubleday-Page, 1924.

Bolton, Herbert Eugene. *Coronado, Knight of Pueblos and Plains*. Albuquerque, New Mexico: University of New Mexico Press, 1949, 1964, and 1971.

————. *Pageant in the Wilderness*. Salt Lake City, Utah: Utah Historical Society, 1951 and 1972.

Brady, Cyrus Townsend. *The Cliff Dwellers Pot*. Kansas City, Missouri: The Crafters, 1911.

Brandegee, Townsend Stith. "Additions to the Flora of Colorado." *Hayden Survey, Miscellaneous Publications, no. 4, 1875*. Washington, D.C.: Government Printing Office, 1875.

————. "The Flora of Southwestern Colorado." *Bulletin of the United States Geological and Geographical Survey of the Territories, 2, 1876*. Washington, D.C.: Government Printing Office, 1876.

Brooks, Juanita. *The Mountain Meadows Massacre*. Revised edition. Norman, Oklahoma: University of Oklahoma Press, 1962.

Butcher, Devereaux. *Exploring Our National Parks and Monuments*. Revised, Fifth edition. Boston, Massachusetts: Houghton, Mifflin and Co., 1956.

California Academy of Sciences. *Bibliography of the Writings of Alice Eastwood*. Fourth Series. Vol. 25. San Francisco, California: California Academy of Sciences, 1949.

Cantelow, Ella Dales and Cantelow, Herbert Clair. "Biographical

Notes on Persons in Whose Honor Alice Eastwood Named Native Plants." *Leaflets of Western Botany* 8, no. 5 (16 January 1957). San Francisco, California: John Thomas Howell, 1957.

Cather, Willa. *The Professor's House,* New York: Alfred A. Knopf, 1925.

"The Cliff Dweller." The Denver (Colorado) *Republican,* Sunday, 22 January 1893.

"Cliff Dwellers of Colorado." Littel's *Living Age,* no. 6 (2 August 1890). Boston, Massachusetts: Littel and Co., 1890. Reprinted from *The Spectator* (A Weekly Review of Literature, Politics, Theology, and Art). Vol. 64, 1890. London, England: John Campbell, 1 Wellington Street Strand, 1890.

Chapin, Frederick Hastings. "Cliff Dwellings of the Mancos Canons." *American Antiquarian and Oriental Journal* 12, no. 4 (July 1890). Mendon, Illinois: S. D. Peet, 1890.

_____. *The Land of the Cliff Dwellers.* Boston, Massachusetts Appalachian Mountain Club, W. B. Clarke and Co., 340 Washington Street, 1892.

_____. *Mountaineering in Colorado.* Boston, Massachusetts: Appalachian Mountain Club, 1889.

Colorado: Public Records, State Archives and Records Service [Denver, Colorado]. Records of the General Assembly: Senate Journal, Nineth Legislative Session, 1893. "The World's Fair," p. 132.

_____. Records of the Office of the Governor: John L. Routt, 1889–1893. *Executive Orders, 1891.* "Appointment of Board of World's Fair Managers," 1 May 1891, bk. 7, p. 128. Vault 12 AB; Stack A, Sec. 1, Shelf 3.

_____. Records of the Office of the Governor: John L. Routt, 1889–1893. *Executive Records, 1891.* "Law Creating Board of World's Fair Managers of Colorado." (Pamphlet) Vault 12 AB; Stack A, Sec. 1, Shelf 3.

_____. Records of the Office of the Governor: John L. Routt, 1889–1893. *Executive Records, 1893. Message of Governor John L. Routt to Nineth General Assembly, 7 January 1893.* Vol. 8, p. 24, Vault 12 AB; Stack A, Sec. 1, Shelf 3.

_____. Records of the Office of the Governor: John L. Routt, 1889–1893. *Executive Records, 1893. Message of Governor John L. Routt and Inaugural Address of Governor Davis H. Waite Delivered Before the Nineth General Assembly, State of Colorado, 10 January 1893.* (Pamphlet, pp. 12–15.)

_____. Records of the Office of the Governor: Davis H. Waite, 1893–1895. *Executive Records, 1895. Biennial Message of Gov-*

ernor Davis H. Waite and Inaugural Address of Governor Albert W. McIntire Delivered Before the Tenth General Assembly, State of Colorado, 1895. (Pamphlet, pp. 34–37.)

————. Register of Warrants Issued from Auditor's Office. Book C, pp. 276–88, 23 November–10 December 1892; pp. 298–299, February–March 1893; Book D. pp. 10–31, March–May 1893.

————. Sessions Laws of Colorado, 1891. Senate Bill 120, "World's Columbian Exposition," pp. 406–409, Bound Volume.

————. Sessions Laws of Colorado, 1893. "World's Columbian Exposition," chapter 167, p. 476, Bound Volume.

————. Tenth Legislative Session, 1895, "Board of World's Fair Managers," 30h Day, pp. 294–95; 52d Day, pp. 474–75.

Colorado Springs (Colorado) *Gazette.* Wetherill advertisement, 5 September 1895.

Cope, E. D. "Report on the Remains of Population Observed in Northwestern New Mexico, 1874." In *Report Upon United States Geographical Surveys West of One Hundredth Meridian.* Washington, D.C.: Government Printing Office, 1879.

Corle, Edwin. *Listen, Bright Angel.* New York: Duell, Sloan, and Pearce, 1946.

Crampton, C. Gregory. *Standing Up Country.* New York: Alfred A. Knopf, 1964.

Cushing, Frank Hamilton. "A Study of Pueblo Pottery as Illustrative of Zuni Culture Growth." Fourth Annual Report of *Bureau of Ethnology* to the Secretary of the Smithsonian Institution 1882–83. Washington, D.C.: Government Printing Office, 1886.

Delaney, Robert W. "This Is the Four Corners." Durango (Colorado) *Herald,* "Annual Summer Four Corners Magazine," 1964.

Douglass, A. E. "Dating Pueblo Bonito and Other Ruins of the Southwest." *National Geographic Society Technical Papers, Pueblo Bonito Series,* no. 1. Washington, D.C.: National Geographic Society, 1935.

————. "The Secret of the Southwest Solved by Talkative Tree Rings." *National Geographic Magazine* 56, no. 6 (1929).

Eastwood, Alice. "Additions to the Flora of Colorado, II." *Zoe* 4 (April 1893). San Francisco, California: Zoe Publishing Co., 1893.

————. "The Common Shrubs of Southwest Colorado. *Zoe* 2 (July 1891). San Francisco, California: Zoe Publishing Co., 1891.

————. "General Notes of a Trip Through Southeastern Utah." *Zoe* 3 (January 1893). San Francisco, California: Zoe Publishing Co., 1893.

_____. *"Gilia Superba, Phacelia Nudicaulis."* *Zoe* 4 (October 1893). San Francisco, California: Zoe Publishing Co., 1893.

_____. "Key and Flora, Rocky Mountain Edition." In *Bergen's Elements of Botany.* Cambridge, Massachusetts: Ginn and Co., 1900.

_____. "List of Plants Collected in Southeastern Utah." *Zoe* 4 (July 1893). San Francisco, California: Zoe Publishing Co., 1893.

_____. "The Mariposa Lillies of Colorado." *Zoe* 2 (October 1891). San Francisco, California: Zoe Publishing Co., 1891.

_____. "Notes on Some Colorado Plants." *Zoe* 4 (April 1893). San Francisco, California: Zoe Publishing Co., 1893.

_____. "Notes on the Cliff Dwellers." *Zoe* 3 (January 1893). San Francisco, California: Zoe Publishing Co., 1893.

_____. "Report on a Collection of Plants from San Juan County, Southeastern Utah." *California Academy of Sciences Proceedings* (2) 6 (August 1896). San Francisco, California: California Academy of Sciences 1896.

_____. "Two New Species of Aquilegia from the Upper Sonoran Zone of Colorado and Utah." *California Academy of Sciences Proceedings* (2) 4 (March 1895). San Francisco, California: California Academy of Sciences, 1895.

"Exposition Art." *Minneapolis Industrial Exposition Annual, 1891.* Minneapolis, Minnesota: n.p., 26 August–26 September 1891.

Faunce, Hilda. *Desert Wife.* Boston, Massachusetts: Little, Brown and Company 1934.

Fewkes, Jesse Walter. "Antiquities of the Mesa Verde National Park: Cliff Palace." *Smithsonian Bureau of American Ethnology Bulletin 51.* Washington, D.C.: Government Printing Office, 1911.

_____. "Antiquities of the Mesa Verde National Park: Spruce Tree House." *Smithsonian Bureau of American Ethnology Bulletin 41.* Washington, D.C.: Government Printing Office, 1909.

_____. *A Journal of American Ethnology and Archaeology.* Boston, Massachusetts: Houghton, Mifflin and Company, 1894.

_____. "Prehistoric Villages, Castles, and Towers of Southwestern Colorado." *Smithsonian Bureau of American Ethnology Bulletin 70.* Washington, D.C.: Government Printing Office, 1919.

Freeman, Ira S. *A History of Montezuma County.* Boulder, Colorado: Johnson Publishing Co., 1958.

Gillmor, Frances, and Wetherill, Louisa Wade, *Traders to the Navajos.* Boston, Massachusetts and New York: Houghton, Mifflin and Company; and Cambridge, Massachusetts: Riverside Press, 1934.

Gregory, Herbert E. *The Navajo Country.* A Geographic and Hydrographic Reconnaissance of Parts of Arizona, New Mexico, and Utah. *Water Supply Paper 380.* Washington, D.C.: Government Printing Office, 1916.

Hammond, Mrs. John Hays. *A Woman's Part in a Revolution.* New York, London, and Bombay: Longmans, Green, and Co., 1897.

Hayden, Ferdinand Vandiveer. *Annual Report of the U.S. Geological and Geographical Survey of the Territories for the Year 1873.* Washington, D.C.: Government Printing Office, 1874.

————. *Annual Report of the U.S. Geological and Geographical Survey of the Territories for the Year 1874.* Washington, D.C.: Government Printing Office, 1876.

————. *Bulletin of the U.S. Geological and Geographical Survey of the Territories, Vol. II, 1876.* Washington, D.C.: Government Printing Office, 1876.

————. *Miscellaneous Publications No. 5, 1875.* Washington, D.C.: Government Printing Office, 1875.

————. *Ninth Annual Report of the U.S. Geological and Geographical Survey of the Territories for the Year 1875.* Washington, D.C.: Government Printing Office, 1877.

————. *Tenth Annual Report of the U.S. Geological and Geographical Survey of the Territories for the Year 1876.* Washington, D.C.: Government Printing Office, 1878.

Henderson, (Alice) Palmer. "The Cliff Dwellers." *Literary Northwest* 3 (May 1893).

Hewett, Edgar L. "Circular Relating to Historic and Prehistoric Ruins of the Southwest and Their Preservation." General Land Office, Department of the Interior. Washington, D.C.: Government Printing Office, 1904.

————. "A General View of the Archeology of the Pueblo Region." *Smithsonian Report, 1904.* Washington, D.C.: Government Printing Office, 1905.

Hogg, John Edwin. "How I Found the Mesa Verde Ruins, as told by Benjamin A. Wetherill." *Touring Topics* 23 (February 1931). Beverly Hills, California: Automobile Club of California, 1931.

Holmes, William H. "A Notice of the Ancient Ruins of Southwestern Colorado Examined During the Summer of 1875." *Bulletin of the U.S. Geological and Geographical Survey of the Territories, Vol. II, 1876.* Washington, D.C.: Government Printing Office, 1876.

————. "Pottery of the Ancient Pueblos." *Fourth Annual Report of the Bureau of Ethnology, 1882–83.* Washington, D.C.: Government Printing Office, 1886.

————. "Report on the Ancient Ruins in Southwestern Colorado Examined During Summers of 1875 and 1876." *Tenth Annual Report of the U.S. Geological and Geographical Survey of the Territories, 1876.* Washington, D.C.: Government Printing Office, 1878.

Hovey, H. C. "Homes and Remains of the Cliff Dwellers." *Scientific American,* 28 October 1893. New York: Munn and Co., 1893.

Jackson, Clarence S. *Picture Maker of the Old West: William H. Jackson.* New York: Scribner's Sons, 1947.

Jackson, William H. "Archaeology." *Annual Report of the U.S. Geological and Geographical Survey of the Territories, 1874.* Washington, D.C.: Government Printing Office, 1876.

_____. *Frontier Photographer Diaries, 1866–1874.* Edited by Leroy R. Hafen and Anna W. Hafen. Glendale, California: Arthur H. Clark Co.

Kansas City (Missouri) *Star.* "After Teetering 1,000 Years, At Last It Falls." By the Associated Press. Farmington, New Mexico dateline. 23 January 1941.

Jones, Marcus E. "Contributions to Western Botany." *Zoe* 4 (October 1893). San Francisco, California: Zoe Publishing Co., 1893.

Kidder, Alfred V. *An Introduction to the Study of Southwestern Archaeology.* New Haven, Connecticut and London: Yale University Press, 1924 and 1962.

Kluckhohn, Clyde. *To the Foot of the Rainbow.* New York: The Century Co., 1927.

McClurg, Virginia D. "The Making of Mesa Verde into a National Park." *Colorado Magazine* 7 (November 1930).

McNitt, Frank. *The Indian Traders.* Norman, Oklahoma: University of Oklahoma Press, 1962.

_____. *Richard Wetherill: Anasazi.* Albuquerque, New Mexico: University of New Mexico Press, 1957.

Mason, Charles Christopher. "The Story of the Discovery and Early Exploration of the Cliff Houses at the Mesa Verde." The Denver (Colorado) *Post,* 1 July 1917, Section 2, p. 6.

Mindeleff, Cosmos. "Cliff Ruins of Canyon de Chelly, Arizona." *American Anthropologist* 8 (1895).

Morgan, Lewis H. *Houses and House-Life of the American Aborigines.* Washington, D.C.: Government Printing Office, 1881.

National Park Service. *Director's Annual Report to the Secretary of the Interior:* 1917; 1919; 1922; 1923; 1924; 1925; 1926; 1928; 1929; 1930; 1931; 1932; 1941; 1945; 1946; 1949; 1951; 1952; 1953; 1954; 1955; 1957; 1960.

Newberry, James S. "Geology of the Banks of the San Juan." *Ex-*

ploring Expedition from Santa Fe to Junction of Grand and Green Rivers, 1859. Washington, D.C.: Government Printing Office, 1876.

Nordenskiöld, G. *The Cliff Dwellers of the Mesa Verde.* Translated from the Swedish by D. Lloyd Morgan. Stockholm, Sweden: P. A. Norstedt and Söner, 1893.

Nuttall, Zelia. "The Atlatl or Spear Thrower." *Peabody Museum of Archaeology and Ethnology.* Salem, Massachusetts: Salem Press Publishing and Printing Co., 1891.

Osborne, Douglas. "Solving the Riddles of Wetherill Mesa." *National Geographic* 125 (February 1964).

Packard, A. S. "New North American Phyllopoda." *The American Journal of Science and Arts* 2 (July–December 1871). New Haven, Connecticut: Tuttle, Morehouse, and Taylor, 221 State Street, 1871.

Peet, Stephen D. "The Great Serpent and Other Effigies." *American Antiquarian and Oriental Journal* 12. Mendon, Illinois: S. D. Peet 1890.

————. "High Cliff-Dwellings and Cave-Towns." *American Antiquarian and Oriental Journal* 18. Mendon, Illinois: S. D. Peet 1894.

Pepper, George H. "The Ancient Basket Makers of Southeastern Utah." American Museum of Natural History Supplement to *American Museum Journal* 2, no. 4, Guide Leaflet no. 6 (April 1902).

————. "Ceremonial Deposits Found in an Ancient Pueblo Estufa in Northern New Mexico, U.S.A." *Hyde Expedition.* New York: Monumental Records, 1899.

————. "The Navajo Indians: An Ethnological Study." *The Southern Workman,* November 1900.

Powell, John W. *Fifteenth Annual Report of Bureau of Ethnology, 1893–94.* Washington, D.C.: Government Printing Office, 1897.

Prudden, Theophil Mitchell. "The Circular Kivas of Small Ruins in the San Juan Watershed." *American Anthropologist* 16, no. 1 (1914).

————. "An Elder Brother to the Cliff-dweller." *Harper's Magazine,* June 1897.

————. *On the Great American Plateau.* New York and London: G. P. Putnam's Sons and the Knickerbocker Press, 1906.

———— "A Summer among the Cliff Dwellers." *Harper's Magazine,* September 1896.

Quick, Eleanor L. "Victim of Well-Planned Attack." The McKinley County (New Mexico) *Republican,* 1 July 1910, Gallup, New Mexico. Reprinted from the *Albuquerque* (New Mexico) *Journal.*

Sharrock, Floyd W. "The Hazzard Collection." *Archives of Archeology,* no. 23. Microcards. Madison, Wisconsin: University of Wisconsin Press, 1963.

Smith, Larry. "The Mountain States Have Fairy Shrimp." *Sunset Magazine* 138, no. 5 (May 1967). Menlo Park, California: Lane Magazine and Book Co.

Stanton, Robert B. *Down the Colorado.* Edited by Dwight L. Smith. Norman, Oklahoma: University of Oklahoma Press, 1965.

State Historical Society of Colorado (Denver). "Major Archeological Collections." Tract compiled 29 November 1962.

Steele, Aubrey L. "The Beginning of the Quaker Administration of Indian Affairs in Oklahoma." *The Chronicles of Oklahoma* 17, no. 4 (December 1939).

Thompson, G. "Notes on the Pueblos and Their Inhabitants." *Report Upon U.S. Geographical Surveys West of One Hundredth Meridian, Vol. II. Part II.* Washington, D.C.: Government Printing Office, 1879.

U.S. Department of the Interior. *Glimpses of Our National Monuments.* Washington, D.C.: Government Printing Office, 1929.

_____. *Mesa Verde National Park Colorado.* Issues of 1912, 1914, 1915, 1916, 1917, 1918, 1919, 1923, 1927, 1928, 1930, 1931, 1932, 1933, 1934, 1935, 1936, 1937, 1938, 1939, 1940, 1941, 1942, 1945, 1948, 1949, 1951, 1952, 1953, 1954, 1955, 1957, 1958, 1960, 1963, 1965. Washington, D.C.: Government Printing Office.

Watson, Don; Lancaster, James A.; Pinkley, Jean M.; and Van-Cleave, Philip F. *Archeological Excavations in Mesa Verde National Park.* Washington, D.C.: U.S. Department of the Interior, 1954.

_____. *Cliff Dwellings of the Mesa Verde.* Mesa Verde Museum Assoc. Ann Arbor, Michigan: Cushing-Malloy, Inc., 1951.

_____. *Indians of the Mesa Verde.* Mesa Verde Museum Assoc. Ann Arbor, Michigan: Cushing-Malloy, Inc., 1953.

Weatherill, Marietta. "When My Trail Crossed Geronimo's, as told to Mabel C. Wright." *Sun Trails* 5, no. 5 (May 1952). Albuquerque, New Mexico: *Sun Trails,* 1952.

Wetherell, Frank. *Families from Village Wetheral.* Des Moines, Iowa: Frank Wetherell, 1948, 1949 Supplement.

Wetherill, Benjamin Alfred. "As I Remember." *Desert Magazine* 8, no. 7 (1945).

Wetherill, Louisa Wade, and Gillmor, Frances. *Traders to the Navajos.* Boston, Massachusetts and New York: Houghton, Mifflin and

Company; Cambridge, Massachusetts: Riverside Press, 1934.

Wilson, Carol Green. *Alice Eastwood's Wonderland*. San Francisco, California: California Academy of Sciences, 1955.

Yale University. *Biographical Sketches and Letters of T. Mitchell Prudden, M.D.* New Haven, Connecticut: Yale University Press, 1927.

UNPUBLISHED MANUSCRIPTS

Arhenius, Olaf. "Gustaf Nordenskiöld" (Biography).

Eastwood, Alice. "Line-A-Day Journal." Alice Eastwood Archives, California Academy of Sciences, San Francisco.

————. "Memoirs." Alice Eastwood Archives, California Academy of Sciences, San Francisco.

Nordenskiöld, Gustaf. "Across Northern Arizona." Translated from the Swedish by George O. Williams. Originally published in the Stockholm *Dagblad*, 1892.

————. "The Cliff Dwellers of the Mesa Verde." Translated from the Swedish by George O. Williams.

Quick, Eleanor L. "A Protest Against Injustice." (Written at Putnam, New Mexico, following Richard Wetherill's assassination.)

WETHERILL DOCUMENTS

Memorabilia, Anna Wetherill Mason:

Letter from Benjamin Kite Wetherill to Marion Wetherill 7h Month 3 1873, copied by Deborah Mason Bent.

Marriage Certificate of Anna Wetherill and Charles Christopher Mason.

Minutes of Meetings to Consider Yearly Meeting House at Lawrence, Kansas, 1t Month 1871 to 10h Month 1873.

Westtown Boarding School History by Sara Roberts Wetherill.

Wetherill Family of Chester, Pennsylvania, History by Sara Roberts Wetherill.

Memoirs, Mary Tarrant Wetherill.

ALAMO RANCH RECORDS

Accounts Payable, 1891–1898.

Accounts Receivable, 1893–1896.

Cashbook, 1885–1901.

Deeds, various dates.

Employee Records, 1886–1901.

Guest Accounts, 1893–1897.

Guest Register, 8 June 1889–15 August 1901.

Horses and Mules Account, n.d.

Inventory, 1880.

Miscellaneous Accounts, 1893–1896.

Miscellaneous Papers, 1880–1899.

Photographs, various dates.

Photography Account, 1892–1894.

Tally List of Cattle, 1886–1887.

Wetherill library.

LETTERS

Aandahl, Fred G. To Martha Wetherill Stewart, 12 August 1960.

————. To Senator Robert S. Kerr, 12 August 1960.

Albright, Horace M. To Martha Wetherill Stewart, 1 June 1933.

Arrhenius, Olaf. To Maurine S. Fletcher, 7 October and 17 November 1964; 28 March 1965.

Baldwin, Hannah. To Mary Tarrant Wetherill, 27 January 1903.

Cantelow, Ella Dales. To Martha Wetherill Stewart, 6 August 1954 to 20 January 1956.

Carpenter, S. W. To B. A. Wetherill, 14 February 1899.

Cowing, Annalee. To Maurine S. Fletcher, 18 November 1964 and 2 January 1965.

Cowing, Agnes. To M. S. Fletcher, 3 January 1965.

Davidson, C. Girard. To Martha W. Stewart, 28 April and 30 August 1948.

Dunkelberger, Luella. To M. S. Fletcher, March 1965.

Eastwood, Alice. To Al Wetherill family, 28 January 1921 to 11 December 1949.

————. To Martha W. Stewart, 15 January 1950 to 22 August 1953.

Edmondson, A. P. To A. Wetherill, 31 December 1898.

Ernst, Roger. To Page Belcher, 22 July 1960.

————. To Senator Robert S. Kerr, 22 July 1960.

Fletcher, Maurine S. To Olaf Arrhenius, 15 June 1964 to 9 June 1965.

————. To Agnes Cowing, 8 January 1965.

————. To Cowing family, 13 November 1964 and 9 December 1964.

———. To Walter J. Hickel, 19 January 1970.

———. To Douglas Osborne, 17 July 1964.

———. To Mary Elzora Bachman Phelps, 3 December 1964 and 23 January 1965.

———. To Stewart Udall, 15 September to 22 December 1964.

———. To N. O. Wood, Jr., 20 November, 29 October, and 20 December 1964.

Lee, Ronald F. To Martha W. Stewart, 15 October 1952.

McLean, Charles H. To B. K. Wetherill, 3 June 1898.

Mason, Alice. To Uncle Al (Wetherill), 29 January 1940.

Mason, Anna Wetherill. To Al and Mary (Wetherill), 16 February 1930 to Christmas 1948.

Mason, Debby. To Uncle Al (Wetherill), 6 October 1939.

Nordenskiöld, G. To Al Wetherill, 21 February 1891 [1892] to 9 May 1895.

Osborne, Douglas. To M. S. Fletcher, 29 July 1964.

Pinkley, Jean M. To Luella Mason Dunkelberger, 9 November 1954.

Phelps, H. E. To Martha W. Stewart, 20 November 1953.

Phelps, Mary Elzora Bachman. To M. S. Fletcher, 18 October 1964 to 16 July 1965.

Prudden, T. Mitchell. To Al Wetherill, 28 March 1902.

Scharnhorst, Judge C. J. To B. A. Wetherill 27 February 1899.

Stewart, Martha Wetherill. To Page Belcher, 2 July and 1 August 1960.

———. C. Girard Davidson, 16 June 1948; 24 August 1948; 24 September 1952.

———. Alice Eastwood, 10 February and May 1918; 10 January 1950 to 29 October 1953.

———. Senator Robert S. Kerr, 2 July and 1 August 1960.

———. Superintendent of Mesa Verde, 24 May 1933; 3 August 1946; 2 July 1960.

———. Chester A. Thomas, 1 August 1960.

———. Hillory A. Tolson, 24 August 1948.

———. Don Watson, 24 August 1948; 26 November 1951; 24 September 1952.

Tarrant, F. D. To Alfred Wetherill, 18 October 1899.

Thomas, Chester A. To Martha W. Stewart, 26 July 1960; 17 February 1961.

Tolson, Hillory A. To Martha W. Stewart, 1 July 1948.

Udall, Stewart. To M. S. Fletcher, 23 January 1965.

Wade, Jack J. To Superintendent of Mesa Verde, 21 July 1960.

Walters, Eleanor Quick. To Martha W. Stewart, 12 December 1947 to 29 May 1952.

Watson, Don. To Martha W. Stewart, 3 April, 24 September, and 12 October, 1952.

Wetherill, B. A. (Al). To Laura Tarrant, 26 December 1886; 24 January 1887.

————. To Alice Eastwood, 1921 to 1949.

————. To Mary and Martha, 1902 to 1949.

Wetherill, B. K. To G. Nordenskiöld, 1 Feby [February] 1894.

Wetherill, John. To Al Wetherill, nearly all undated to near 30 November 1944.

Wetherill, Marion. To Alice Eastwood, 18 September 1916.

Wetherill, Richard. To G. Nordenskiöld, 28 April 1892 to 6 July 1895.

Wood, N. O., Jr. To M. S. Fletcher, 6 October, 16 November, 4 December 1964.

MAPS

Note: The maps used were for reference only. The maps in the text are not to scale.

Army Map Service (AOSX), Corps of Engineers, U.S. Army. *Sheet NJ 12–9 Cortez, 1953–55*. Washington, D.C.: United States Department of the Interior Geological Survey, 1962.

Army Map Service (GE), Corps of Engineers, U.S. Army. *Sheet NJ–12 Grand Canyon, 1959*. Washington, D.C.: United States Department of the Interior Geological Survey, SX 10–62.

Army Map Service (BESX), Corps of Engineers, U.S. Army. *NJ 12–12 Shiprock, 1954*. Washington, D.C.: United States Department of the Interior Geological Survey, 1963.

Bauer, Clyde Max. "Professional Paper 98," Plates 64, 65, and 69. *Contributions to the Geology and Paleontology of San Juan County, New Mexico*. Washington, D.C.: Government Printing Office, 1916.

Berry, R. W.; Ecklund, C. A.; Marshall, R. B.; Tatum, Sledge; Urquhart, C. F.; McKinley, C. P. *Soda Canyon Quadrangle, 1911–12*. Additional trails, springs, and reservoirs added 1933 by Indian Office. Washington, D.C.: U.S. Department of the Interior Geological Survey, 1954.

Berry, R. W., and Ecklund, C. A. *Topographic Map of Mesa Verde National Park, Montezuma County Colorado, 1910–1911*. Washington, D.C.: U.S. Department of the Interior Geological Survey, 1915.

Besley, E. and Co. *Topographical Map of Colorado 1889*. Denver: 1889.

Chittendon, Geo. B. "Preliminary Map of Southwestern Colorado Showing the Location of Ancient Ruins." *Bulletin of the U.S. Geological and Geographical Survey of the Territories 2, 1876.* Washington, D.C.: Government Printing Office, 1876.

Fischer, Emil B. *Map of Southwestern Colorado 1893*. Compiled, drawn, and copyrighted, 1891. N.p., n.d.

Gleissner, Max J. *Partial Revision of Geological Survey by R. W. Berry and C. A. Ecklund, 1926*. Washington, D.C.: U.S. Department of the Interior Geological Survey, 1954.

Gregory, Herbert E.; Heald, K. O.; Pogue, J. E.; and Emery, W. B. *Geologic Map of the Navajo Country Surveyed in 1908–13*. House Document, 64h Congress, 1t Session. Washington, D.C.: Government Printing Office, 1916.

King, Harry. *Annual Report of the Bureau of Ethnology, 1880–1881*. Washington, D.C.: Government Printing Office, 1883.

U.S. Geological Survey. *Mesa Verde National Park*. Administrative Map, 1916. Washington, D.C.: Government Printing Office, 1917.

Utah State Road Commission. *Utah*. Official Highway Map, 1958. N. p., n.d.

Index

Numbers in boldface indicate photographs.